BEYOND CONTENT

UNCOMMON INTERVENTIONS

WITH

PEOPLE IN CRISIS

Philip Perry, Ph.D

SYNERGY LIBRARY

Calgary, Canada

1990

Published and Distributed by Synergy Library
P.O. Box 61142, Kensington Outlet
Calgary, Alberta, Canada, T2N 4S6

Canadian Cataloguing in Publication Data

Perry, Philip Eric, 1943-
Beyond content

Includes bibliographical references.

1. Crisis intervention (Psychiatry). 2.
Change (Psychology). 3. Self-actualization.
I. Title.
    BF637.S4P47 1990   158'.1   C90-091633-8

ISBN   1-895359-00-7

Cover design by Kelsey Lundmark

ACKNOWLEDGEMENTS

I am deeply greatful to so many countless colleagues who have encouraged me to go beyond my illusions of limitation and my tendency to procrastinate. Of particular note has been the kind and generous contribution of Wood's Homes in the form of secretarial support, as well as giving me the time off to write this manuscript.

Also, I am indebted to the many challenging workshop participants I have encountered over the years who have pushed me towards becoming more precise, as well as provocative, in my attempts to reveal workable ways of intervening in the crisis of others.

Finally, I would like to acknowledge Susan Ogilvie for her persistent and enthusiastic support, as well as sensitive caring during the heavy writing times and to Alice Fador who over and over again reaffirmed my commitment to extracting value out of fully exploring the essence of living through one's pain.

FORWARD

Why are you so unhappy?
Because nine-tenths
of everything you think, feel
and do is for yourself
and there isn't one!
Wei Wu Wei

I suppose it begins with one small urge - to make sense of our world. In making sense, we gather experience and think thoughts and form understanding. We take this understanding out into the world, we try to share it or exercise it with others and in so doing create new understanding. If we're fortunate enough our nervous system allows us to form certainty out of our understanding - to predict and see how things work. Such certainty then gives rise to power and personal competency. To know things yes, but also to do things, demonstrating how our understanding fits into and shapes our life with others.

Then something unexpected happens. Bad luck, someone else's differing thoughts, our own failed certainty or life just running into us and our belief about things is shaken. Perhaps our understanding is shown to be too small for the task at hand. If something bad or unexpected goes on long enough we call it a crisis. A crisis is life pointing out what we don't know or haven't learned yet. It mocks our certainty and throws our power back in our face. I guess this seems cruel, but if we pause for a moment and consider there is in fact another side. Crisis or life, is also a teacher, pointing out our next steps or lessons. Crisis, if not life in general, would remind us, again and again, that we are simply in process, moving along, expanding understanding, exchanging one temporary/useful certainty for another and co-creating or shaping life with others. This is sometimes referred to as the transpersonal perspective.

Transpersonal is that which is left when one has dropped words, specified thoughts, understanding, certainty and the attempt to enforce certainty through the power it engenders. It is a "state" that rests beyond specified experience or thought. Perhaps it is best understood as an openness to the raw material of the moment; it _is_ understanding and certainty in service, even bondage, to the moment, not the other way around. Santanya, the philosopher, has said, "it is better to find interest in the changing seasons than to be hopelessly infatuated with Spring". So too the transpersonal abandons fixed point and instead flows with and revolves around the changing seasons of life, experience and the rise/fall of the moment. It is not that certainty is wrong, only that certainty is never right enough.

Life as an ongoing experience of one normative crisis after another, either rubs our nose in or gently leads us toward the truth of the transpersonal. You see when all is said and done what do we really know, for certain <u>and</u> how long does knowing this really matter. It seems rather than pursue certainty and specificity of belief, life and/or crisis invites us to cultivate a sense of powerful uncertainty, brilliant curiosity and active tentativeness - the essence of transpersonal experience.

But how do we get this? What's required and where do we look? Generally those in the 'know/now" make fun of us and tell us there is no place to look and nothing to get. In fact, some say that to try to capture the transpersonal is to lose it for to think, understand, become certain etc., about the transpersonal is not possible. While it might on occasion catch us, we can never really capture it. So what can we do?

Long ago, a Tibetan lama was asked this same question and he responded by suggesting that though we can't catch it, we can do certain things to allow it to catch us. We can bait the trap, so to speak, with certain actions, attitudes, practices and beliefs. In and of themselves these activities or attitudes have no intrinsic value, but as bait for the transpersonal they have great use.

This book then represents "bait", i.e., practices, beliefs, actions, etc. that invite the union of crisis with a transpersonal perspective. It is geared to those who would, as the title suggests, seek to practice uncommonly creative work with people in distress. The essence of the work is that beyond beliefs, theory and reified professional learning lies an open fertile space within which creative practice can take place. It provides structure not as <u>the</u> way, but <u>a</u> way to awaken the practitioners own liveliness and creativity. Its goal is not to place the crisis worker in bondage to new ideas, models or techniques, but set the practitioner free from the positive obstacles theory represents. For this reason it vacillates between theory and the world of ideas <u>and</u> practice and one's own experience. The transpersonal is not thoughtless nor mindless, but thought/mind in service to the necessity of the moment. It refers to certainty/understanding as an Act; those sets or pre-dispositions which give us direction in life (page 95) and tries to point out, no matter the content nor redeeming quality an Act is just an Act, not to be abandoned nor censored, but recognized for the all and "no-thing" that it is.

Though specific, even detailed the book is an Act, not to be modelled upon nor copied, but incorporated as directions into one's own Act in order to go beyond the givens of crisis or more conventional solution. If successful, it will not simply provide another cook book for crisis work, but instead evoke in its reader their own transpersonal experience.

Jon Amundson, Ph.D.

TABLE OF CONTENTS

LIST OF FIGURES

LIST OF TABLES

PROLOGUE

A JOURNEY BEYOND CONTENT

Without question these are frightening times for human beings throughout the world. More than any other time in history, humanity is threatening to run away with itself as it seeks to avoid problems rather than choose to have our difficulties foster growth, mentally and spiritually. Most of us are well aware of the growing pollution problems,
increasing acts of world terrorism and the horrendous world poverty and starvation problem. It seems in our effort to avoid suffering we create more suffering. This journey that mankind has embarked upon is obviously insane. Unfortunately, many of us sit back and operate as if there is nothing we can do. In fact, the byword for most these days is to **"cope"** with life, and the best that life ever gets is temporarily better always to be followed by disillusionment and more suffering.

Even though the world looks to be on the brink of self destruction, it is evident a perceptible ground swell movement is slowly building a critical mass of energy. This movement is bent on exploring and uncovering new ways that human beings can actualize their aliveness towards constructive ways of being. This movement is not born out of the isolated and unappreciated genius of a few. A silent majority is producing a gradual collective awareness that a conspiracy is needed. This conspiracy as Jean Houston (1982) suggests, is challenging our collective dullness and our seemingly fatalistic intent to repeat our mistakes and be limited by our beliefs. Her book, **The Acquarian Conspiracy**, chronicles the unfolding conspiracy by referring to it as the "rhythms of awakening". Unquestionably and irreversibly, we are becoming more and more aware of ways to transform our experiences of crises. Leading the way on **The Road Less Travelled**, (Peck, 1978), are those who choose to rise above being preoccupied with chaos and to actively confront crises in search for opportunities. To such people, life has not changed necessarily. Rather, the relationship to things in their lives has. Jean Houston (1982) aptly refers to them as "people of the breakthrough". They are everywhere. Quiet, creatively persistent and always prepared to include you.

This book is an invitation for you, the crisis intervener, to begin the journey along this road of transformation others have travelled. It is designed to shake you out of your sleepwalking and to liberate those unused parts of yourself. The aim is for you to develop a new or renewed quality of attention both personally and in your life work as a crisis intervener.

Please understand this book does not provide a blueprint for the way it should be. It does not give the reader a prescription for transformation. Rather, it simply asks you to be an explorer as you are able to and to expand your capacity to understand naturally without force. This is not a book to teach you by manipulating you to think other than the way you do. It is not necessarily about you getting better or acting differently as a crisis intervener, nor is it prescriptive. Although, this may well be the outcome. This book is about freedom from suffering and helplessness as it focuses on one's sources of competency. Interestingly enough, this way of exploration has been around for the past ten thousand years or more. Once you tempt yourself to reconnect to this more or less forgotten way, it will be difficult to turn back. The way you intervene will never be the same. In any event, it's up to you to take the journey and to experience the trip.

Enjoy the experience!

INTRODUCTION

MEANING OF BEYOND CONTENT

Beyond Content is a slogan for transformation. In contrast to traditional change focused crisis intervention, transformation focused crisis intervention literally means to rise above or go beyond ordinarily imposed limits or boundaries - transcending form or the circumstances of a crisis. For example, anyone who has experienced a crisis transformation, will know that the circumstances of their existence, such as their job, their living situation, their physical health and their socio-economic status do not necessarily change. What shifts is the availability of alternative ways to perceive the forms of our existence. This enables us to relate and respond to our circumstances with greater flexibility and with a felt sense of being more "in charge" of our aliveness. In this respect, Beyond Content and transformation are intertwined contextual concepts the meanings of which can at best be only approximated through words. In any event, let's review its possible meaning in greater detail.

Beyond Content is about evolution rather than revolution. It's dialectical; it blends or absorbs differences rather than clashing with them. It is confrontation **with** rather than confrontation **against**. It is not formless wishy washy liberalism or idealistic futurism. Rather, it is for active and effective development of powerful new patterns evolving from chaotic life events. It focuses on the correlation of opposites. In this sense it is not a matter of destroying old patterns so much as it is about using them to unfold new patterns or pathways. It is about coming from solutions rather than getting to them. It gravitates towards stability and seeks order out of chaos. It is about connecting with an evolving self organizing synthesis of natural wellness.

Beyond Content is about going beyond mediocrity, reductionism and sanctification of our ignorance. It avoids hanging on to beliefs, dogmatism and polarization. It is about taking quantum leaps by-passing methodical and change-resistant mechanical thinking. Yet, Beyond Content is not necessarily about changing our thinking. It is simply a framework for change allowing change to occur naturally and productively. Beyond Content, as already alluded to, operates just outside of language as language is insufficient to facilitate creativity. Rather, language really only serves to pattern our existing knowledge.

Finally, although not conclusively, Beyond Content is based on the understanding that the inherent nature of our existence is embedded in **unconditional competency** and that the power in crisis can be harnessed. Mastering this power using our competencies is the primary goal of the Beyond Content approach to crisis intervention. In this regard, the essence of our underlying competencies is perhaps best summarized by Jeremy Hayward (1984):

> Beyond all philosophies of good and evil, of righteousness and sin, of morality and immorality --beyond all theories of human development and human behaviour, all potential theories of conservatism, futurism and liberalism--the human being has a basic unconditioned competent nature. (P.8).

Operating from this viewpoint, the Beyond Content Model addresses human competency by focusing on "what works" and "what makes a difference". It assumes we all are capable of manifesting our own unique brand of competence regardless of our crises.

THE CHALLENGE

Beyond Content Crisis Intervention is written to challenge you in many ways. You may well explore uncharted waters; and at times they will be perceived as hazardous. Many of your currently held beliefs, opinions, attitudes and thoughts will be challenged. At times, what you read may seem contrary to your experience or reasoning. At other times, what you read will crystallize and focus for you what you have intuitively known, yet have not found a way to practice or make clear to others. What is right or wrong and what is fair will come up for you as will other issues such as integrity, commitment and caring.

More specifically, it will challenge your thinking and viewing about how to balance the polar opposites of life crises. As well, it is designed to challenge your illusions about helping others and distorted viewpoints about **getting better** as both a crisis intervener and as a person in crisis. It is intended that the format challenge your intuitive side, your competency side and your capacity for genius.

As the format is beyond traditional methodical training, you will be asked to explore ways of thinking that may be unusual for you. Edward DeBono (1972) suggests our old way of thinking is outdated, archaic and passe'. What we now need, he says, are new thinking tools. In this respect, Beyond Content involves a shift in perspective towards a new or different paradigm. This shift is like the turning of a coin where one side represents creation and satisfaction and the other side represents dissatisfaction and coping.

On the other hand, this paradigm is inclusive of what you already know and does not suggest that you abandon anything. It speaks to a re-mapping or re-patterning of your experiences, resulting in the enrichment of an ever deeper, ever more encompassing understanding of oneself and others.

Some of you will find this "work" book useful in problem solving, others may not. Some will find it awkward at first. It is written to include **YOU** in the process of crisis exploration as well as

---

the client you serve. While it is not designed to frustrate the reader, the reader will inevitably be, from time to time, somewhat frustrated with knowing exactly how these concepts can be incorporated and practically understood.

It is not meant for the faint of heart or for those who are content with the status quo. Some of you may retreat from the vulnerability of exploring your own unknown territory, preferring instead in a limiting way the sanctities of our conditioned reality. If this is the case, the book is really not for you.

BOOK DESIGN

The book is divided into five sections. It begins with six chapters covering the basic building blocks of the Beyond Content model, along with suggestions on how to make use of this model. The next three sections use the Beyond Content crisis intervention model to explore the vast and expansive crisis territory from three different perspectives. Section II starts by offering five chapters on specific symptom-based crisis topics, such as self harming behaviour and substance abuse. Section III shifts towards demonstrating the impact that the Beyond Content model can have on families and relationships. Section IV goes on to clarify how might this model be used in different community or institutional environments. The final section addresses ways and means for crisis interveners to support skill maintenance, as well as to further develop their own crisis intervention competency. In a concluding way, the last chapter entitled, **The Step Beyond**, offers some reflective and speculative thoughts on the implications of this emerging paradigm of crisis intervention. Following a basic retrospective overview comparing this model with what is standard fare in the crisis intervention field, a discussion is entertained outlining the what are some of the shortcomings of this model, what risks are inherent taking the Beyond Content journey, and how to further support those who actively desire to pursue the quest of their own personal development.

This "workbook," is intended to be a basic reference manual for periodic review of your own evolving thoughts and insights as a crisis intervener. As such, the chapters function in an interdependent way and tend to build on one another.

While some attempt has been made to offer an intellectual understanding through identifying, in a semi-scholarly way, the wisdom and sorcery of others, the primary intent is to offer as practical guide as possible. The model has been developed from experience as well as from the mind. I am more interested in your testing out what has been said than in your being impressed with historical knowledge. Consequently, not every concept or principle is backed by references. At the end of some of the chapters are suggested reading references for further study and exploration for those so inclined.

Some space is also provided for note-taking and for the exercises related to the training material. Throughout the book, crisis intervention concepts are blended with practical examples followed by exercises. Reading the material is not sufficient to give you a working understanding of the model, as the book will soon demonstrate. These exercises give you an opportunity to relate both personal and interpersonal life circumstances reflecting crisis situations.

THE PRIMARY AIMS

This book has four primary aims. These are:

1. To demonstrate how a somewhat provocative crisis intervention model enhances (expands) the power and effectiveness of the crisis intervener, regardless of professional persuasion.
2. To assist crisis interveners in clarifying their purpose in serving others.
3. To assist crisis interveners by refining their present skills and by offering preparatory, as well as maintenance skills that foster the dynamics of competence.
4. To foster the exploration of new mind/body territory, using crises as opportunities to go a step beyond our present-day conditioning.

MAKING IT WORK FOR YOU

This book will no doubt challenge you to go beyond your complacency and your mind's tendency to be disorderly, as well as its predisposition to being lazy. It is meant for those wanting to go beyond the ordinary. You are encouraged to actively explore with self-discipline ensuring that you use your mind rather than have it run you. The book will work when you commit yourself to completing the exercises, practising the model, and confronting yourself when you don't. The ultimate quality of your work depends on your willingness to confront your barriers and those barriers placed before you by your crisis work.

Tempering this viewpoint is the suggestion that you use the book to periodically prepare yourself for anticipated interventions or simply to prime yourself for incubating innovative intervention ideas. In this vein, Beethoven was known to have said, "Nothing comes to me today, we shall try another time." Make the information work for you in the same vein that Beethoven suggested, allowing yourself the privilege of letting your natural wisdom to percolate in its own time.

NOTES

_____

_____

_____

_____

_____

_____

_____

_____

_____

_____

_____

_____

_____

_____

_____

_____

_____

_____

_____

_____

_____

_____

_____

_____

_____

_____

_____

_____

SECTION I

BEYOND CONTENT CRISIS INTERVENTION

This first section includes the first six chapters and focuses on describing the contextual and the practical aspects of an evolving model of crisis intervention. Beginning with a brief review of some of the historical underpinnings of crisis theory an effort is made to trace the forces that have converged generating the impetus for the Beyond Content crisis intervention model. The components are then then gradually revealed as a working format for this model.The first chapter includes a statement of purpose, a definition of crisis as a cornerstone of the model and a description of ten foundation principles.

This section continues with a second chapter on how four identified forces of competency are interwoven together into a wellness fabric. It goes on to outline how these forces can be activated by self actualizing crisis intervenors using a contextual formula as guiding pathway through the crisis territory. This formula is repeatedly used throughout the book with many examples of different crisis scenarios.

Chapter three describes a number of self preparation tasks for crisis intervenors and invites the reader to try them on. Included are exercises in competency identification, crisis intervenor purpose generating, self observation, actualizing psychological neutrality, power walking body charging and listening.

Chapter four explores issues related to crisis intervenor skill maintenance and enhancement. Specifically addressed are concerns related to crisis teamwork,crisis debriefing and crisis consultation.

Chapter five presents a three pronged approach to sizing up a crisis. As a simultaneous approach to assessment and intervention predominating perceptual modes, Acts or life roles and crisis states of integrity combine to form the front end of the intervention formula presented in Chapter Three.

The last chapter in this section offers a consolidating overview of how the information in the first five chapters can be used in a composite way. In particular, a primary emphasis is placed on experiencing how to use the crisis states of integrity as a differential yet dynamic guide for intervening no matter what the crisis.

CHAPTER ONE

AN EVOLVING MODEL

One doesn't discover new lands without consenting to lose sight of the shore for a very long time ...

- Andre Gide

HISTORICAL OVERVIEW

Crises and crisis intervention are as old as mankind itself. Yet, only in the last few decades have we seen the evolution of crisis intervention theory in practice. In response to ever-mounting discontent with expensive, hard-to-access and poorly fitting traditional psychotherapies, novel crisis-intervention approaches have started to appear.

These approaches, in opportunistic ways, have emerged alongside a robust new force in psychology referred to as the humanistic movement (Goble, 1970). Forged out of the psychodynamic, behavioural and cognitive movements, the humanistic movement, sometimes called the "third force in psychology" had its embryonic beginnings in the Mental Health Clinic movement in the western world. One milestone in the development of crisis intervention as a treatment of choice occurred when a European psychiatrist, A. Querido, opened a Psychiatric First Aid Station in Amsterdam in the early 1930's. This early forerunner of the modern day community mental health centre provided fertile ground for the growth of crisis intervention theories. Operating from an environmental perspective, Querido offered outreach services in the community as well as more traditional treatment services. His Aid Station assisted people in their own homes, coordinated efforts with other social service agencies, and maintained a liaison role with other community professionals. In the process, Querido (1968) also advocated strongly for client self-sufficiency as well as community self-sufficiency by endeavouring to get clients to mobilize personal and community supports.

Clearly, Querido's pioneering efforts have had a profound effect on the evolution of community services and crisis intervention methodology. In obvious ways, the current mental health system gives evidence that his principles of intervention enjoy widespread usage today.

Perhaps better known as a cornerstone for the theoretical and clinical understanding of crisis intervention is Eric Lindemann's classic work with 101 bereaving relatives and friends of the Boston Coconut Grove 1943 fire. This fire took almost 500 lives. Lindemann (1944) observed that acute grief followed a sequential and somewhat predictable pattern. In an effort to gain mastery over their grief, survivors went from (a) a state of mental disorientation to (b) preoccupation with the past along with general apathy to current circumstances to (c) acceptance of loss and finally to (d) expression of normal or pathological grief reactions. The remarkably uniform, identifiable, and predictable behaviourial pattern led him to the conclusion that provocative "preventative intervention" could be implemented to minimize the possibility of a serious and prolonged psychopathological reaction to grief.

Clearly this viewpoint has set the stage for others (Caplan, 1964; Parad, 1965; Rapoport, 1963) to explore life crisis situations. The aim of this exploration was to determine ways to intervene in accordance with the behaviour manifested and with the possible behaviourial stages associated with that type of crisis.

If Querido excavated the ground and Lindemann laid the cornerstone for a crisis intervention theory, then Gerald Caplan established the foundation. Following in Lindemann's footsteps, Caplan further developed a theory of crisis intervention and articulated protocols for clinical practice. Caplan's theory was also influenced by Eric Erikson's (1963) work on psychosocial stages of development. His appreciation of Erikson led him to include what he called "developmental crises" as a key component of his crisis theory. In this respect, it will be useful to comment on Caplan's theoretical premises as they acknowledge individual differences in learning, growth, and socio-cultural life styles. The primary components of Caplan's theory are as follows:

1. A crises results when an individual's "emotional homeostasis" is upset and habitual problem-solving activity fails to restore the balance. Caplan refers to habitual problem-solving activity as "coping".

2. A crisis that is accidental or situational rather than developmental is nevertheless responded to in accordance with the individual's current developmental awareness of the perceived precipitant of the crisis.

3. A crisis proceeds through four distinct phases. They are:

    i)   Initial efforts to reduce tension through habitual problem-solving tactics;

    ii) After the failure of habitual problem solving efforts, disorganization occurs accompanied by trial-and-error problem solving tactics;

    iii) **Next** a breakthrough can occur resulting from novel problem-solving attempts or a redefinition of the problem is achieved **or** a resignation or discounting of the crisis occurs;

iv)   Finally, however if breakthrough is not achieved, breakdown can occur resulting in major personality disorganization as the crisis continues and seems unsolvable;

Caplan further suggests that crises are generally self-limiting and will be resolved in one way or another in a period of one to five weeks. Moreover, crisis outcomes are normally the result of the actions taken by the person in crisis and by others and not the result of the nature of the problem, the individual's personality, or her experience (although the latter factors influence the outcome).

Caplan's theoretical work established a solid foundation for other crisis theorists (Rapoport, 1962; Taplin, 1972; Parad, 1968), who have elaborated, modified, and refined it. For this reason, Caplan is often seen as the modern- day father of crisis-intervention theory.

It is important to note that Caplan's theoretical premises, while they do not enjoy wholesale acceptance, are remarkably compatible with those of psychoanalytic and ego psychology, behavourial theory, humanistic and existential psychology. Even more importantly, Caplan (1964), clearly acknowledges that a crisis can be an opportunity for personality growth as well as a time of increased vulnerability to psychopathology. He suggests that, for a crisis to be successfully resolved, the usual patterns of behaviour must be transcended. Such transcendence can lead to a re-organization of the personality at a higher level of functioning. The inclusion of this perspective in crisis theory has served to crack open the door to consideration of what Maslow (1962) refers to as the "self actualizing potential" arising out of a crisis.

Maslow, well known for positing an heirachy of human needs, established a "turning point" in the field of psychology when he urged that an understanding of human needs required going beyond a problem focus. His viewpoint suggested that we all, regardless of our traumas and life circumstances, possess the potential to become self-actualizing at any given moment. He specifically argued that it was much more efficacious to examine clinical need by probing into what works, rather than what was wrong or problematic.

Breaking away from traditional problem-focused viewpoints Maslow nevertheless supported a synthesis as well as a developmental approach to growth. In this context problems are not to be avoided. Rather, they are to be embraced as essential aspects of growth. Often they serve as a catalyst for necessary and natural evolutionary development. Unlike other developmental models, (Erikson 1963; Kohlberg, 1969; Piaget, 1958), Maslow also boldly suggested the conditions for self-actualization. He indicated that, while self actualization normally requires time to develop in life, it could be achieved outside of the restraints of time. In his view, we are all "covered up self actualized beings".

Since Maslow's milestone efforts to integrate traditional viewpoints into the unfolding and coalescing field of humanistic and transpersonal psychology, there has been a proliferation of crisis-intervention models. Many of these models have acknowledged the potential for self-actualization; yet the models that include self-actualization are largely prescriptive in orientation and are based upon symptoms of illnesses with only illusions of wellness possibilities. The "coming from" problem focus still dwarfs the "coming from" solution focus. This perspective has more than likely been generated from these models having originated out of social, political and professional action based on the increasing complexities of our contemporary social fabric. Further, these models tend to be grassroots developed and environmentally or territorially specific. They tend to represent rising concerns over suicidal rates, child abuse trends, family violence and breakdown, homelessness, drug and alcohol abuse, AIDS and generally, social/cult cultural deterioration. Many of these models have emerged out of social work practices reflecting the mounting concern over the deterioration of our social fabric along with growing disillusionment with high cost traditional medical and psychological as well as institutional intervention.

CURRENT STATUS

Crisis intervention as a mode of service is seemingly evolving into the treatment of choice in many community and mental health social service settings. Witness the fast-developing free-standing networks of walk-in clinics, store-front clinics, and even emergency mental health clinics operating out of hospitals. Many of these services cut across traditional lines of service to offer a quick-access, no frills, relatively cost-effective service to those in crisis. Walk-in services are the current fad: They are being developed within many fields, such as law, dentistry, and medicine. As an alternative to office-bound counselling services, we are seeing a number of developments: Street work or outreach programmes, home support programmes, emergency shelters or crisis units, and mobile crisis teams.

Walk-in services are not the only trend that offers an alternative to traditional institutional services. There is currently an increase in the number of crisis call lines with well-defined target populations, such as AIDS sufferers, sexual-abuse victims, and domestic-dispute victims.

There is a downside to these developments. The new services are used in an ever-increasing number of ways; yet few people understand how to use them effectively. One reason for this is that the new services tend to have rather vague and poorly defined frameworks. The services often overlap, and lack of coordination results in misuse or abuse. In some respects, these services are like band-aides covering a sore when more substantial intervention is needed. Often they cover up real need by adhering to coping strategies whose implicit aim is to achieve temporary well-being.

Nevertheless, these services have enormous potential and can, in some cases, serve as powerful and impactful alternatives to psychotherapy. What is needed are more models that, instead of opposing or ignoring current theories or using them in confusing ways, offer broad-banded encompassing frameworks. Such frameworks should have built into them principles of continuity across service arenas. In the true Maslow spirit, "full humanness" could be the context that embraces human crises as challenges rather than as problems.

TRANSPERSONAL EMERGENCE

As we have seen, the field of crisis intervention has primarily evolved through successive infusions of ideas drawn from a wide variety of traditional theories of therapy. Conspicuously absent from our current conceptualization are approaches to crisis intervention that address transpersonal possibilities such as self actualization, transformation or transcendence. This relatively new paradigm of psychology, sometimes referred to as the "fourth wave" in psychology, (Assagioli, 1965; Grof, 1988; Wilber et al., 1986), has not yet offered an operational model of crisis intervention. Nevertheless, it is this transpersonal movement that promises major breakthroughs for those who wish to produce more than temporary well-being through their crisis intervention work. Supporting this premise is the widely accepted viewpoint that the transpersonal movement has indeed largely evolved out of breakthrough experiences with crises. Ironically, it seems we all do our best work when our back is against the wall! Consequently we need look no further than our successes in crisis intervention to gain an awareness of the major contributory aspects of the transpersonal perspective.

A reflective review of some of our crisis successes might reveal a number of noteworthy emerging transpersonal principles. To begin with, the desired goal of change as an outcome of a crisis seems to happen naturally when turning points are reached in a crisis. Once a person in crisis lets go of their resistance to the way things are in the moment, many possibilities surface when otherwize there may appear to be none.

Even more provocative is the notion that the way out of a crisis is through it! What almost aways happens in a crisis is that we respond in a frustrated, anguished manner in search of ways to protect ourselves from any further loss and to avoid pain. We do so by ignoring, or at the very least, overlooking the possibility that there is anything to be gained from the crisis. Yet, more often than not we end up enduring long suffering rather than short suffering as a result of our ignorance. In other words, by avoiding and ignoring we actually experience more pain in the long run. This suggests we can easily become hopelessly addicted to suffering in search of the condition called "no pain".On the other hand, when the pain or even perceived pain is great enough, that is, when we are not willing to tolerate any more, our willingness to take action spontaneously generates breakthrough options. Those who are awake to this cycle of abuse we put up with recognize early on in the cycle, the wisdom of using or transforming one's crisis pain into a resource to be learned from.

Another principle suggests that despite the fragmentation and alienation that is experienced in a crisis there is a natural undercurrent force of integrity that surfaces in all of us. This quest for unity is often expressed in the reoccurrent desire to be at peace with oneself and others personally, interpersonally and sometimes spiritually. It seems this state episodically comes to the surface at various junctures of a crisis and becomes optimally manifested when reinforced by others.

Complementary to this principle is the notion that there is something in all of us that seeks freedom from suffering knowing that deep down we yearn to play, create and recreate. When we are open to listening to the fact we are prisoners to our own beliefs and attitudes and to the form things must take in our lives our intuition tells us freedom comes from letting go of our rigid attachment to form and content and our limiting beliefs.

Another transpersonal principle is revealed during a crisis when self observation is activated. Those who discover that a crisis actually generates a powerful opportunity to accelerate "working on oneself" benefit from uncovering increasing flexible ways to dissolve their crisis. Put another way, disciplined self observation during critical turning points or crises can also awaken us to alternative ways of being where suffering actually becomes an ally.

Yet another transpersonal principle potentially surfaces from a crises when a successful outcome unconditionally demonstrates that our competency is virtually limitless and that our potential is massive and remarkably underutilized.

Pioneering exploration by Fritz Perls in gestalt therapy (1968), Roberto Assagioli in psychosynthesis (1965), Stanislav Grof in altered states of consciousness (1988), Francis Vaughan (1979) in intuition and John Welwood (1979) in spirituality, to and name a few, have substantiated several of these transpersonal principles for inclusion within a crisis intervention model. To date, some bold and provocative crisis interveners have used several of these principles in their interventions, though this work has been inconspicuous in comparison with the work using ordinary systemic-based perspectives. As Marilyn Ferguson (1980) already pointed out, a silent yet profoundly important conspiracy is emerging as practitioners increasingly gravitate towards strategies grounded in transpersonal concepts. This conspiracy is receiving powerful intellectual support from a major paradigm shift in the arena of science. Notably, the fields of physics and biology are offering potentially converging or complementary principles that allow a transpersonal perspective to be cognitively understood and pragmatically practiced. For extensive and up-to-date accounts of the scientific aspects of transpersonal psychology, see Capra (1980), Ferguson (1980), and Wilber (1986).

EXERCISES - CHAPTER ONE

1. Write a paragraph that outlines what you think or know of a transpersonal approach to crisis intervention. Comment on what you need to know in order to assist you to make more effective use of this framework.

2. Identify in point form your beliefs about crisis intervention as they might limit assisting others or alternately how these beliefs might aide others in crisis regain a balance or state of homeostases.

3. List what you need to know at this point to develop your competency as a competent crisis intervener.

4. Start a crisis intervener competency journal and commit yourself to using it to record your experiences of unfolding competency in crisis situations.

SUGGESTED READINGS

1. For a more scholarly review of crisis theory, and particularly for a comparison of three primary theoretical perspectives, (behavioural, psychoanalytical and systems) of the family, refer to Umana, R.F., Cress, S.J. and McConville, M.T., **Crisis in the family**. New York: Gardner Press, 1980.

2. For a comparative overview of practical ways to implement a transpersonal approach to counselling and pscyhotherapy, refer to Hendricks, G. & Weinhold, B. **Transpersonal appraoches to counselling and psychotherapy**. Denver: Love Publishing Co., 1982.

NOTES

NOTES

CHAPTER TWO

A BEGINNING TEMPLATE

What we know about our world is often what someone else has trained us to think and believe about it. The task of growth is not to learn something else, but to erase the distorted knowledge we already have so we can see the world inside and outside afresh.

- Gay Henricks

The time is now ripe . . . [for] a "full spectrum model" of human growth and development.

- Ken Wilber

THE TRANSPERSONAL BASE

As already mentioned, the model I am proposing adopts an expansionistic, open-ended, or transpersonal viewpoint. Beyond our mechanistic conception of reality, beyond our preoccupation with time as a linear process, beyond our restricted view of cause and effect, there lies a sleeping giant. This giant in all of us, which might be what Carl Jung (1957) referred to as our "collective unconscious," knows no boundaries and operates from a sense of wholeness. Through cognitive operations, we limit this power within us, minimizing its capacity to produce results for us in our lives. Nevertheless the pathway towards our expansion is through our cognitive crises, our conditioning, and our developmental layers of self.

The way in which self-actualization and transcendence occur can potentially be conceptualized by use of Maslow's (1971) model of a hierarchy of needs. A condensed version of this hierarchy is depicted in Figure 1. The needs are like rungs on a ladder: One is no better than another, all are important, and all are interconnected. Transcendence, the state where we surrender into an expanded sense of self, grows out of self-actualization. Before these two higher needs can be met, our lower

---

needs must be satisfied to some degree. Given we meet some of our lower needs, we are then capable of connecting with these higher states at almost any time in our lives. As Charles Tart (1987) suggests, transcendence is "state specific." In other words, it is part of our natural, inbred inheritance; it exists within us in some form all of the time. To move towards transcendence requires that we continuously let go of our traumas, making our load in life lighter so that enlightenment can naturally occur.

Transpersonal, in the broadest, most definitive sense, means "through, to connect, to go beyond the personal." In Latin, the root meaning of **personal** is **persona** or **mask.** Psychologically speaking, our mask or set of masks, as the case may be, figuratively represent the form our personality takes. In other words, put together a number of masks, and you get a distinct,describable personality. The combination of **trans** with **personal** may then be interpreted as meaning "to go beyond our personality."

Certain transpersonal states of being go by the names of precognition, retrocognition, clairvoyance, intuitiveness, forecasting, out-of-body experiences, peak experiences, and so on. Essentially, the transpersonal is a state of being that goes beyond the skin boundary of our body.

According to Ken Wilber (1979), there can be many levels of identity available to the individual. Wilber proposes that these levels of identity thread together, forming a "spectrum or rainbow-like affair" of distinct observable realities. Figure 2 shows a modified version of his spectrum of identities, designed to depict this spectrum in a way that suggests that every form of identity emanates out of what he calls "unity consciousness." Thus unity consciousness is seen as the baseline of our existence. One might say that we originally come from unity consciousness, then we are conceived into the transpersonal realm, and then we slip out of this realm, in a developmental way, to the other levels of the identity spectrum.

Life as we know it, then, begins in the lower portion of the "egg" identity spectrum (Figure #2), somewhere within the transpersonal bands. Exactly where depends on the social and cultural factors of our existence and our own subjective opinions. As can be seen, the beginnings of the waving boundary line within the transpersonal bands is broken up suggesting the transpersonal realm is largely experienced as non dualistic reflecting our tenous capacity for holistic living or beingness. However, our initial transpersonal state quickly dissipates as we establish a skin boundary line between self and not-self during the first few years of our life. The first or primary boundary (the solid wavy line in the total organism/environment realm) gets drawn between the total organism and the environment. We draw this boundary as our organism becomes threatened by experiences of physical discomfort, injury, or abandonment. In effect, we learn to distinguish figure (our organism) from ground (the background around us). In other words, "What is inside my skin is me, and what is outside my skin is not me."

As we continue to evolve, we learn to make gradual distinctions within our organism as our embryonically developing mind "maps" out a fledging identity based on our significant experiences with life. Now the boundary lines are drawn within our skin rather than just at the edge of it (the ego/body realm). The progressive refinement of identity that goes on is in fact a narrowing process in which we develop an image of ourselves by externalizing what is not us and inwardly contracting

FIGURE 1

MASLOW MODIFIED

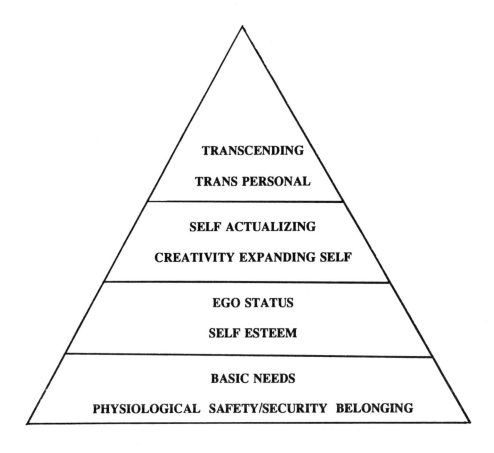

TRANSCENDING

TRANS PERSONAL

SELF ACTUALIZING

CREATIVITY EXPANDING SELF

EGO STATUS

SELF ESTEEM

BASIC NEEDS

PHYSIOLOGICAL SAFETY/SECURITY BELONGING

to a mind view of self. In this respect, the mind disconnects from the body such that the body begins to become something that we have and carry around as an appendage to the mind. Consequently, it is possible, through conditioning, to live more or less exclusively within the mind and at most to allow the body to be used for pleasure and ignored when it sends messages of pain. As Ken Wilber states, "even St. Francis referred to his body as 'poor brother ass' and most of us do indeed feel that we just sort of ride around on our bodies like we would on a donkey or an ass."

By the time our body fully matures, our self-identity normally does not embrace the organism in its entirety. Rather, we tend reluctantly to accept our bodies as a never-quite-adequate container for our ego.

Finally, as precipitated by life's unresolved traumas, we succomb to the realm of persona/shadow. This is where parts of the mind or ego generate an ability to disown other unwanted parts of the ego. For example, we may draw a boundary line between who we think we are (our self-image) and what we do not accept about ourselves, such as the tendency to be inconsiderate of others. In so doing, we disconnect our image of self from these unwanted aspects of self, even to the extent that we project them onto others and think that these traits actually emanate from others rather than ourselves.

As we construct these different boundary lines between our possible identities, we move up towards our "self created image prison." On the other hand, the boundary line can be re-drawn given that we consciously seek to re-capture our wholeness through efforts to dissolve the barriers which we have erected. As mentioned these barriers are frequently the result of unresolved crises in our lives.

To summarize, Figure 2 suggests our identity and personality is forged throughout life only to ultimately be revealed as an illusion given we awaken and recapture essence of wholeness. Unity consciousness, as Wilber sees it, is not something we rise to; rather it is something that we are grounded in. Although we contract out of it as life progresses, we can, with effort and sometimes by stumbling, move back toward it and towards our natural inheritance through consciousness-raising experiences. Some contemporary psycho-technologies, which aim at producing self-awareness and consequently self-integration, can create opportunities for us to connect with unity consciousness.

The spectrum-of-identity model also suggests that each level of identity includes all those above it. In this respect, the transpersonal levels may be viewed as including all other realms. The transpersonal levels also endeavor to expand upon the other realms (Wilber, 1979), and to link them to unity consciousness. The transpersonal actually seeks to co-exist with any other belief system, even though the bewildering array of psycho-technologies generated from the realms above it are often circumstantially conflictual with one another.

Fitting the psycho-technologies alongside the different identity spectrum realms is an attempt to clarify how they can optimally connect with the person in crisis at their identity crisis level. So, it could well be that from an orthodox Freudian point of view what is manifested in a crisis may be sex and aggression; from a behaviorists' point of view a search for reinforcement and an avoidance of punishment; and from the humanist point of view, the exploration of our own self-actualization potential. All, in orderly fashion, have a goodness of fit and can be relatively complimentary with one

FIGURE 2

IDENTITY SPECTRUM

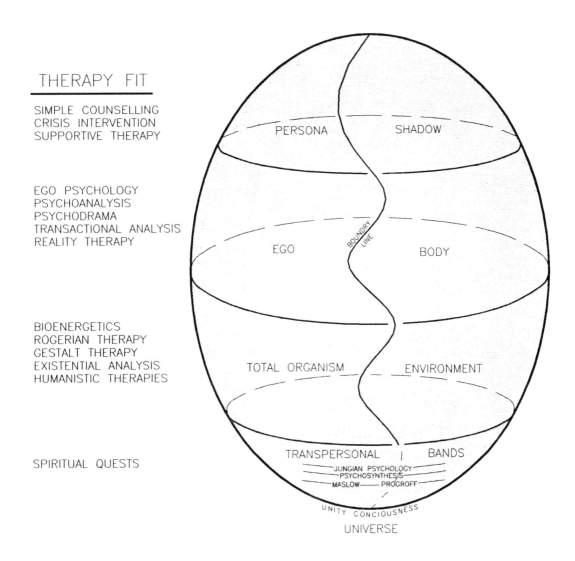

THERAPY FIT

SIMPLE COUNSELLING
CRISIS INTERVENTION
SUPPORTIVE THERAPY

EGO PSYCHOLOGY
PSYCHOANALYSIS
PSYCHODRAMA
TRANSACTIONAL ANALYSIS
REALITY THERAPY

BIOENERGETICS
ROGERIAN THERAPY
GESTALT THERAPY
EXISTENTIAL ANALYSIS
HUMANISTIC THERAPIES

SPIRITUAL QUESTS

PERSONA   SHADOW

EGO   BOUNDARY LINE   BODY

TOTAL ORGANISM   ENVIRONMENT

TRANSPERSONAL | BANDS
JUNGIAN PSYCHOLOGY
PSYCHOSYNTHESIS
MASLOW —— PROGROFF

UNITY CONCIOUSNESS
UNIVERSE

*   Adapted from Ken Wilber's Spectrum of Consciousness, (**No boundary**, Los Angeles: J.P. Tarcher, 1979).

another in the service of a crisis.

This is not to say that a particular theory cannot address and recognize all levels of identity. When a crisis intervener recognizes the optimum fit of theory with the level of identity, they can blend as appropriate their predominant theory with the most suitable therapeutic process. Thus, the boundary lines between our identity layers can be permeated by any persuasion resulting in breakthroughs to a higher level of wholeness.

For a more comprehensive overview of this spectrum and its therapeutic linkages please refer to Wilber's book **No Boundary**. This book has profound implications for the helping professions in the way it sheds light on the gaps in our continuum of care.

Drawing together our self actualization and transcendence needs within a spectrum of evolving identities creates a beginning contextual base having heuristic value for crisis intervention. It serves as a template for the development of a blueprint for the Beyond Content transpersonal crisis intervention model.

OUR TRANSPERSONAL CORE

Following from the identity spectrum model, it may be useful to think of ourselves in a more personalized way as having a number of different layers. Like an onion, these layers might generate out from a core as spheres of identity. Figure 3, in an approximating way, shows our core emotions to exist at the centre of our identity. The core emotions depict, in humanistic terms, our natural state which operate spontaneously as unbridled energy. The core represents our living and evolving essence. Emotion is simply created by motion. The core represents the space where all life energy resides and where our connection with unity consciousness begins. It is the space where creativity, competency and natural action exist. While we know it exists, we cannot really describe it. When we, in virgin manner, operate from this space, we intuitively know it is something that connects us transpersonally to those around us.

The next layer operates at the boundary between organism and environment. This layer emerges as our organism develops in response to our environment. For example, our body uses energy to maintain its integrity. It can do this by severely tensing the muscles depending on where it senses it needs protection from stress. Rigid and sustained constriction of the muscles create a barrier that interferes with the natural expression of the core energy. Acting like a wall, the muscles trap our natural expression and warp or distort the body in the process. Obviouslt then, one of the most effective ways to free ourselves from pent up emotions is to alter the physical state of the body. Clearly it is difficult to maintain a depressed state when you are made to laugh or when your body is highly activated. Once again, motion creates emotion.

The next layer develops when the mind and body split and the ego develops as a control centre that endeavors to survive the effects of the inability to tap into our core energy and the consequent body distortions (for example, headaches, hyperarousal, and psychosomatic illnesses). This mental layer develops as we mature and on the positive side, it serves to assist us in solving problems and navigating around danger. The down side of the mind is that it also distorts our ability to see things

FIGURE 3

LAYERS OF SELF

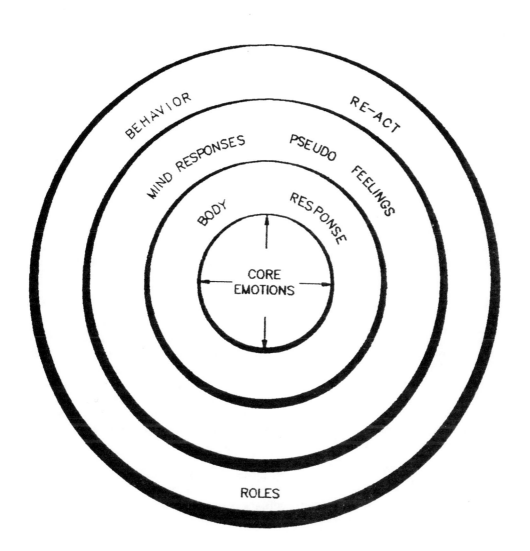

as they are, especially when we are disconnected from our core emotions. The mind calls upon our conditioned thinking, our built-up prejudices, our outdated beliefs, and our opinions and uses these to defend itself against owning our core emotions. The defense Insert Figure 3 often surfaces as pseudo feelings; for example, we will pretend to be angry when really, underneath, we manifest fearfulness. Or, to mask excitement, we portray a pseudo feeling of boredom or depression, because our mind has been conditioned to conceal our true emotions for fear of rejection. This fear is historically based and often not totally realistic in the current moment. Pseudo feelings take the form of guilt, depression, blame, shame, boredom, resentment, jealousy, frustration, and so on. In a distorted way, they mask as real emotions or body feelings and eventually justify themselves as being a necessary defense system.

The outside skin or layer is our observable personality or persona. It is the layer that is behaviorally evident as our act or role in the moment. When this layer develops, we no longer are consciously aware of our true nature and we "re-act" out of our past conditioning in both constructive and destructive ways. Once a well- established act is in place, we tend to avoid our problems, disown them as our shadow, and defend our need to do so. Chapter six on Sizing Up a Crisis, offers a more thorough explanation of more precisely how our acts or roles get developed from crises and how to detect them.

Taking a snapshot overview of our self, it can be seen at the core is a condition of oneness or natural integrity. As we move out, we become more and more fragmented and screened off from our natural core essence. To live "in life" transpersonally is to know we must continuously draw upon our core energy to cut through and dissolve the never-ending reinforcement of the layers of our conditioning.

THE MODEL AS CONTEXT

Consistent with the spectrum of identity, the Beyond Content Model draws from many theoretical arenas and is perhaps best described as meta-theoretical. In an effort to integrate theoretical principles from different perspectives into a holistic framework the Beyond Content Model deductively, as well as inductively, attempts to weave together a tapestry of what works. By no means does the model suggest that it is **the** pathway to ultimate truth. The search for truth allows the model to take on form so as to be of some practical value. The model is formed out of many workshops given on crisis intervention, pilot research projects, personal observation of crises, experiences running numerous crisis programmes, and my own transpersonal explorations.

The Beyond Content crisis intervention model is, in many ways, somewhat foreign to traditional ways of thinking. Firstly, it proposes that crisis, in its form or structure, takes its status from the way in which we view it. In other words, the observed pattern of a crisis is a reflection of patterns of one's own mind. Consequently, as mentioned earlier, it speaks to multiple viewpoints and offers many entry points from all crisis arenas. In this way, the model metaphorically operates "from the seat of the pants." We can all own it and put on it our own design or stamp of uniqueness.

Secondly, the "seat of the pants" model of crisis intervention understands a crisis as a dynamic inter-connected web of events. No one part is more fundamental than the other.

Thirdly, the crisis in this model cannot be broken down into fundamental entities or component parts. It comes from the viewpoint that humans, regardless of their stress, are less fragile than we think and are capable of harmonious and holistic development of all of their potentials. It attempts to encompass the full spectrum of human growth and development, and it endeavors to weave together different, even contradictory, viewpoints into a network which reflects the possibility of a mutually enriching synthesis. In theoretical terms, this model adheres to Jung's (1957) concept of "coincidence of opposites," in which explicit opposites are made into implicit allies.

Finally, this model, as alluded to in many ways already, represents a shift from the predominant crisis intervention paradigm of "coping" or "managing" to a more encompassing competency based paradigm. This refreshingly distinctive new way of thinking of crises, has been stimulated by the scientific, cultural and socio-psychological crises of our time. These crises are actually showing us the way to break through our long standing and engrained professional rigidity and "stuckness " with archiac problem focused intervention approaches. This transpersonal and humanistic perspective of crisis intervention offers a rough proto-typical control panel for connecting with the actual beneficial sources of energy existing within every crisis. The desired outcome to be achieved is a transformation of upsets into opportunities.

The way to understand this contextual model is to experience it. As a contextual model, it is meant to offer beginning levels of transpersonal intervention that step slightly beyond traditional thinking. Finally, it is meant to be dynamic, ever-evolving, and wide open for others to fine-tune or alter in accordance with their own self-actualization needs.

THE PRIMARY PURPOSE

It seems that most models for crisis intervention are problem-focused so that solving problems, helping others change for the better, and helping them out of their helplessness, are familiar goals for most crisis interveners. Generating a purpose out of these conditions becomes challenging, to say the least, and almost inevitably results in some statement suggesting that "coping" with life's dilemma's or "getting over" the crisis is the aim of intervention.

At the transpersonal end of the crisis spectrum, the intent is to go beyond ordinary imposed limits; to tap the often forbidden territory of universal spirituality or essence and to reach for the core of competency within those in crises. At the risk of getting semantical, this is done by primarily serving or assisting rather than helping others. To serve is to give without conditions, in ways that are actually experienced as a privilege by the intervener. Serving is a humbling experience where credit for serving is not a requirement. Serving with a flavour of support does not carve out results, it manifests them. Together, serving and assisting reflect the foundation in their aliveness, curiosity and natural state of abundance. In so doing, the primary purpose of this intervention model is to:

ASSIST and SERVE those in crisis to re-capture a state of balance by mobilizing their un-used potential for restoring their natural competency, self sufficiency, and a continously expanding sense of significance.

To use this model requires enormous courage on behalf of crisis interveners, as it tends to shake up the status quo. Tremendous pressure exists around us to minimize our potential (Ferguson, 1980; Peck, 1978), despite our true nature and buried intent to actually self-actualize this purpose statement. This definition is meant to be dynamic, as is the model. There are as many ways to view it as there are unique viewpoints.

THE CRISIS CONTEXT

A crisis can mean many things to many people. Therefore defining it becomes a real challenge. One of the first rational efforts to do so was made by Kaplan (1974), who defined a crisis as "upset of a steady state". This was a state where there seemed to be no immediate solution using the presently available problem solving skills. Such circumstances, he suggested, resulted in confusion and disorientation. This somewhat linear and temporal definition enjoys wide spread acknowledgement, especially in the fast-developing field of crisis intervention.

From a general literary viewpoint, **Webster's Dictionary** suggests that a crisis is a "turning point". In the interests of drawing from the many parts of the spectrum, it also is intriguing to discover that the Chinese word for crisis, wei-ji, involves the interplay of two concepts - danger and opportunity. Literally translated, the definition is approximated by the phrase "a crisis is an opportunity riding on a dangerous wind." Consistent with their dynamic view of life as a duality represented by the negative **Yin** and the positive **Yang**, the Chinese view a crisis as stimulus for transformation.

It is obvious from the literature that there have been many frustrating attempts by theoreticians to define crisis. Schulberg and Sheldon (1968) commented in their review of this literature that "one cannot help but be struck by the arbitrary, varying and even illusive qualities currently associated with the term..." "It ...remains for the most part diffident in definition, popular in usage and ambiguous in value." Nevertheless, despite the risks of forming either a too inclusive or too exclusive definition of a crisis, a synthesized or blended combination of the above definitions is posited:

CRISIS

AN OPPORTUNITY RIDING ON A DANGEROUS WIND . . . .

A Crisis is an upset (a danger) that produces many turning points (opportunities) for natural change or for a transformation of the crisis circumstances.

The transforming part of the definition suggests that while not all the damage from the danger of a crisis may be alterable, the way we view or hold the outcome may be. This definition of crisis,

---

contextually speaking, allows a crisis intervener to view human suffering as a fluctuating, ever changing pattern where opportunities for personal and inter-personal evolution continuously present themselves.

THE CONTEXTUAL PRINCIPLES

Stemming from the primary purpose and the above definition of crisis are a number of major contextual principles offered as a beginning map for this transpersonal model of crisis intervention. Though these principles serve individually as pathways, they are interconnected, and in many ways overlapping. The principles are as follows:

1.   ON CLIENT-DEFINED CRISIS
2.   ON COMPETENCY
3.   ON CRISIS AS OPPORTUNITY
4.   ON IMMEDIACY
5.   ON WHAT WORKS
6.   ON NEUTRALITY
7.   ON AUGMENTING
8.   ON BLENDING
9.   ON INCLUSIVENESS
10.   ON SELF ORGANIZING

This list is by no means exhaustive. Rather, in keeping with the model's expansionistic and transpersonal perspective, the principles at best only approximate the model. They are not intended to limit or put boundaries on the model, only entry points into it. As well, these principles can be expanded upon without loss of meaningfulness or increased in numbers in accordance with the model's evolving nature. To clarify their intent, each will be briefly commented upon.

1.   ON CLIENT-DEFINED CRISIS

This principle really speaks to the wisdom of allowing the person or persons experiencing the crisis, regardless of how serious the crisis is from our point of view, to have their point of view acknowledged. In this way, you acknowledge that for one person an event may be a significant crisis, whereas for another it may not. For example, being laid off from a job for one person may be viewed by one person as a catastrophe and by another as an opportunity to explore a new career long sought after, yet not pursued. Some clients may embellish a crisis, seemingly exaggerating it beyond proportions. It may well be clear to the crisis intervener that malingering or gross exaggeration suggests that a particular declared crisis is less than critical. Nevertheless, when the client defines the crisis, attention is paid in accordance with the client's underlying need rather than her declared need.

Allowing a person to have her crisis, to define it in her own way, offers her the opportunity, psychologically, to break away from her conditioning, repetitive, disabling behaviour and her "stuckness". The more the client recognizes that she is defining her own crisis and that her definition can alter as she becomes clearer about the nature of her need, then the greater the possibility that this client will use the crisis intervener as a valued resource at strategic turning points during the crisis

---

event. Consequently, the client more quickly experiences the crisis intervener as an ally rather than as a rescuer. In this respect, the crisis intervener goes along for the journey rather than directs the trip!

This is not to say that the crisis intervener would not actively respond to someone who was self-harming or in a life-threatening situation. Rather, acting to minimize any further loss, the crisis intervener would respond by actually using or capitalizing upon the client's resistance or "stuckness" as a resource for fostering stability and relief from the crisis. In other words, instead of primarily responding to the content of the crisis, the crisis intervener would take an active role in discovering ways to legitimize the crisis resistance. Then the crisis intervener would seek out ways to transform the resistance into a competency resource for dissolving the present trauma. This suggests that assessing and diagnosing the clinical or treatment need is secondary to the first and foremost need of reducing the risk level while preserving the client's integrity.

The transpersonal crisis intervener acknowledges the point of view of the person in crisis as a start point for intervention. While the client's definition may be perceived as off base, confusing or covertly concealing another issue, the challenge is to encourage the client to uncover her real need. This can be done by having the client examine her resistance or stuckness evident in the dialogue with the crisis intervener. Clearly, this does not mean that the crisis intervener avoid sharing the truth or allow herself to become sidetracked with secondary concerns. The crisis intervener simply recognizes that the quickest pathway to crisis dissolution is by focusing attention on the client's present state of being.

2.   **ON COMPETENCY**

All too often we nod our head when it is mentioned that a crisis intervener ought to accentuate strengths or competencies of an individual in crisis and use them as resources. Actually, what happens more often that not is that there is a tendency to gravitate or be drawn towards a problem focus, thereby resulting in only superficial attention to the strengths of the individual. What is needed is to go beyond just identifying strengths and to actively promote development of the strengths. To do this, the crisis intervener must stay focused on and committed to the individual's well being, not ill being.

Once the person's strengths are energized, the crisis intervener would encourage that they be mobilized and acted upon to reduce the crisis anguish. In a process sense, the crisis intervener would also do well to model these competencies. Such modelling could serve to **inspire** the individual to use her competencies to go beyond her crisis anguish.

A transpersonal crisis intervener becomes naturally intrigued with creative ways to re-contextualize or transform maladaptive or problem-labelled behaviour so that it represents strengths and competencies. Some examples of how problem labels may be brainstormed into competency labels are listed in Table 1.

Using these as examples of creating competency labels that fit the resistance of the moment, the crisis intervener can gain a perspective of the resistance that acknowledges the worth of the client at the same time that it legitimizes the crisis. Frequently this is all that is needed to connect with the primary source of crisis pain.

TABLE 1

PROBLEM LABELS TRANSFORMED

PROBLEM LABELS			**COMPETENCY LABELS**
- MANIPULATIVE	AS	-	SOCIAL SKILL
- UNRELIABLE	AS	-	FLEXIBILITY
- DOMINEERING	AS	-	LEADERSHIP
- HISTRIONIC	AS	-	CREATIVITY
- CALLOUSNESS	AS	-	PRAGMATISM
- SUSPICIOUS	AS	-	INSIGHT
- REACTIVE	AS	-	SENSITIVITY
- STUPIDITY	AS	-	PLAYFULNESS
- AGGRESSIVENESS	AS	-	CHALLENGING
- PATHETICNESS	AS	-	RE-CHARGING
- IMPULSIVENESS	AS	-	RISK-TAKING

3. ON CRISIS AS OPPORTUNITY

This principle previously alluded to as integral to the service purpose, is gaining in popularity, especially with those crisis interveners who are intrigued with humanistic or transpersonal possibilities. This underlying principle facilitates the intervention approaches being actualization based rather than getting sidelined into a rescuing mode of intervention. Taking the view that a crisis offers a turning point, a point at which new resources and potentials can be cultivated, allows the crisis intervener to create an atmosphere of assurance and competence. In this way, a breakthrough, rather than further breakdown, is actually achievable.

By virtue of the crisis being a temporary state of confusion, an upset of a steady state, the opportunity exists to search for new and renewed crisis dissolving possibilities that were previously not evident. The crisis is also a point where resistance to change naturally drops leaving room for change to occur. Using the remaining resistance as a source of change, the crisis intervener can the probe for illuminating possibilities. While the altruistic or idealistic flavour of this principle might seem suspect to the seasoned, perhaps overly conditioned crisis intervener, the elements of pragmatic value become realizable when all the principles are experienced as an interwoven blanket of care and intervention.

As the crisis intervener focuses on the opportunity aspect of a crisis, this focus automatically communicates encouragement that the crisis can be handled, that something can be done about it, and that much can be learned from the experience that sooner or later will be invaluable to the person in crisis. The intent here is not to offer false assurance that everything will work cut; instead, it is to recognize that a "breakthrough can follow a breakdown."

If one subscribes to the view that health is really a multi-dimensional phenomenon involving inter-dependent physical, psychological and social aspects, then freedom from suffering can come from many levels. This is to suggest that there are many pathways to pursue and that a crisis simply telegraphs or profiles some of those pathways. Consequently, a crisis can be an opportunity for the human being to engage the strengths of one or more dimensions of their healthy self to counteract their unhealthy dimensions. As Capra (1982) suggests, "The organism may also undergo a process of self-transformation and self-transcendence involving stages of crisis and transition, resulting in an entirely new state of balance." Consequently, growth and development can be natural outcroppings of a crisis, even to the extent that it leaves a person at a higher level of integrity than was enjoyed prior to the crisis.

4. ON IMMEDIACY

A person experiencing a crisis, however short-lived, has in a confused way reached a point where there appears to be no alternative courses of action or no apparent immediate relief from the crisis. Such a person tends to flounder and reach out in indiscriminate ways. The crisis intervener, able to respond to another's crisis, can make a significant contribution by creating a sense of responsiveness to the immediacy of need. Whether it be on the telephone or through direct contact, the crisis intervener acts in a way that acknowledges that the "here and now" state of circumstances is all that counts.

When a person in crisis experiences the crisis intervener as being fully "there" with them, there is a sense of immediacy of response to their difficulties. Experiencing this sense of being with the other, of having nothing between, tends to re-instill a feeling of significance and renewed sense of competency. Linking with the person in crisis by exuding a sense of urgency and immediacy draws her towards revealing and recognizing previously discounted competencies. These competencies can then be readily mobilized by the client as her confidence to act gets reinforced by an increased felt sense of significance. Thus, assisting and supporting in a crisis becomes present based and action-oriented, rather than historical and passive.

The flavour of responding is not time-bound. In other words, when a crisis intervener is with the person in crisis fully and completely, the sense of urgency around time seems to be suspended. A crisis interaction could last as short a time as five minutes or as long as a number of hours and still be perceived by the crisis intervener as not time-bound. Even scheduling frequent, but short intervention sessions can be perceived as characterized by a sense of immediacy. In a sequential, building-block manner, these sessions could significantly re-affirm the importance of the person's perceived crisis need. The crisis intervention work ought not be limited by the traditional restraints of time commonly represented by the limitations of the therapeutic hour: Crises are primarily circumstance and perception-determined.

5.   ON WHAT WORKS

Adopting a "what works" perspective reflects the transpersonal state of allowing explicit opposites to become implicit allies (Jung, 1960; Krishnamurti, 1980). This is to say that when the focus shifts away from getting caught up in either what is wrong or what needs to be right, both right and wrong can be seen as two sides of the same coin. The one really determines the other. Therefore, exploring them both; allowing them to coincide as integral to one another frees the crisis intervener so that many pathways can be travelled towards crisis resolution. When the attitude of "what works" prevails the crisis intervener can become curiosity driven rather than problem focused driven. This kind of an attitude is present when a crisis intervener's curiosity generates beginning intervention questions such as "what's good about this crisis?" or "What's not perfect about it yet?" or "What do I want to do to have to have the person in crisis to re-establish a balance in their life?" This state of being recognizes that a person in crisis is most often stuck in a view that their circumstances are either right or wrong. Holding onto a position that things are either right or wrong actually creates crises in the first place. While it may seem nearly impossible not to adopt either of these positions, a third position, inclusive of right or wrong yet outside of them, is where the real power to change the circumstances exists. Operating from this state is incredibly exhilarating, as it weaves together the right and wrong positions of others. Floating freely between position and opposition, the crisis intervener allows this condition to be a state of grace whereby her vision becomes correlative. This is to suggest they can perceive aspects of opposition as contributing in a converging way to produce what would work in the crisis circumstance. According to Carlos Castenadas, (1974), this is the path of the razors' edge - a balancing act on the thinnest and sharpest of lines.

6.   ON NEUTRALITY

Another primary twine of the contextual crisis intervention fabric is the often misunderstood principle of neutrality. As with the nature of all contextual principles, this one is also challenging to describe and clarify. Coming at it from what is **not** seems to have the most value. First of all, it is **not neutrality in action.** It does not mean the crisis intervener acts as an insignificant blob of mush, leaving everything as it is, letting demise occur. In the crisis moment and place, the crisis intervener responds so as to minimize error and to stabilize the crisis as quickly as possible. Guided by the generally accepted notion that short suffering is preferable to long suffering, the crisis intervener's content and form responses are far from neutral. The context of response is nonetheless qualitatively neutral.

Psychological neutrality is different from time and place neutrality. The latter is quite simply not possible in day-to-day reality. Psychological neutrality is a perspective that endeavours not to change those in crises, regardless of how outrageous their behaviour might seem. Minimize error, yes-change, no. The neutrality sought here, while it is grounded in the natural wish for a sense of mutual connectedness, is not much interested in the problem per se, only in the way the problem manifests itself with the person in crisis. Psychological neutrality takes no sides, and, for this reason, it is not weighed down by the obligation to assess who is right and who is wrong, what is good and what is bad. What works, rather than what is right or wrong, is the guiding beacon for this psychologically tuned neutral crisis intervener. Remarkably, this perspective can make the work of a crisis intervener relatively easy and quite straightforward.

Of course, this manner of being begs the question, "How do you do this in the moment of chaos?" "How do you let things fall apart without jumping in and saving those who are obviously blinded by their own state of survival?" Obviously, special training is essential if this principle is to be experienced as having value. Exercises are offered in Chapter Four on self-preparation to assist the crisis intervener sustain a psychologically neutral stance.

In conclusion, neutrality is that space where one's true value to one another begins to be known. It is the space where creative intervention flourishes. In this space, the crisis intervener can perceive a multitude of possible ways to go beyond the rigidity of roles, egos and boundaries erected between self and others. To create a context of neutrality requires the crisis intervener trust her natural state of integrity, acknowledge her competency with confidence, and practice observation of others (as well as herself) without judgement. Most importantly, the continuous monitoring of her own self-awareness in the process of assisting others in crisis enables the crisis intervener to stay tuned into the context requirements of psychological neutrality.

7.   AUGMENTING

This principle advocates that the crisis intervener serve more or less as an unexpected **resource** to those in crisis rather than being perceived as a primary **source** of resolution. **Augmenting** means to add on, primarily by acting as a catalyst that stimulates those in crisis activate their own resources in order to produce a more stable state. To augment with neutrality leaves the crisis intervener uncontaminated and primed to be used as a catalyst over and over again.

Augmenting is often experienced by the crisis intervener as a privilege. For a brief and impactful period the crisis intervener can show in the lives of those who are anguished and pain stricken without a responsibility to change anything. It becomes a unique and extremely challenging opportunity to be alongside others in their troubled times and to discover ways to contribute without giving advice and taking responsibility for needed change. Augmenting happens naturally, spontaneously and usually without effort. Quite often it means nothing more than to be in attendance fully awake. Countless times crisis interveners who have simply allowed themselves to do nothing other than listen have been startled by proclamation of acknowledgement by those they were assisting.

Augmenting is a simple process, often all it requires is to allow the circumstances of the crisis to dictate what action is required by the crisis intervener. It reflects a mature attitude of just being there in the moment, willing to assist yet seemingly unattached to having to be responsible for the outcome of the crisis.

8. ON BLENDING

This principle is closely connected to the principle of augmenting. Blending suggests that the crisis intervener offer a profile no more important than the most significant resource available to the individual in crisis. In a natural and unobtrusive way, the crisis intervener blends in with the individual as well as with the environmental resources uncovered through the intervention process. By so doing, the crisis intervener serves to stimulate the person in crisis to weave together the more sustaining environmental resources into a resilient fabric that supports her to regain a state of self-sufficiency. The crisis intervener who disappears as a personality and surfaces as a behind the scene energizer can then exit leaving no lingering need for dependence on outside competency.

Blending is a humbling enriching process recognizes a holistic self determined framework of competency need to be self determined. Those in crisis ultimately need to own the changes they make and to experience being in charge of the resources they call upon to assist them regain their competency.

9. ON INCLUSIVENESS

As blending recognizes the availability of other resources to a person in crisis, inclusivity addresses the value of activating these resources. The crisis intervener should become highly sensitized to the background of a crisis as well as with the crisis foreground. Ever mindful (as the Polish semanticist Korzybzi (1966) suggests) that the "map is not the territory," the crisis intervener should seek to uncover and include as many resources within the crisis territory as possible. While doing so the crisis intervener would be careful not to get stuck or side tracked with either the figure or ground. Pragmatically this means to include and make valuable such resources as neighbours, relatives (distant or otherwise), valued material objectives, best friends, religious affiliations, or other group connections. The list can go on and on.

One's environment is indeed incredibility rich with resources however, latent of covered up they may be. This principle is easily overlooked when the crisis intervener becomes trapped in the melodrama of the crisis foreground. Inclusiveness requires a conscious shift in mind set. When enacted this principle offers yet another interconnecting thread linking the proceeding light crisis principles into powerful crisis intervention fabric.

10.   ON SELF-ORGANIZING

This principle of self-organizing recognizes the inherent capacity of the human organism to achieve homeostasis or balance (Jantsch, 1980). In obvious ways, we continuously and automatically self-regulate as we naturally draw resources from our surroundings. Simultaneously a process of dissipation or gradual erosion of our form also occurs.

Practically speaking, the crisis intervener should recognize that the threshold of falling apart is a turning point for self-organizing to begin to occur. The form that self-organization takes largely depends upon new awarenesses instilled at these turning points. The crisis intervener who is mindful of self-organizing tendencies can capitalize on the catalytic potential of the turning-point junctures which often occur many times during a crisis. Using patience and timely intervention to align herself with the self-organizing energy in both its dissipative and growth forms the crisis intervener stays in tune with nature's way. In some ways, the crisis intervener is like the surfer, who patiently organizes around each crest of a crisis wave. Then, acting at the right moment the challenge is to transform the turbulence of the wave into harmonic motion.

From another viewpoint when the principle of self-organizing is allowed to naturally occur the crisis intervener quickly becomes redundant. The crisis intervener who is aware enough to recognize the natural healing rhythms will know when to start withdrawing before they unwittingly dampen or inhibit self organization from happening.

Some waves can be ridden fully, some for a moment, others not at all. In other words, when the turbulence passes the crisis intervener would be wise to allow self-organization to chart its own course.

EXERCISES - CHAPTER TWO

1.   Which core emotions do you express the most, least?

2.   Whatever core emotion you restrict or inhibit (fear, anger, joy, sadness, excitement) the most, how does it effect:

        a)   your body as it displays pain or pleasure;

        b)   your mind as it attempts to avoid pain and seek pleasure;

        c)   the development of pseudo feelings such as resentment, boredom, depression, apathy and so on;

        d)   your behaviour as an act or re-action.

3.   Take a wallet sized card and type out or print in bold block letters the ten crisis intervention principles. Use this card as a quick and ready conditioning cue card that you can refer to at your wallet open to viewing as you would keep a picture visible for repeated viewing.

4.   Identify five problem labels you would recognize as characteristic of yourself and transform them into competencies.

5.   Reflect back on three major crises in your life and identify what opportunities they produced for you that have impacted on your life in powerful opportunistic or growthful ways.

6.   Identify two occasions when you didn't do anything seemingly of value yet those you were assisting in crisis claimed to have benefited from your assistance. Comment on whether some of the crisis intervention principles such as Self Organization or Psychological Neutrality were prominant in producing the results experienced.

SUGGESTED READINGS

1. Crisis interveners and mental health workers seeking alternative transformational models to effect physical and emotional healing are encouraged to review the edited book by Stanislav Grof and Christina Grof entitled **Spiritual emergency: when personal transformation becomes a crisis,** (Los Angeles: J.P. Tarcher, Inc., 1989). This compilation of ground-breaking articles written by leading edge psychologists, psychiatrists and spiritual leaders reveals pathways through the maze of spiritual materialism and social, as well as cultural neuroticism.

2. As already mentioned in this chapter, Ken Wilber's, **No boundary**, is a must for those looking for new, easy to grasp framework that explains in simplified terms how different philosophical intervention models address various levels of human suffering. Wilber guides the reader step-by-step through a composite overview map of human consciousness, offering specific exercises designed to clarify the nature and practice of these different therapeutic intervention models.

3. For those managerially-minded or willing to extrapolate ideas from fields other than mental health arenas, Tom Peters' book, **Thriving on chaos**, (New York: Harper and Row, 1987), is incredibly provocative. This straight forward handbook powerfully and persuasively introduces up-beat crisis mastery approaches for those who seek to turn business upset into opportunities.

NOTES

NOTES

CHAPTER THREE

FROM SOURCE TO SORCERY

In the end, we can never be given knowledge by others: we can only be stimulated. We must develop our own knowledge.

- Charles Tart

THE DYNAMICS OF COMPETENCY

Competency by its very nature is quite elusive. For the ego-driven self it is indeed an unreachable goal. Your ego-mind is your best friend but it is also your worst enemy. Not only because it has vested interest in limiting what you believe you can do but also because it has a way of selling you short. Crisis interveners in particular, continuously wonder whether what they are doing is acceptable. Sometimes they may even feel as if the "blind are leading the blind." The irony is that the more one searches outside of oneself, the more elusive this need called competence becomes. Even though many crisis interveners "intuitively" know that competence is subjectively determined, their conditioning has them operate as if competence had to be "some thing", a skill or an ability that they ought to strive to master. Most, if not all of us, can refine a skill or an ability, yet we still labour under the illusion that our success has to be measured against others as well as against our own ego-driven, never-to-be-satisfied, self-imposed yard stick of competency.

Webster's New World Dictionary says that "to be competent is to be capable, sufficient, adequate." The Latin root, "competere" means to "strive or seek together for." Combining these two interpretations, competency could potentially mean "being sufficient and capable of striving for harmony and balance with your environment and your mind as well as your body."

In reviewing various descriptions of competence, Maslow (1962) views competency as a reflection of our current self-actualizing state. On the other hand, Satir (1988), suggests that certain learnings are universally necessary at various junctures in our lives and that these learnings constitute personal competency. She identifies these learnings as experiences with:

* Self Differentiation
* Relationships
* Self-Esteem
* Power of Productivity
* A Loving Way of Being

In developing the Beyond Content perspective on competence, the descriptions by Maslow and Satir, combined with many experiential insights and learnings, have contributed to produce a somewhat blended conceptual framework for competence. This particular framework has four primary competency components which are as follows:

1. **INTEGRITY**
2. **MISSION STATEMENT**
3. **CREATIVE INTENTION**
4. **SELF-MASTERY**

As energy forces these components can coalesce or interconnect producing a powerful platform from which a crisis intervener's competence can be actualized and experienced. An attempt will now be made to outline the nature of each of these forces and how they can be interwoven.

1. **INTEGRITY**

The first and perhaps primary force of competence is **Integrity**. Integrity simply means wholeness or completeness. Integrity is embedded within us all as a true underlying desire. It struggles to manifest itself through our search for genuineness, despite our tendency to be recognized as if we need to be more than what we are. Operating with Integrity is underscored in Shakespeare's Hamlet when Polonius says "This above all: to thine own self be true, and it must follow, as the night the day, thou canst not be false to any man." Figure 4 attempts to depict the spiralling nature of integrity when it arises out of our core state of naturalness. Beginning with the state of natural integrity we can evolve to higher states of integrity when we commit ourselves to such a journey. This type of journey beyond the content of our lives is rarely travelled by very many, as it requires an enormous effort and commitment to want to evolve beyond our perceived limits. These evolving or higher states exist in a condition of grace; and, while they are rare, they are actually achievable by everyone.

Our primary or natural state of integrity almost invariably becomes blanketed by the socially reinforced roles we adopt in our lives. Conditioned to avoid failure or loss in life our ego driven roles seek to insulate us from truly mastering our failures and learning from our losses. Nevertheless, our natural state of integrity forms the bedrock of our existence and, like a dormant volcano, is always available to us.. This core force within us all, is recognizable as our inherent desire to be real and to genuinely act out our various roles in life without pretence. Being a doctor, psychologist, social worker, crisis intervener or any other human service professional is clearly understood as adjunctive or secondary to who we really are. The natural state recognizes that life is just the way it appears to be. There is an active acceptance of others just the way they are as well as an enthusiasm for making connection based on the perception that others are mysteriously interesting. You know when you are in a state of natural integrity, when you spontaneously promote and advocate for yourself as well as for others. You easily tune in to the primary frequencies that form the basis for a harmonious existence with others and your environment. Any boundaries between you and others tend to melt, or disappear as you connect in empathy, caring, and appreciation for others. Jean Houston (1982) refers to this experience as having "leaky boundaries "where we naturally resonate with one another."

To move towards extraordinary levels of integrity requires a willingness to "wake up" from our consensus trance (Tart, 1987) and give up your preoccupation with modest achievements. It requires that the crisis intervener jump into the void of the unknown, to awaken the giant within, knowing that there is more than enough of you to go around. This state which goes beyond our primary narcissism is fuelled by the notion that sufficiency and indeed abundance rather than impoverishment and scarcity actually exist. It is the state where we **manifest** ourselves through a project or mission that encompasses others and our environment. This state is uncommon since it requires extraordinary effort to stay on track with the bigger purpose and not to become sidetracked with one's internal pseudo-survival needs. In this context we **can** actualize our competence.

On yet another level altogether, integrity at its zenith recognizes the immense responsibility we all have for life - every moment of it. This is the condition Smothermon (1982) and many others refer to as empowerment.

The truly empowering intervener is not wed to any particular outcome and seems to achieve results just by being there. Their humility abounds as they readily exude a desire to share whatever power they haves with others. Ironically, their "power of being" grows the more they give of themselves to others. As this happens, so does their sense of responsibility and compassion.

The empowering intervener, through persistent self-exploration, recognizes their own impurities, their own desires, their own clingings. As well, mindful of one's shadow or one's unconscious strivings which inhibit wholeness, they keep a constant vigilance for signs, especially for those indicating that clients or even they themselves are taking the advice offered too seriously. They seek liberation for themselves as well as for others. They support **everyone** winning and attaining freedom from suffering. In so doing, they foster a "culture of care" in every crisis situation that is unique in its opportunistic flavour.

Above all, the empowering intervener communicates to the client that who they are, regardless of the circumstances is acceptable to them. The client does not have to be better than she is or different than what she is at this time. In fact, while the circumstances under which she exists or her behaviour may be less than perfect, she as a person, in a very unique way, is still perceived as competent. This felt sense of being significant or competent is both intuitively and or unconsciously experienced in powerful enticing ways by the client. Empowering integrity manifested by the crisis intervener allow them to align in almost magical ways with the client's hidden or partially buried

FIGURE 4

TRANSPERSONAL INTEGRITY STATES

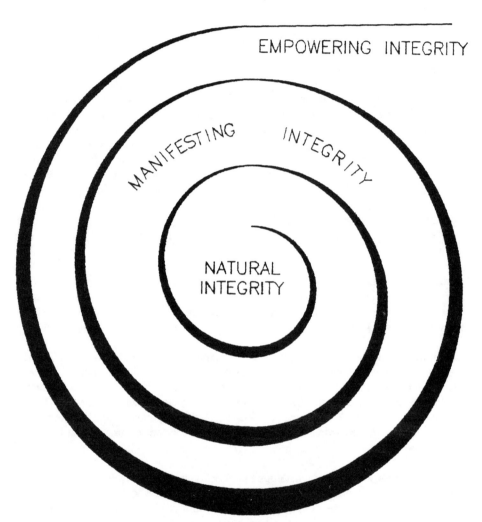

EMPOWERING INTEGRITY

MANIFESTING INTEGRITY

NATURAL INTEGRITY

THE TRANSPERSONAL REALM

genuine intent to have her life make a difference - to discover in some way, how to actualize her worth in the world. The empowering state is challenging, quite exhilarating and appealing. Others in crises are instinctively drawn to the empowering crisis intervener.

2. MISSION STATEMENT

It is wonderful to dream great dreams, as many crisis interveners do, having become clear and having worth granted to whatever it is that they do. Yet in this upside down era of uncertainty and unpredictability realizing one's dreams requires a willingness to act with a ferocious commitment to using the power in chaos to formulate a battle plan. Having a battle plan or mission with clear goals attached is a fundamental key to life long success. While most people have goals they tend not to be driven by a well thought out resilient mission statement. Quite often these goals tend to be impotent and even conflictual with one another. For example, some have goals related to helping others that suggest that getting others to "cope" with their upsets is the best they can achieve. Actually they want to achieve more with the person in crisis but they are unclear and overly cautious fearing failure if they step out into the unknown without some guiding purpose.

It has been my experience that less than ten percent of us are clear about **why** we do what we do. Even fewer know exactly **how** to go about attaining goals that reflect an underlying mission. Although no simple explanation exists for why writing down a mission statement is power generating, this act of focusing seems to trigger off our creative juices. We seemingly, in mysterious ways, both consciously and unconsciously become driven towards our desired outcomes when we take the effort to record and continously refine our mission and goals. Somehow a well worked out mission statement embedded into our daily life generates an expanding sense of confidence. This process stimulates our natural competencies to take each upset that comes along as "grist for the mill" and compells us to **act** on our desired goals. When we diligently and persistently generate awareness of our mission, we produce what Max Planck, a Nobel Laureate in Physics, called "a quantum tunnelling effect." This effect is akin to the brain cells making a blueprint supporting the mind to automatically follow an imprinted plan of action. In this way new thoughts tend to associate with this blueprint, synchronizing into patterns rather than in fragments, conditioning our mind to take action. Having an energized mission statement can generate a laser-like channel for one's integrity to operate.

Linking Integrity with Mission Statement

In our natural state of integrity, which is the state we start out with in life, boundaries between us and others are virtually non-existent. We easily commune with others, instinctively knowing we are somehow related in some metaphysical way. When the essence of "I AND THOU" (Martin Buber, 1970) is experienced between ourselves and others, it is easy to unfold a purpose or mission statement that promotes you, the crisis intervener, in relationship with others. Your mission naturally is to share yourself, your experiences, your insights and your desires to promote harmony within and between others.

If, per chance, we take up the challenge to go beyond ourselves and desire to promote wellness and self-sufficiency within a community context, our mission statement or purpose can become one of empowerment of others. In the rarefied air of empowerment, our integrity gets a chance to shift

---

towards considering missions in life that are more universal, and that leave no one out. The mission might begin by encouraging others to link up with your actualizing state of integrity and thereby stimulate recognition of one's own competency possibilities. In this respect, you might actively, tirelessly, and with unfettered enthusiasm, give to others the power of your competence. To empower others with a mission is to connect with their extraordinary capabilities. When this happens, it is experienced as a profound privilege.

Figure 5 attempts to reflect how a mission statement or a purpose can unfold a spectrum of competency levels, all inter-linked and emanating from one's holistic or core personal competency. It can be seen that this spectrum also aligns with the spectrum of identities outlined in Chapter Two, Figure 2. A mission statement is therefore meant to accentuate every layer of personal competency and to be congruent with one's continuous search for a meaningful purpose in life. For example, you might wish to predominantly aspire to a healthy mind-and-body focus in your intervention by encouraging those in crisis to achieve a more balanced physical and mental state of being. Your purpose would then likely lead you to model physical and mental well-being and to focus upon exercises and interventions that are both physical and mental. Therapy, breath control exercises, meditation, hypnosis, and other physical experiences are some ways that have been developed to address mind-body competency.

Developing a Mission Statement

Crisis interveners not only want to be clear about the purpose of their work, they are also driven by a desire to find meaning in what they are doing as they are doing it This effort to go beyond the more mundane circumstances of a crisis is fueled by a desire to generate an action-oriented purpose larger than one's self. Consciously, they know that, as Nietzsche (1952) suggests, he who has a **why** to live for (or clear understanding of their purpose) can bear almost any **how**.

In clarifying their mission statement, competent crisis interveners intuitively know that there is no all-encompassing authority in the field of crisis intervention. In fact, no authority or system has ever demonstrated universal workability. They know, too, that if they are to ensure against manipulating their clients and against having their clients manipulate them, clarity of purpose is essential. The old adage "a man who stands for nothing falls for everything" may well be the outcome for those who act without a mission statement.

So, they generally begin by outlining to themselves a mission statement as it exists at a given moment. Knowing that evolution of their awareness is continually taking place, they review their statement often throughout any given year. As they do so, they may ask themselves the following questions:
    Is this purpose or mission workable in my environment, or is this idealistic?
    Is it broad enough to include everything I do?
    Is it clear enough to be explained and understood by clients and colleagues?
    Is it simple, and can others support it?
    How is it connected to my current state of integrity?
When the answer to any of these questions is "no" or is unclear, they re-focus until the answer fits their current stance as a crisis intervener like a glove.

FIGURE 5

MISSION STATEMENT
THE FORCE OF PURPOSE

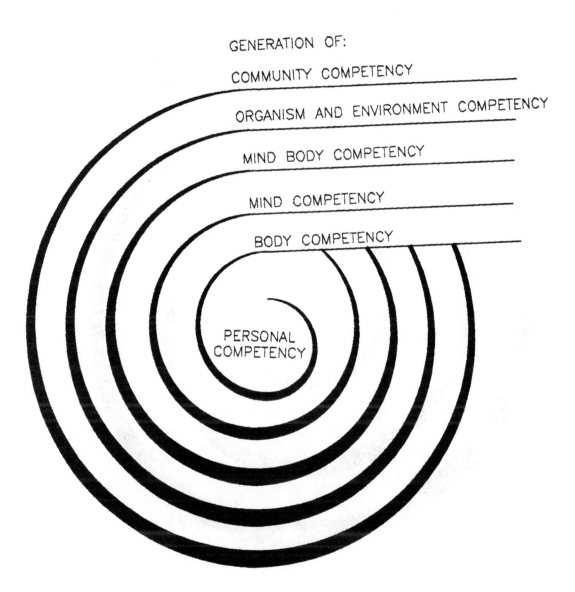

GENERATION OF:

COMMUNITY COMPETENCY

ORGANISM AND ENVIRONMENT COMPETENCY

MIND BODY COMPETENCY

MIND COMPETENCY

BODY COMPETENCY

PERSONAL
COMPETENCY

FIGURE 6

CREATIVE INTENTION

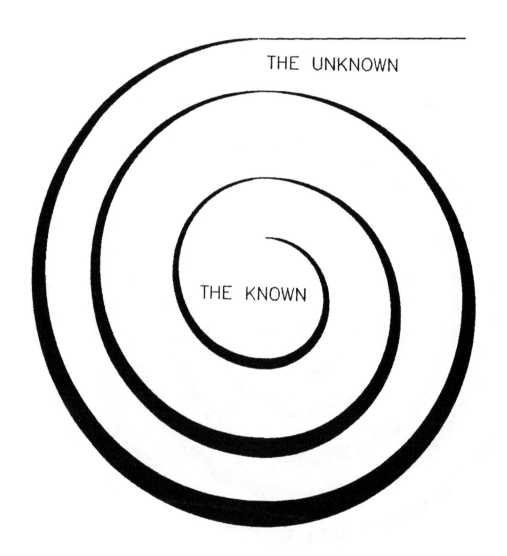

THE UNKNOWN

THE KNOWN

3.   CREATIVE INTENTION

So, what on earth is creativity much less creative intention?   Countless explorers have attempted to capture the meaning of creativity only to find it illusive. Volumes of books abound on this subject as many seek to master an understanding of the creative process.   Nonetheless, paradoxically the more we attempt to find, teach, or master creativity the more it seems to become intangible. Not to be deterred by this challenge the combination of creativity and intention as an unlikely dual concept seeks to boldly reveal and make use of the true nature of this creativity paradox. It does so by recognizing the utility of this paradox as a "coincidence of opposites" with the power to shed light on how one might manifest creativity.   Therefore, the concept of Creative Intention suggests that both "thought-less" spontaneity and "thought-full" willingness can actually collaborate in meaningful ways. Put in another way, Creative Intention seeks to tap into the well of Infinite Intelligence by combining the spontaneity of imagination, and intuition, with goal directed, logical thinking. This concept reflects the power that can be manifested when both sides of the brain become activated at the same time.

On a practical level, as the concept might suggest, Creative Intention does not occur voluntarily. For Creative Intention to operate at will it needs to be backed up by a vision or a mission about what one wants to achieve in their work. Without a vision and a plan to achieve this vision creativity happens haphazardly and in dissonant ways. On the other hand, the state of creative dissonance, in contrast to Creative Intention, happens voluntarily and it only offers splinters of creative possibilities that seldom produce sought after breakthrough achievements. It could be said this state flourishes without any effort whereas Creative Intention requires diligent and persistent effort. Moreover, Creative Intention is driven by a focused dissatisfaction with the way things are (therefore the need for a mission).   On the other hand, creative dissonance **tolerates** dissatisfaction and a perceived **uncontrollable** condition of creativity. This more common state of creative dissonance germinates from the individual's pre-disposition towards "being in charge" of what they are doing before they can create. In contrast, Creative Intention germinates from a pre-disposition of "not having to know" what to do when engaged in creative acts. The state of creative dissonance at best allows the crisis intervener to stumble forward. The ear markings of this state are often expressed in limited beliefs such as:

*   To be spontaneous is to be frivolous
*   Creativity cannot be mastered - it happens by choice
*   Creativity is a matter of luck
*   It's more important to be practical than anything else.

These and many other limiting beliefs run rampant in our culture, minimizing the possibility of creative intention being cultivated as a power source of achievement. Therefore, the challenge for the transpersonally minded is to diligently transmute negative or restricting beliefs into expanding beliefs. For example, such transmutations might occur as:

*   Play is work and work is play
*   Every upset produces an opportunity
*   The more mistakes the bigger the success

* What works is what counts
* When in doubt just go for it
* There is always a way to make a difference
* Everyone counts even when they don't want to.

Consciously conditioning one's thinking with these expanding beliefs sets the stage for creative intention to operate. It is through daily practice of attempting to inculcate expanding beliefs that crises become turning points. These turning point possibilities result in creative breakthroughs when driven by intention or desire to actualize one's vision or mission.

Countless examples exist of inventors, artist scientists and even those in the helping professions who were driven by a tenacious intent to achieve something called a vision. Often it is only when they reach a turning point of exhaustion before a breakthrough occurs. It is this very persistence that **incubates** ideas in the brain and it is the willingness to momentarily let go of trying that brings alive the intuitive and creative capacity of the brain. This turning point state is similar to the state one often experiences in a crisis. To practice harnessing the power of creativity and intention so that you can actively and wilfully create results in your work some steps are suggested. These steps are:

1. Armed with a clear mission or vision of the outcome you seek in a crisis event that adds value to those in chaos, consciously activate a mind set that you can create a significant outcome.

2. Free your mind from internal chatter and relax your body by focusing on the image of the outcome you seek from any particular crisis event.

3. Allow this image to unfold in your mind's eye as if it had already been achieved.

4. As you continue this process allow your right brain to guide your left brain suggesting that images of opportunities will and can surface at any given moment as you observe the space between your thoughts.

5. Now engage your left brain and evaluate what creative possibilities your minds eye has put together with your imagination.

6. Put together a mental plan of action around what you can do in this particular crisis situation. Allow this plan to unfold as quickly as possible and check it out with your right brain's sense of intuitive comfort with this plan.

7. Allow both your right and left brain to align by letting your emotional states release ideas that seem to pop out between your thoughts.

8. Finally, it is absolutely essential that you do not leave a plan that has developed in this creative process without taking some immediate action. Be willingly courageous and habitual in your practice of this process.

This process of creative intention can take as little as a few minutes or it can go on for forty minutes or more depending on your state of relaxation. Therefore, it can be entertained both within a crisis situation or even at a time chosen for reflection and review of a post trauma situation. Those wanting to practice different ways of working on this right and left brain process will find Jean Houston's (1982) book, **The Possible Human**, an excellent resource offering many stimulating and quite provocative exercises.

In summary, assuming a "not knowing stance" is the hallmark sign of those who demonstrate creative intention. It is significant to note that Virginia Satir (1988) acknowledges this condition of being challenged by and not rendered helpless by the unknown as a pre-requisite for competency in crisis intervention. Creative intention is the power source that allows the crisis intervener to go beyond acceptance of "pat" answers or providing solutions based upon similar experiences from other crisis situations. It is the dynamic source of competency that generates the necessary enthusiasm for the crisis intervener to discover uncharted pathways through the realms of human chaos.

Integrity, Mission and Creative Intention

When coupled with a natural state of integrity and a corresponding mission statement, creative intention surfaces in the form of adventurous curiosity. The crisis intervener, becomes intrigued with the nature of relationships as a compassionate witness of the crisis event rather than as a co-sufferer. In both compassionate and passionate ways, the crisis intervener creatively learns to melt the boundaries that distance people from one another. Connecting with those in crisis armed with creative intention a state of natural integrity and a driving purpose tends to stimulate them to exercise their own competence. The combination of these power driving forces, like a powerful river, allows the crisis intervener to effortlessly flow with those in crisis and to simultaneously stimulate their desire to take action and gain power out of the chaos.

4. SELF MASTERY

Self-Mastery is the fourth force of competence and it is predominantly driven by an inner-directed willingness to be **responsible** for one's actions. Self-Mastery is the power state that starts to flow when you awaken to the realization that it is up to you to demand that life, humanity or circumstances give you what you what, and that you are totally responsible for what you get. As well as the ability to respond, self-mastery is further manifested by actions of **accountability, commitment** and **discipline**. When these four ingredients are combined together they generate an empowering state of self-mastery as depicted in Figure 7. More specifically accountability in self-mastery simply means the ability to be counted on, to follow through with one's declared responsibility. It means to do what you said you were going to do, to be on time, to follow through with some action or to produce what you committed yourself to produce. This requires discipline, which is really quite simply the willingness to focus your energy. As Scott Peck (1978) suggests in his book **The Road Less Travelled**, discipline is the basic tool that we need to solve life's problems rather than avoid them. In a definitive sense, it means to learn new ways; and to do so is to experience a transformation of one's conditioning. Finally, the willingness to learn or to discipline oneself is actualized by a commitment to follow through with some action. This completes the cycle as commitment regenerates responsibility and all interconnectively reflect self-mastery.

Integrity, Purpose, Creative Intention and Self Mastery

Tying self-mastery in with the other three forces offers the crisis intervener a powerful framework to reinforce staying "on track" and to produce significant results. It generates a condition of being able to serve others in clear, unimpeded, and non-sacrificial ways.

Like a vortex (Figure 8), these combined forces can draw out of us our natural competencies and, at the same irresistibly as an inspirational model, draw others towards uncovering their own competencies. Actually these forces stimulate one's **spirit** or **essence** forcing others to evaluate their competencies in the light of yours. They have the synergistic potential of causing a breakthrough in our ego-bound conditioning leading to self-actualizing experiences states of being crisis interveners. At higher levels of integrity, the combined forces can enable the crisis intervener to proactively forecast future possibilities and to produce results that are at times magical.

ACTUALIZING CRISIS INTERVENER COMPETENCE

Moving now with a clearer sense of the energy forces of competence and what they can be for the crisis intervener, it's appropriate to outline a pathway these forces can travel in actualizing or making real our competence. Numerous practical approaches exist in prescriptive form pointing the way (Rogers, 1974, Satir, 1987, Truax and Carkhuff, 1976, Houston, 1982). Extracting from some of them and synthesizing what I view to be essential characteristics, I now offer this pathway in the form of an acronym. First, though, it's important to note that the mapping I offer is far from isomorphic with the territory. At best, it offers a simulated and simple-minded roadmap for travelling within the complex and intricate arena of human crises.

Clearly, most crisis intervention training formulas, when applied prescriptively or methodically, diminish our brilliance and restrict our vision. So, having been thus cautioned, please examine, explore, and use it as an acronym that, from time to time, guides you. Also this formula can be enriched in its value when accompanied by the acknowledgement of the 10 crisis intervention contextual principles outlined in the previous chapter The formula is as follows:

SOURCE FORMULA

S : SHARING
O : OBSERVING
U : UNCOVERING
R : RESOURCING
C : COMPLETING
E : EXPANDING

This acronym, the word **SOURCE**, itself has extraordinary meaning. It's virtually indescribable as it can mean so much more than words can communicate. It's a word that contains all words. It's really Beyond Content, the essence of this book. It is the ground of our being. It is what underscores the meaning of our existence and our suffering.

FIGURE 7

SELF MASTERY

MAKING USE OF WHAT WORKS

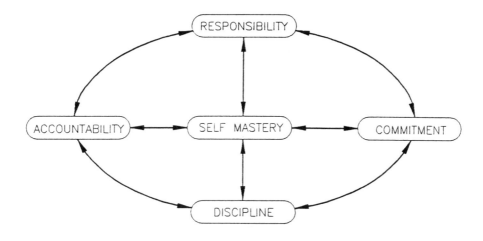

FIGURE 8

THE DYNAMICS OF COMPETENCY

AN EVOLVING MODEL

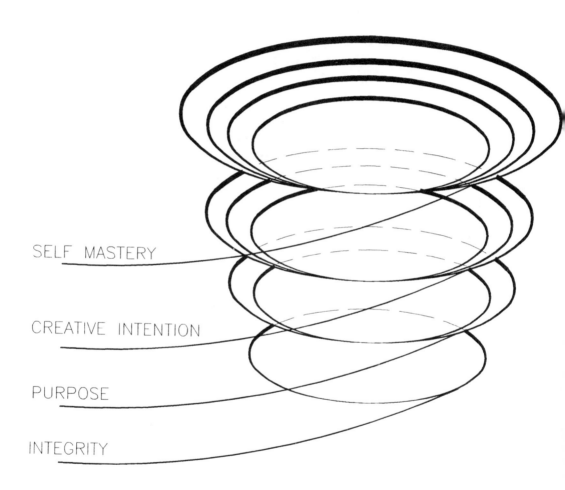

SELF MASTERY

CREATIVE INTENTION

PURPOSE

INTEGRITY

The self-actualizing crisis intervener knows deep down that we are all manifestations of some source and that the challenge is for all of us to recapture, uncover, and revitalize our connectedness to our natural competency. To do this, we need to step outside of our conditioning and to recognize that we are the **source** of our experiences and are ultimately responsible for them. The self-actualizing crisis intervener, regardless of her beliefs, attunes to this state of awareness as the background of her intervention.

The steps required to use the **SOURCE FORMULA** are in many ways simple and quite obvious. Nevertheless, while they are easily understood, they tend not to be practised despite our best intentions. What is necessary is for the crisis intervener to make a deliberate and conscious effort to use them despite residual resistance. In so doing, the crisis intervener can take transitional steps towards actualizing their competencies.

SHARING

To begin with, crisis interveners engage with others in crisis by sharing themselves in exactly the way they appear. While they may be in the role of a psychiatrist, psychologist, social worker, nurse, probation officer, teacher or child care worker, they know that these roles are adjunctive. They share themselves just the way they really are, and they do not pretend to be anything other than who they are at that moment.

They share by exuding an aura of being at peace with themselves. She does not get overly concerned about what others think of her. She knows that by sharing herself, she can (as George Leonard [1978] suggests), reveal and uncover her natural resonance with another. Sharing in its truest form is not restricted to talking or to using any one of our perceptual modes. It's contemplative yet active, receptive, yet interactive. Sharing essence as well as content in present-based awareness becomes experienced as lively communication.

A really competent self-actualizing crisis intervener has very little to teach. She is most powerful through sharing who she is (not her history) with others.

At the front end of a crisis, the crisis intervener shares by modelling self-mastery through concerted action. When others in crisis need assistance to prevent further escalation of the crisis event, the crisis intervener, first and foremost, shares by firmly requesting others to be guided by the instructions she offers. Often the crisis intervener will look for someone, either someone present or a significant other readily available by telephone, to take a leading role in stabilizing the current state of chaos. Firm, self-assuring, and controlled sharing is used in short, yet impactful ways, then is quickly abandoned as those in crisis reconnect to the resources around them and to their natural self-mastery capability. This crisis-entry form of sharing guides, rather than directs, using all the available environmental resources to augment the competency-sharing experience.

OBSERVING

The overriding question, according to Krishnamurti (1970), is "Are we capable of looking without distortion?". When one looks, what one sees is the figure or image of the person out there as it fits within the framework of one's experiences. These experiences are based on what is brought to awareness as knowledge. The observer, then, is a reservoir of knowledge; but our images filtered through our storehouse of knowledge imprison us and distort what we actually see. We tend to analytically see through the filter of our past and therefore we primarily see image fragments. Observing in this way is tiring, causing us to see even less. Often our remedy for this is to label what we see. Thus we can awaken to go on to other images, especially when we are in a role of being the crisis intervener with the other in crisis. Other peoples' crises trigger off our memory banks so much so that we more often than not operate from our conditioned past in an effort to avoid or reduce pain and to promote pleasure. Once again, then how do we exercise "primary observation" or (as the sorcerer Don Juan, in Carlos Castenadas' [1981] **The Eagle's Gift**, calls it) our "second attention"? Observing with a fresh mind, without division, requires a quiet or empty mind. When you see, says Don Juan the sorcerer, everything is new and everything is extraordinary. He goes on to say that seeing is different from looking. Seeing or observing requires discipline. It is the discipline of seeing with soft eyes when the background is incredibly alive and the people in the foreground are unusually luminous. Looking, on the other hand, does not require discipline; it's simply tiring.

Observing requires a shift in our perception so that we awaken, even if only momentarily, to the awareness that life is filled to the brim and that boredom under these conditions is impossible. Observing, as alluded to earlier, is about continuously integrating figure and ground so that a "correlative vision" - a vision where patterns are perceived over and above objects - becomes possible.

This way of seeing is unifying and can be learned through such exercises as dis-identification developed by Roberto Assagioli (1965) and focusing developed by Eugene Gendlin (1978). Both these exercises are described in greater detail in the next chapter on Self-Preparation.

Observing others beyond an image- or cognitive- oriented way is much like Zen seeing. It requires a willingness to allow the body and the mind to work in cooperation with one another, producing what Gendlin (1978) refers to as a "felt sense." This felt sense is a body/mind integrated response often practised in the martial arts such as Tai Chi and Aikido. When it is experienced, this response generates the capacity to attend to what is not yet verbalized. It is important to note that logical thinking, in the form of images, conceptual viewpoints, or interpretations, are not left out. Rather, exercising "felt sense observation" allows the observer to freely try on all different kinds of conceptual approaches without being restricted to any one of them.

To get a beginning sense of this way of seeing (which we are all capable of), wait until the next time you are on a public bus or in some waiting room with other people; then observe what is going on by de-focusing. This really is to let your awareness include the background, rather than any one object or person in the foreground. Most people de-focus unconsciously in such circumstances. In this instance, do it consciously, and what you observe may well come alive for you in an unusual way. It will be like seeing for the first time, when our curiosity seems to be insatiable.

In summary, observing in this context is multi-modal. It involves all of the senses spontaneously contributing to clarifying and coalescing the crisis intervener's evolving awareness of the crisis moment. A "felt sense" of the crisis pattern as a gestalt draws the crisis intervener to flow naturally toward **uncovering** hidden or buried issues underlying the crisis.

UNCOVERING

To uncover is to actively explore the boundaries between various states of our consciousness which Ken Wilber talks about (See Figure 2 on page 24). More specifically, it is to probe and root out the underlying causes of our crises and how we perpetuate and even desperately cling to them. The self- actualizing crisis intervener knows that the person in crisis is marooned between two states of consciousness. Seeking new ways of combining energy, the crisis intervener, like a warrior, stalks the caverns of lost awareness. With soft, transparent, coalescing energy, the crisis intervener reveals the crisis boundaries and endeavors to create opportunities for those in crisis to leap out from under the weight of their self-imposed limitations.

Recovering one's competence is often an ordeal of mammoth proportions. The uncovering process, even when it is laced with caring, often results in those in crisis retreating back to a previous state of being. Hooked by our social conditioning, we often hang onto our crises for fear of losing control. Becoming vibrant again is sometimes too much to ask for and can be exceedingly frightening. Uncovering, getting at the heart of our neuroses, may not be what the person in crisis wants. It is highly likely that most people in crisis want just to be more adequate in their neuroses. Therefore, the crisis intervener compassionately and sensitively uncovers inhibiting boundaries to awareness in accordance with the clients' willingness to experience these boundaries. Such provoking reveals the cover, then supports the client to dissolve it as she can be inspired to do so.

RESOURCING

The processes of sharing, observing, and uncovering get the crisis intervener to first base. When a crisis intervener naturally and spontaneously shares, observes and uncovers, she automatically discovers resources which previously may have been overlooked. The environment is incredibly rich in resources, some quite powerful and others seemingly insignificant. Quite often these resources have been discounted or discolored by failed attempts to use them effectively in the past. The challenge for the Beyond Content crisis intervener is to transform them to make them re-appear with their inherent essence of value jumping out as renewed, revitalized resources.

Also, the crisis intervener looks for opportunities to awaken the client to resources that are buried or discarded within herself. Since sleeping often seems preferable to being awake, the successful crisis intervener never shies away from the many escape routes used by the client. Even a clients' sleep-walking state can be used as a resource. Carefully massaged, a clients' dream-like state can be used to tantalize the hunter within, to recognize that their sleeping giant has a soft, yet strong, elusive aura. When stimulated, the sleep-walking state has the power to free the client from archaic restraints.

COMPLETING

By its very nature, a crisis has two sides: a position on something and opposition to it. Losing a job but not wanting to, drinking but not wanting to, withholding or lying but not wanting to, and other such scenarios can precipitate a crisis where no longer does one's past resources adequately relieve the tension and stress. This "stuckness" is characterized by a pronounced resistance to what

---

one opposes at the moment so as to protect oneself from any further loss.

The primary aim of a Beyond Content crisis intervention approach is to allow the crisis to reach a **turning point** so that other sides of an issue can connect with each other in utilitarian ways. Thus, a turning point is the juncture of opportunity within a crisis situation. As T.S. Eliot (1935) shares, ". . . except for the point, the still point, there would be no dance . . ." Once the resistance is fully acknowledged and can be perceived as a potential energy source for crisis dissolution, the dance towards harmony becomes possible as the duality of the crisis begins to fade away.

These junctures or turning points can be reached simply by having the experience of being fully listened to by a crisis intervener. Or, they can be reached by coming to a point where one is willing to consider letting go of resentment, prejudice, "hurtness," or other by-products of perceived or actual loss. It is at these points that Completing an intervention becomes possible. Completing is the step taken around the corner of a crisis, which reveal aspects of the true nature of what one is resisting. It is this process that allows what we resist to become an integral part of our vitality and wholeness.

Completing becomes a possibility when the crisis intervener detects tell-tale signs of letting go. Often this occurs in the form of a sigh of relief, when breathing becomes less laboured and restricted. Sometimes it is telegraphed by shifts in perceptual functioning, such as when suddenly the person in crisis makes eye contact for the first time, or unfolds her arms or acknowledges your presence as a resource when previously she seemed oblivious to your presence. At this juncture, the competency attribute, **Creative Intention,** can be beneficially triggered by the crisis intervener as the driving force towards exploring the increasingly evident number of pathways through the crisis maze. **Creative Intention** serves in the way that Roberto Assagioli (1974), the founder of Psychosynthesis, described as "the power to play with opposites and establish synthesis." Aided by **Creative Intention,** the process of completing takes the condition of "being of two minds" and melts the two minds into one. Completing is surrendering to the power of seeing value in our resistance and seeing how to gain self-mastery over our resistance. It is as if we give permission for our right and left brain to balance each other off.

These momentary, yet many times occurring, states of being are the moments every crisis intervener anxiously awaits. Unfortunately, they are easily passed over or overlooked as the crisis fallout drives the crisis intervener to distraction. When we confuse Completing with changing or making better, the tendency is to manipulate, which clouds our capacity to detect **turning points** when they arise. When we become preoccupied with diminishing the resistance of the person in crisis, we often inadvertently reinforce it. As a consequence, turning points occur less often.

Being fortunate enough to connect with a turning point is a cause for a celebration. To celebrate the person in crisis at this point is to inspire her to experience her vibrancy through doing something with her resistance. This "being" through "doing" can be augmented by encouraging her to align with her so- called good side or her intuitive and integrative side and to "animate" it. Her competencies, reinforced and activated, can then transform the experience of tension into the "felt sense" of excitement.

However, it requires disciplined practice to use the productive side of competencies to counteract the debilitating side of our survival tactics. The regressive and archaic effects of our survival tactics are often overwhelming, as they restrict action and encourage a way of coping based on avoidance, denial, or repression. To shift out of this trap and to go beyond our conditioning, requires extraordinary commitment and diligence. Completing, therefore, is a highly conscious process which endeavors to challenge our conditioning with action which is counter-conditioning. Such committed effort might take the form of the person in crisis practising forgiveness in a disciplined, repetitive way, until it becomes natural. Or she might practice listening to someone else without interrupting even though she is easily plugged into disagreeing with what has been said.

Disciplining yourself to practise takes a willingness to use the mind rather than let it use you. Allowing creative intention to be the "will power" is akin to having the right brain provide the framework to make information coming from the left brain workable. The crisis intervener who inspires the person in crisis to practice actualizing their strengths facilitates the completing process becoming an empowering experience.

Completing is simply doing something about the mechanics surrounding the crisis. It paves the way for a transpersonal connection to be made. Finally, completing experiences are like lighted steps on the journey towards **Expanding** into unity consciousness.

EXPANDING

We either expand or contract in life; and ultimately we contract at least physically through death. More often than not, a crisis causes us to contract or to hold the line on things. In keeping with the principle that a crisis is also an opportunity, Beyond Content crisis interveners seek out expanding possibilities every step of the way in a crisis situation. To expand is difficult - we are like rubber bands in which strong forces fight against expansion. It takes energy to expand a rubber band and to keep it expanding. The self-actualizing crisis intervener operates as if ultimately the only way to go is to expand to our limits without breaking, knowing that the rubber band called life will break away eventually. Why leave it partially unused?

Practically speaking, an expanding focus encourages the individual to go on from a steady or stable state rather than to build on top of a temporarily resolved crisis. Allowing the crisis of the past to dissolve and dissipate requires a willingness to cut the ties that bind us to the past. What's next, aided by the competency force of **Creative Intention,** can then consume the individual's awareness, allowing her to break new ground and explore new territories.

Expanding is the hard work of miracles. Ultimately, though, nothing is ever lost. Contracting is an alliance with deadness.

EXERCISES - CHAPTER THREE

1. Comment on the four forces of competency by rank ordering them in accordance with how they have been significant for you. Which one would you desire to make more use of and what are your reasons.

2. List two or three people you know personally or by reputation who make extraordinary use of these competency forces. As possible role models which competency force do they present strongest in?

3. Reflect back on a personal crisis that wasn't satisfactorily resolved for you. Systematically apply the **SOURCE** formula retrospectively. Identify what, if any, different results could have been achieved by any one of the **SOURCE** steps.

4. Identify four limiting beliefs that you have such as, "I can't study very well, I am too young and inexperienced to be working with other people's problems, I am not a flexible person," and so on restrict action and diminish or reduce competency. Now outline the behavioural actions you take to ritualize these beliefs so that they control you. Identify how these limiting beliefs have cost you in the past and what cost they will likely have for you in the future.

5. Identify four expanding beliefs that you make use of as a crisis intervener. For example, an expanding belief might be every crisis produces opportunities for change. Another might be you believe the more people in crisis are non-competent, the more they really can benefit from your commitment to serve and assist. Now take these expanding beliefs and identify at least three crisis events where you were able to transform a problem label into a competency label. Describe specifically how you used the problem as resource to move the person in crisis towards self healing.

SUGGESTED READINGS

1. J. Bandler and R. Grinder in **Frogs to princes** (Utah; Real People Press, 1979), provide a fascinating account of out-of-the-ordinary approaches to unfinished crises based on workshop experiences. This book described concepts and exercises based on neurolinguistic programming; a psychotechnology based on the clinical works of Milton Erickson, M.D., the modern day father of clinical hypnosis.

2. M.Y. Brown has compiled a useful compendium of psychosynthesis awareness exercises for practicing counsellors in her book **The unfolding self**: Psychosynthesis and counselling (Los Angeles: Psychosynthesis Press, 1983).

3. An exceptional and extraordinary comprehensive work by Eugene Kennedy, **On becoming a counsellor** (New York: Seabury Press, 1977) is an indispensable guide for those working extensively with people in crisis. It offers ways in which a counsellor can use the energy of her own understanding in a measured yet impactful way.

NOTES

CHAPTER FOUR

ON AWAKENING:

SELF PREPARATION TASKS FOR
CRISIS INTERVENERS

Knowledge is a function of being. When there is a change in the
being of the knower, there is a corresponding change in the nature and
amount of knowledge.

- Aldous Huxley

THE TASKS

As already mentioned, the training of crisis interveners is largely based on symptom-related problems, particularly the high profile concerns such as suicide, self-mutilation, substance abuse, child abuse, and delinquency. Quite elaborate intervention protocols have been identified in prescriptive fashion in an attempt to **delineate** crisis problems and offer a security blanket for the generic crisis intervener. Almost negligible effort has been made to introduce training methods for crisis interveners that focus on how to stimulate and accentuate their own vibrancy or potency. In other words, the dynamics of competency are not well articulated into training experiences. Yet, on the other hand, a growing body of self awareness and competency knowledge, like a groundswell, has surfaced from a variety of human service disciplines. This knowledge is now readily available in countless self-help books and workshops on self-actualization. Some of these practical and revealing processes can now be more readily adapted to potentiate the crisis intervener's impact in a crisis.

It is highly likely, though, that the many centering techniques have only been half-heartedly tried by those in the crisis-intervention field. When we come upon them indirectly, they tend to be "one time" experiences that startle or awaken our core self for a short while. Then they soon get lost and swept away in the powerful currents of our automated conditioning.

Realistically, being exposed to the tasks to be shared here is not likely going to do much for a crisis intervener unless considerable effort is dedicated towards practising them. When such effort is made, the crisis intervener can experience a sense of rejuvenation and a feeling of expanded ability to challenge upsets encountered.

You are invited to begin exploring for yourself the utility of these tasks by first of all getting a feel for them through experimentation. Then, decide if you are willing to commit yourself to disciplined practice. If at any time you discover that they no longer work for you, give yourself permission to discontinue and do something else for a while. In this way, if you decide to try them again, they will not be overly contaminated by half-committed attempts to make them work.

This chapter offers four major tasks that serve to prepare the crisis intervener for entering into the crisis arena. The first task is designed to awaken and activate the crisis intervener's unique forms of competency. The second task acknowledges the value of generating a personal mission statement that is congruent with one's current desires and experiences. The third task offers perception-checking suggestions that assist the crisis intervener to remain true to their purpose and to stay connected to their competency. The fourth task offers practical experiences in how to generate a state of psychological neutrality, using the SOURCE formula outlined in the preceding chapter.

1.   ACTIVATING COMPETENCY

Many of us have heard of the well known "A" and "B" personality types. In contrast to these a budding "C" personality type is beginning to reveal itself. The "C" stands for **competency,** and the type "C" personality can be described by numerous characteristics that manifest competency. Interestingly enough, most of these characteristics can be named by words beginning with the letter "C", as we see in the list in Table 2 on the following page.

Through regular, even daily, preparation with these competencies, the crisis intervener can prepare a solid wellness or transpersonal awareness base. To begin preparation, simply choose one of the characteristics each day, like a vitamin pill, and pop it into your consciousness in the form of an image anchor, a feeling anchor, or even just let the word trigger off meaning for you.

As an example, take the characteristic **calm** and connect to an image of yourself when you were extraordinary in your calmness in an activity that required you to be competent. Skiing, stopping a fight, writing an exam, or putting out a fire, are some of the examples of what might be considered. Often it is even more powerful to reflect on an image of someone you know who exercised extraordinary calmness in a crisis situation. Then, simply incorporate the desirable attributes or mannerisms this person displayed into your own unique way of being competently calm.

TABLE 2

COMPETENCY CHARACTERISTICS

CONFIDENT	CHEERFUL
COMMITTED	CONVICTION
CALM	CONSISTENT
COURAGEOUS	CREATIVE
CHOICE-MAKING	CONCENTRATOR
CONCRETE	CONSTRUCTIVE
CHALLENGING	CONCEIVING
COMMUNICATIVE	COMMUNAL
COMPASSIONATE	COORDINATING
COOPERATIVE	CHILDLIKE
COHERENT	CHANGE-MAKER
COMPLETING	CENTERED
CARING	CLEAR
COGENT	CANDID
CAPACIOUS	CONTEMPLATIVE
CONTROLLING	COMPELLING
CHARISMATIC	CAPABLE
COLORFUL	COMICAL
CAPTIVATING	CONNECTIVE

Images seem to work best as anchors for most crisis interveners, so you ought to consider taking the entire list and generating a visual anchor to list beside each characteristic for quick and easy application on a daily basis.

Once you "engage" your awareness with one of the characteristics, reflect on how the attached image can be embodied within you for the day. Let the image be a guide for your mind to instruct your body to act congruently with the characteristic for the entire day. This process takes only a few minutes each day to implement. The dividends are quite remarkable.

Other possibilities to consider are to write the word and image in your daily diary or on reminder notes for your work place, your bathroom, your refrigerator, or anywhere that can serve as a frequent visual reminder of your competency in this area. Change them often, as they tend to lose their lustre and impact as our mind seeks to go to sleep taking our competencies for granted after an initial effort has been made to activate any one particular competency. Revitalizing yourself by every day planting a new characteristic and associated anchor in your awareness guards against daily upsets and ingrained survival patterns. This activating process can open doorways to your inner core space where all competencies reside. So, you are urged to mobilize your desire for self-mastery and allow yourself to overcome the natural tendency to let your past conditioning rule you.

The dynamic nature of self mastery is such that its machinery functions best when placed on automatic pilot. In this way, when a crisis does occur, the crisis intervener is already primed to respond with at least one oasis of competency.

2.   PURPOSE GENERATING

A crisis intervener to remain competent and powerful must continuously develop and clarify a purpose or Mission Statement making it realistic and practical. All too many self-proclaimed crisis interveners are unclear and even ignorant of their primary purpose for intervening outside of what they know as defined by their job mandate. Ask yourself, are you able to spontaneously share your purpose without defending it? Personally, I am quite struck by how the vast majority of crisis interveners I have encountered across all fields (including hospitals, police, corrections, and mental health and child care settings), who do not know how to begin to share their purpose or mission. In fact, it has been a rare occurrence to encounter crisis interveners who can speak with clarity and potency about their purpose.

Examining your purpose is comparable to evaluating your effectiveness as a crisis intervener. Though we hear much talk of the importance of purpose clarification, we see very little action. We seem to unquestionably agree that there is a need for self-exploration and self-examination. Yet we let this need take a back seat to the rigors of our daily work. For those who are willing go beyond their own defensive posturing to tackle their unknown or buried views, the rewards are substantial.

When the crisis intervener is armed with a clear purpose, a synergy of confidence contagiously effects those whom they encounter in crisis. This confidence allows those in crisis to use the crisis intervener in much more than a hit and/or miss manner. A consciously evolving purpose offers a foundation of extraordinary value, as it is just this clarity of purpose that those in crisis are lacking.

Crisis interveners who examine their own resistance to achieving clarity of purpose become increasingly sensitive to the underlying causes of those crises that they are attempting to assist with. The clear-minded crisis intervener tends to radiate an assurance that escape from the darkness of crisis is indeed possible if one dares to risk exploring their crises by looking within oneself for the answers. By not exploring ourselves, we project our unmet selves upon those we encounter. At the same time, we become the opaque screens for the projections of others. In some respects, we mutually incarcerate one another by our stale personhood, by our "helper-helped" social hierarchy and the static rituals that go along with it.

I invite you to go beyond your resistance, at the same time allowing it be a source for tapping into your deep reservoir of courage and commitment to self-explore. So, give yourself permission to put pen in hand and begin writing out your own purpose statement.

Before beginning, you may wish to spend a brief few minutes preparing yourself. You can start doing this by creating a visual picture of someone you know who, in an extraordinary way, exemplifies clarity of purpose in his lifespace. It could be anyone from an Olympic athlete to a profound teacher or even a parent, colleague, or friend. Let their image cast light on you, stimulating your confidence and self-assurance, especially in your recalled effort to intervene in crisis.

Now, give yourself a fifteen-minute time slot to record whatever thoughts come to your mind revealing your current understanding of your purpose. To assist you, you may wish to have some empowering music in the background, such as Pachebel's Kanon in D Major, or some other equally creatively stimulating music that you favour. On your journal paper, write the date, the time and your current position as a crisis intervener, whether it be that of a teacher, consultant, practitioner, or trainee.

In doing this exercise, suspend your internal judgement of yourself, and let your emerging viewpoint provide a scaffolding upon which you can build your clarity of purpose.

As your curiosity and interest in examining your purpose grows, you could begin by jotting down your thoughts in an unrestricted, free- floating manner, trusting that your intention will creatively serve you. So, begin.

For those who benefit from a guiding framework, you may wish to complete the following questions:

As a crisis intervener,

1. My purpose is to serve the community through (by) _____

_____

_____

_____

_____

2. My purpose is to serve families through (by) _____

_____

_____

_____

_____

3. My purpose is to serve individuals through (by) _____

_____

_____

_____

_____

4. My purpose is to develop my personal capacity to _____

_____

_____

_____

_____

Continue and add any other comments you may wish to make regarding your purpose as you let your mind flow accordingly. To refine your purpose statement, refer to the section in Chapter Three on Mission Statement, especially to the questions that competent crisis interveners might ask themselves to clarify their purpose in serving others.

In many ways, crisis intervention is a high-wire act. It involves a balancing of energy and effort, of concentration with receptivity, of wisdom with compassion, of awareness with mercy, of insight with letting go, and of appearances with what lies beyond appearances. Without question, the first and most important task of any crisis intervener is to be and continue to remain clear about their purpose.

Write down now, if you will, a date on which you would like to review your purpose. I might suggest that you pick a date and put it into your journal or appointment book if you have one. Then, on that date or close to it, the commitment inside of you will want to re-state your purpose. For example, I have found it quite useful to first re-state my purpose before referring back to the original statement I have written today. In this way, a sense of one's vision and movement can be experienced. As a final note affirming the constructive and positive intent of this process, the words of the Zen master Susuki Roshi are particularly noteworthy, "Everything is perfect but there is always room for improvement."

3.   ON SELF-OBSERVATION

Given that you have grounded yourself by means of a **beginning** or an evolving mission or purpose statement, it is then really essential for you to practise observing your current, ever-changing state of being. Engaging in the process of self-observation offers the opportunity for crisis interveners to clarify their integrity state. As well, self- observation can increase self-awareness in ways that significantly facilitate and enhance personal congruence. Self-awareness can also minimize the confusing or even deleterious impact that a crisis intervener's own issues will have on others in crises.

In another important way, self-observation efforts can act like incubation periods, allowing crisis interveners to recapture a "creative" or "intuitive" edge. There are countless examples of intervention breakthroughs that have resulted when crisis interveners took the time to explore their own self-awareness as a prelude to exploring with those in crisis.

Crisis intervener can use self-observation to watch how they connect with their own "activated competencies" or, alternatively, how they are minimized by super-ego injections such as "You don't deserve to recognize yourself as competent in this area yet." Self-observation reveals where our energy wants attention but is blockaded. This process can alert the crisis intervener to these subtle roadblocks and lead to removal of inhibition and release of energy. Self-observation as a "noticing" process is like scientific data-gathering, in which facts are observed as objectively as possible. It is not a process that involves analyzing, judging, or assessing. When those mind functions occur, self-observation simply notices that they are going on, without trying to change them.

Finally, by being **personally** familiar as well as practised, in a self-observing way, with the Beyond Context process, (involving the SOURCE approach, the dynamics of competency and the contextual principles of crisis intervention), you can actively and progressively synergize your usefulness with others in crisis. By so doing, you honour the process by allowing self-awareness to augment other-awareness.

One of the first steps to take in self-observation is to prepare yourself for inner exploration. It is suggested that you simply find a quiet space and begin to listen to your inner dialogue. Listening to one's inner voice isn't easy, as our mind likes to wander a great deal, introducing random and disconnected thoughts and even seemingly blanking out from time to time. So, to assist you, I offer some multi-modal or observational "tuning in" guidelines to use when you begin to activate the SOURCE approach with yourself. These guidelines grow out of the notion of the layers of one's self, described in Figure 3, Chapter Two, page 25. You may benefit from reviewing them again before you continue. Now for the guidelines.

* Listen for your ACT or the role you play in life that runs you, such as being a victim, a rebel, a tyrant, or a rescuer. More later on how to detect and describe these Acts both in yourself and others.

* Listen for your mind's opinions, biases, beliefs, reasons, justifications, and judgments. Just listen to them with curiosity, without having to do anything about them.

* Tune in to body signs of tension, hyper-arousal, or discordance.

* Listen for pseudo-feelings, such as boredom, guilt, depression, frustration, and nervousness.

* Tune in and examine primary feelings, such as happiness, sadness, anger, fear, and agitation.

* Listen for silent awareness--an awareness that seems to stop time and offers a balance or linking of insight with outsight.

It is my experience that most talented and experienced crisis interveners can more or less make cognitive sense out of these guidelines. Yet, when it comes to putting them into practice, various degrees of confusion abound. So, to prepare you to make optimum use of these guidelines a series of exercises are offered using the SOURCE approach as an operating framework. These exercises are designed to "prime your awareness pump". It is instructive to note they basically arise from one of the Beyond Content contextual crisis intervention principles, the one known as "psychological neutrality."

4.   ACTUALIZING PSYCHOLOGICAL NEUTRALITY

What is this concept called "psychological neutrality"? Is it really achievable, much less, practical to use in a crisis situation? This often misunderstood contextual principle (Chapter Two, page 34) of the **Beyond Content** model of crisis intervention gets lost in the world of opposites we live in.

To trust its value requires going beyond thinking in opposites. As briefly mentioned in Chapter Two, it requires the crisis intervener to adopt the position of taking no sides. In this respect, the crisis intervener does not become weighed down by having to assess who is right or who is wrong or what is good and what is bad. Stepping outside of this polarizing dilemma, the crisis intervener weaves the "What Works" contextual principle together with the "Psychological Neutrality" contextual principle, allowing what works, rather than what is right or wrong guide to be one's guide.

To be actualized, psychological neutrality needs to be consciously practised; otherwise it surfaces in seemingly unpredictable ways, and its value can easily be overlooked. Therefore you are invited to experiment by practising with a series of exercises designed to sensitize your conscious ability to generate this state of being on demand and with ease. Each one of these exercises needs to be repeated often. Practising them allows for the natural emergence of this skill during a crisis with others or even during a crisis of your own.

So, you are urged to go beyond your tendency to be complacent and to commit yourself to practising mastery over this concept. Do not dismiss the exercises or go over them lightly. They are meant to help prevent you from clobbering yourself with your own abundant, sometimes misguided energy. They are designed to help educate you to yourself and to awaken your natural power to make an impact on others in turmoil. If doing them is a problem for you, may I jog your memory by asking you to refer to your purpose; and may I encourage you to mobilize your competency forces of **Self-Mastery** and **Creative Intention**. If your ego continues to resist, fearing perhaps a loss of control, simply allow your interest to unfold in its own time. As. E.E. Cummings suggests: If you can be, be. If not, cheer up and go about other peoples' business doing and undoing unto others until you drop.

Exercise #1: Power-Walking

In preparation for neutrality, it is useful to regain or to uncover a sense of vitality with one's body. The intent here is to awaken yourself to the flow of your inner natural rhythm and to "ground" your energy so that your body and mind are in harmony with one another. Most of us are painfully aware of how our mind and body compete or are simply out of touch with one another. This mind/body dissonance makes it impossible to be neutral, as we tend to be continuously distracted by our own fragmentation and our preoccupation with our boundaries.

Begin this exercise by slowly walking around in a quiet space of your own choosing. As you do so, allow your attention to gently rest, giving permission for the environment around you to pass by you as if you were not moving, rather that things around you were. This is somewhat like being on a train in a train station. As the train begins to pull out ever so slowly, it appears the train alongside you is actually moving instead of you in your train. Sometimes you can get this sense in a stationary automated car wash. Even though you know you are stopped, it appears as if you are doing the moving instead of the carwash machinery around you.

As you continue to walk slowly, with soft, accepting eyes, a rhythmic movement of the environment may be detected. You remain quite alert, observing everything yet focusing on nothing. A sense of solidness within is counter-balanced by a sense of free-floating fluid movement within your environment.

As your mind comes in and out of its memory banks, you may reflect on how you might generate this state of physical and mental neutrality while arriving at the scene of a crisis. From a physical perspective, it is useful to know that walking as if pulled or drawn towards something from a centre point (just below the diaphragm) of our body generates the potential for power-walking. This type of walk is peaceful and at the same time quite impactful, as all your energy tends to resonate from your core.

Continue walking this way until giving yourself permission to let go of judgments, opinions, and any resistance that seems to interfere with your being in neutral as you walk. Thank yourself for whatever you get out of this experience.

Practice power-walking as often as you can, so that you can remain consciously alert without being preoccupied. This state is akin to that of a stag at bay, ever alert, totally vibrant, moving gracefully as it grazes. It is a state in which the mind and the body mutually tune into one another, allowing you to experience being fully present in the moment.

Exercise #2: Body Charging

For this exercise you may wish to find a comfortable spot to lie down or to sit. Lying down seems to work best for most. Now simply close your eyes; and then, in your own time, make a fist out of your left hand. Take a deep breath clenching your left hand into a fist, then gradually exhale, letting go of the tension in your fist at the same time. As you do this, notice your breathing, the sound it makes and how it alternately charges the body as you breathe in and lets go of the body's tension as you breathe out. Breathe in again, letting air fill you up like a bellow. Then notice how exhaling leaves behind a pulsating satisfaction that gradually radiates throughout your body.

As you continue breathing and making fists, allow the energy to feel as if it is radiating from the abdominal area to all parts of your body. Do this without judgement, just noticing, as a witness, where it flows freely and where it seems to get stuck or to bypass parts of your body.

Observe the energy flow downward to the toes, to the very tips, taking any excess tension it can pick up along the way and allowing it to leak out into the surrounding environment. Observe it flow and radiate to the ends of your arms and hands, to your neck and to your scalp, perhaps leaving a tingling sensation at your extremities.

As you continue to breathe out, allow any distressful thoughts as they appear on your mind's screen to softly flow out and dissipate into the environment like smoke rising. From moment to moment, you may notice how difficult it is for the "wandering monkey mind" to stay with the body even if it is for brief periods of time. Because you are a curious sort of person, it may strike you as some kind of mystery that the mind tends to wander no matter how diligent you may be in concentrating on what you are doing. Perhaps the thought has occurred to you: If you are not in your body, then where might you be? Charging your body and mind in this way can leave you refreshingly alert and ready to explore new territory.

Exercise #3: Sourcing Self

Having experienced the self-awareness exercises, you may also be able to more easily resonate with the "tuning in" guidelines already mentioned. Now, continue by reviewing the "tuning in" guidelines again, surrendering to your current heightened mind/body awareness. Gradually, perhaps referring to a cue card outlining the SOURCE formula, reflect on these building-block steps. It is also a good idea to refresh your memory about the various layers of the "self" (Figure 3, p. 27) before continuing.

It is sometimes useful to begin the process of sharing with yourself by means of a dis-identification exercise adapted from the field of Psychosynthesis. To do this, consider committing the following to memory:

I am a mind but I am not just my mind as I am continuously changing my mind.

I am much more than my mind.

I am my body but I am not just my body as my body is always changing.

I am much more than my body.

I am my emotions but I am not just these emotions as they are constantly in flux.

I am much more than my emotions.

I am much more than all that I know.

Knowing that I don't know is my opportunity to be fully alive and explore.

Once you have the essence of the above passage in your wareness, you can choose to vary it, using some of your own words. It is also useful to recite this process aloud to yourself. This simple, yet powerful process, when repeated several times to yourself, can also be used during crisis situations when you find yourself getting caught up or entangled in the chaos. Taking a short breather from the crisis situation and dis-identifying can assist you to re-capturing your composure and to activate appropriate competencies.

Next, start by sharing with yourself by giving your inner mind dialogue free reign. In so doing, observe and listen for discord, recognizing that as much as three-quarters of what we say to ourselves is based on discordance. As you listen for discordance, mentally record how it manifests itself for you throughout the various layers of the self (Figure 3). For example, your "tuning in" lets you recognize your behaviour. You become aware of how your behaviour is conditioned from previous experiences. You may even have glimpses of how automatic and perhaps unconscious you operate to sabotage yourself getting any benefit out of inner exploration as your mind wanders off track and becomes dis-interested in revealing your inner discordance.

At the next layer, the mind, you may hear your voice say "you really don't need to do this" or "A Beyond Content model won't work or at least won't work except for advanced professionals or already enlightened people."

At the pseudo-feeling level, it is possible that you hear yourself say that you're bored now and want to go on to something else or that you are frustrated because you can't seem to clearly understand what you are now feeling. As you begin to uncover layers of yourself, you may discover body responses, such as your heart is beating rather fast, that the muscles in your neck are extremely tight, that your eyes are tiring fast, or alternatively that you are wide awake.

Finally, when you tune in to primary feelings or your core emotions, they will seem to well up in the moment and to operate as if they were all of you. Being primary feelings, they either open the door to your core self or they quickly vacate for a pseudo feeling cover-up in order for you to avoid being vulnerable.

Tuning into your core is seldom experienced because you simply cannot get there by avoiding any of the other layers (Figure 3). You can, however, let yourself into this holistic space by including all other spaces within it. YOU know you're in this space when your state of being is indescribably visionary, clairvoyant, or intuitive. The state seldom lasts any more than for a few brief moments. Nevertheless, it can be experienced by anyone, and most often we reach it by stumbling into it.

To uncover some, but not all of your layers is to be expected. Make certain that you can identify your thoughts about the layers uncovered. Keeping your thoughts in mind, let any resistance around those thoughts be revealed and legitimized.

Once you accept your thoughts as having some validity, you can begin to play at making different patterns with them, as if you were external to them. In so doing, you can shift them towards new possibilities. Your thoughts then become intriguing resources. This re-patterning process can facilitate a breakthrough whereby the layers of yourself begin to constructively and congruently interconnect. The boundaries between your layers then begin to fade, and a more holistic sense of self begins to emerge. Attaining a state whereby you become connected to your core self requires self discipline and the willingness to persevere. Perhaps worthy of remembering are the words of the master, Lao Tsu:

> Knowing others is wisdom;
> Knowing the self is enlightenment.
> Mastering others requires force;
> Mastering self needs strength.
> Tao Te Ching XXXIII

Completing this exercize allow yourself to **expand,** letting your natural competencies unfold without being overly attached to them. A state of self-abundance starts to pervade you as you expand towards letting your thoughts drift away. You become amusingly aware that you have an abundant storehouse of thoughts always seeking to be known and then let go. Our next thought, fueled by enthusiasm and competence, might be to engage others in empowering ways.

TASKS SUMMARIZED

The first task of activating one's competencies opens the door to getting in touch with or having "a felt sense" of one's core essence. The second task of generating a purpose or mission statement allows one to be clear about what track to take with one's competencies. The third task intertwines with the first two and serves to reinforce the crisis intervener stay awake by actively listening to one's mind thereby revealing layers of oneself. The fourth task of practising psychological neutrality offers a context for the first three tasks. Practising psychological neutrality can assist us to operate **from** our core Self. This process gives us a fourth way to act on our competencies and to observe others as well as ourselves from a more "holistic space".

SELF OBSERVATION PREPARATION SHEET

Use this sheet as a model for recording the self-explorations you make by use of the exercises in this chapter. Given that you chose to repeat these exercises, you may wish to make several copies for continued use.

SHARE, OBSERVE, AND UNCOVER

Current Behaviour _____

Current Thoughts _____

Body Sensations _____

Feelings _____

RESOURCE, COMPLETE AND EXPAND

Primary Competencies _____

New Possibilities _____

EXERCISES - CHAPTER FOUR

1. Identify four competencies you actively demonstrate as a crisis intervener. Take each competency characteristic and make a sentence out of it such that is speaks to your way of demonstrating this competency. One example might be "I am absolutely committed to creating as many choices as possible for those in crisis."

    Write down these four sentences in your Competency Journal at the very front or even on the front cover. Now make a commitment to yourself to condition yourself daily with these statements by saying them over and over again to yourself. Do this religiously and you will be absolutely amazed with the shift in awareness you experience with the power of your competencies.

2. Review your purpose statement again and listen to your mind for agreement and notice if your body is physically aligned (accepting) of this purpose for the present moment. If your body seems to react with tension, focus your tension on this tension and keep asking yourself what message is your body attempting to communicate about this purpose.

3. Write down (in your Competency Journal) your experiences with the exercises designed to prepare you for generating a state of psychological neutrality. Commit yourself to practicing these exercises of power-walking, body charging, and sourcing self at least once a week until you begin to do them naturally.

SUGGESTED READINGS

1. One of the best practical resources for self-observation is Eugene Gendlin's book, **Focusing** (New York: Bantam Books, 1978). It offers a new way of getting easily connected with our core essence through a "holistic" process referred to as "felt sense." This incredibly powerful manual is perhaps best described by Marilyn Furguson in the Introduction as she says:

    Focusing is at once richly complex and surprisingly simple. It's mental and kinesthetic mysteriousness in its capacity to summon buried wisdom, holistic in its respect for the "felt sense" of a problem. An effective method in itself, it is also valuable in conjunction with a variety of psychotherapies,. . . In short, Focusing works for any for of "stuckness."

2. An extraordinary account of ways to self-observe and to connect with a transpersonal state of being is offered in **Waking up** (Boston: New Science Library, 1987), a new and easily readable book by one of the foremost authors of consciousness states, Charles Tart. It is a must to read for anyone serious about exploring how to actualize their competency.

3. For those wishing to become more familiar with Psychosynthesis processes, techniques and theories, a good place to start is to read two books by Roberto Assagioli, **Psychosynthesis** New York: Penguin Books, 1965) and then The Act of Will (New York: Penguin Books, 1974). A practical manual on skill development for therapists by Molly Young-Brown, **Counsellors and teachers** (Los Angeles: Synthesis Press, 1983) is also worth reviewing.

4. A working book on self-awareness exercises for would be Sorcerers. Arising out of the Gestalt therapy field and worthy of consideration is John O. Stevens **Awareness: Exploring, experimenting and experiencing** (Utah: Real People Press, 1971). As a unique "self-help book," it offers tools that can deepen your awareness of yourself as you are now.

NOTES

NOTES

CHAPTER FIVE

SIZING UP A CRISIS

Only parts suffer not the whole . . .
The art of Seeing cannot be cultivated. It does not occur as a result of
gradual growth. Actually, when perception, expressions and actions
are all one, then Seeing occurs.

- Krishnamurti

A THREE DIMENSIONAL APPROACH

Often a crisis snowballs into a full blown episode in a moment. In these circumstances it is quite common for a crisis intervener to get swept into a crisis situation where they themselves become at risk or at best ineffective. This can happen even to quite competent and seasoned crisis interveners. It happens especially to those who seek to develop rapport or to intervene via their authority before they establish what environmental supports exist, what degree of risk to self and others is present, and to what extent those involved legitimize the crisis intervener as a resource. There have been countless incidents when well- meaning professionals or para-professionals have stepped into a crisis situation without first of all sizing up the situation. To say that this is undesirable is not to say one's position, mandate, and capacity to care should be disregarded. Rather it is to say that, except in life-and-death situations where immediate action is obviously required, mishaps can be short-circuited through pausing to size up a crisis. Before describing this three-dimensional approach to sizing up a crisis, I'd like to point out some basic guidelines for a crisis intervener to consider at the very beginning of the intervention process. These entry guidelines are at best suggestions. They are meant to be implemented only in accordance with the unique nature of each crisis scenario. Their utility depends upon the crisis intervener's presence of mind, her perceptual acuity, and the moment-to-moment she has on those in crisis.

Initial Guidelines

1.   When entering a crisis, adjust to a soft or receptive observational approach. In contrast to the critical, evaluative eye, this way of seeing attends to the background scenario or crisis territory while merely monitoring the foreground chaos. The background becomes alive as the crisis intervener's curiosity seeks to clarify and highlight resources available in the crisis field. Allow your eyes to scan the crisis environment, being sensitive not to give the impression of being too penetrating. This type of observation, as mentioned already in the Self- Preparation chapter, requires a willingness to somewhat de-focus, in a contemplative way whereas we automatically tend to become even more focused with our critical eye.

2.   Maintain or create space between those involved as well as between them and yourself that is at least three to four times the normal socially acceptable interaction distance. Do so immediately and with the humble assurance that what you are doing is best for everyone. Such space is a requirement if you are to implement a soft or receptive observation. When those in crisis are too close to one another or when the crisis intervener moves in too close too soon, it often inhibits or restricts movement and reduces escape-route possibilities should the crisis escalate.

3.   Adopt a quiet, contemplative stance when presenting yourself in a crisis situation. Contrary to what most people think, contemplation is action rather than inaction, although it accentuates knowing and being rather than seeking and becoming. Keep your body alert, and maintain an open stance with hands loose and arms to your side. Take care to notice when, or if, you fold your arms, and then re-posture.

4.   Notice your breathing, and allow yourself to breathe fully and deeply without effort. Re-adjust your breathing every few moments in keeping with the desire to stay ready, yet calm and non-threatening.

5.   In circumstances in which physical threat is perceived possible, place your feet about eighteen inches apart and staggered so that one foot is behind the other. This allows you to side step or turn away without abruptness and without having to back up. Do not look down at the ground or down at those in question. Keep your eyes moving slowly from side to side, focusing on objects behind and to one side of the person at risk for violence. Move slightly to one side so as not to be a potential "face to face" target for aggressive outbursts.

6.   Intervene physically as a last resort, ensuring that all other resources within the environment are used first as appropriate. Blend back into the background at the earliest possible time after direct intervention and scan for new resources that become available in the immediate crisis territory. A more comprehensive and in-depth review of violence and how to intervene is presented in Chapter Eleven.

7.   State your purpose in a simple, yet non-defensive way as necessary to gain entry into the crisis territory and clarify your purpose for those who appear to be confused and unclear. Even for those who know your mandate, it is often important to share your intentions once

---

again, as each new crisis situation may well create crisis intervention assumptions that have not been clearly established.

Once the crisis intervener acceptance into the crisis situation and her legitimacy has been acknowledged, then a more detailed sizing up of the crisis situation. Basically, a three-dimensional approach is embraced within the first half of the **SOURCE** formula and involves discovering:

1.   How those in crisis function **Perceptually**.

2.   To what extent are they lacking in **Integrity** by being fragmented or disconnected from aspects of themselves.

3.   How their identity is being manifested as a role or an **Act** in life.

When all three perspectives are interwoven, they offer a "holographic" like viewpoint, rich in clues that can lead the crisis intervener towards harmony-producing intervention.

The approach to sizing up used here is qualitatively different from a deductive assessment of crisis situations. In contrast to dissecting a crisis to determine faulty areas, this approach attempts to discover how a natural holistic state of being can be uncovered and mobilized to support a re-capturing of competency. In this sense, it stresses connectedness, relationship, coherence, organism and wholeness as opposed to the fragmenting, over-differentiating, and compartmentalizing forces of traditional crisis assessment.

The first dimension to be examined includes the three dominant perceptual modes--seeing, feeling, and listening. Although this perspective, as will become evident, addresses functioning aspects of the brain, it is not an attempt to split the unsplittable and thereby defeat the holistic intent of this crisis-intervention mode. After a cursory and somewhat comparative review of some attempts to differentiate various aspects of the human being's functioning existence, I shall attempt, through a metaphor, to clarify how the sizing up of functioning parts in a crisis situation can occur within a synthesizing, holistic framework. If the human being is to be conceived as being a whole as well as a set of parts, at the very least, our words need to convey patterns, pictures, and schemata depicting the whole.

1.   **MODES OF PERCEPTION DIMENSION**

Many attempts have been made to split the thinking and developing mind. Charles Hampden-Turner (1982) offers a comprehensive visual overview of these many attempts that demonstrate their simplicity, their converging natures, and their complementarity. Anyone intrigued by the now popularized left brain-right, brain cognitive/spatial differentiation and the mind/body issue as it relates to various disciplines will likely find this review invaluable.

On the practical side, Virginia Satir (1982) is well known for her simple approach to descriptively classifying people in crisis as blamers, placaters, and super-rationalizers. These primary categories align quite well with the primary perceptual modes, seeing, feeling, and hearing. I suggest that during a crisis one of our perceptual modes (and one of Satir's categories) predominates while the others go into a submissive or impoverished state.

From a perspective that is more theoretical and philosophical yet equally practical, Charles Tart (1987) identifies three aspects of the brain, suggesting that they exist in varying degrees of balance and imbalance. Our three-brain nature he identifies as being the intellectual, the emotional and the body-instinctive. In crisis situations, our three-brain beingness is off balance, resulting in overloads, distortions, deletions, and over-generalizations. However, in some cases, extraordinary growth and power can come from specializing in one particular perceptual dimension over the others. The rewards may be significant, and one's behaviour may be socially sanctified in narrow ways. Yet, in many other circumstances, such off-balance specialization can cause suffering or generally be useless.

Tart goes on to suggest there is a state of being which is virtually indescribable although we know it exists. This state of being or transpersonal centre balances all three brains and is guided by what some refer to as our intuitive capabilities. This holistic mind, which he refers to as the "fourth dimension brain," can be activated through disciplined practice of self-"re-membering", a process of putting back together our component parts by conscious sensing, looking, and listening.

The three operative brains he refers to tend to correspond with Satir's classification and with the primary perceptual modes. For comparative purposes, they are as follows:

TABLE 3

COMPARISON OF PRIMARY MODES

PERCEPTUAL MODE	SATIR CATEGORIES	TART'S THREE BRAINS
Visualizer	Blamer	Body/Instinctive
Feeling/Kinesthetic	Placater	Emotional
Auditory	Super Rationalizer	Intellectual

It is possible for the crisis intervener to recognize how one perceptual modality may predominate over the others by noticing the personality traits. For example, a blaming stance coupled with visual references, such as "I see you always being a victim" or "It doesn't look to me that you care about me" signal a perceptual or body-instinctive brain-dominance. Visualizers seem to have a need when in crisis to see concretely before they believe. They tend to look with penetrating eyes, and they use their hands in somewhat obtrusive or threatening ways. They also like to see all of you and others in crisis situations.

On the other hand, placaters in crisis situations tend to go by their feelings or emotional state, screening information so as not to become even more internally distraught. They are easily overloaded as they re-cycle their emotions, leaving very little room for new information to enter. Consequently they tend to minimize eye contact and exude a sense of being overwhelmed and "intranced" by their emotions. Their interaction with others is restrictive and tends to placate or down-play the need for action. Unable to get angry, they become overly frightened by their experiences. The phrase "I don't know what to do" is commonly heard from a person kinesthetically predisposed.

Finally, the super-rationalizer or the intellectualizer cues in to the meaning of words, how they are spoken, and what logically makes sense to her. She tends to be highly critical, immune to emotional stimulation, and in need of time to "think things out" in a crisis situation. She will often repeat what you say, either to themselves or out load, to buy more time to think up a response. Overall, she tends to be highly deductive reasonable, and logic-bound.

It is probably obvious to you by now that the other human senses have not been addressed. Actually, little is known about how they interplay with the three primary modalities. However, we do know that the senses of taste and touch can trigger off historical data in our memory banks. Perhaps these senses can uncover a new frontier and assist us in completing unfinished business by enabling us to recall repressed or buried information.

As a means of further clarifying how the various perceptual modes inter-relate in crisis situations, let us imagine that the human being is something like a "new age" multi-modal movie camera. In addition to sight and sound capabilities, this camera would be blessed with what might be best described as a feeling monitor. But the really extraordinary aspect of this camera would be its capacity to synthesize all three perceptual modes. This feature might loosely be referred to as an intuitive lens. It would have the unique ability to continuously process information called up from the camera's film or memory banks along with new information from the other perceptual lens and the feeling monitor. Further, it would have the ability to re-programme the camera's memory bank and to open and close the lens apertures. Functioning like a master mind our intuitive lens would draw upon already stored information and, in a synthesizing way, link it with the continuously flowing new sources of information from the external world. It might also be useful to think of the intuitive lens as having synergistic capabilities to take bits of information and increase their value as they become harmonized into a holistic pattern.

Unfortunately though, our intuitive lens is grossly under-utilized and quite dormant. In fact, it is often forgotten or simply ignored because its usefulness is not fully understood or appreciated. Consequently, when our camera's memory banks get overloaded with conflictual or antagonistic information from either the visual or the auditory lens, the feeling monitor immediately sends a message to the appropriate perceptual aperture to constrict or shut down. Sometimes chronic overload causes the feeling monitor to malfunction, with the result that one of the perceptual apertures actually stays stuck wide open. Without an actively functioning intuitive lens to counteract this stuckness the camera tends to become imbalanced and will ultimately malfunction. Persistent episodes of this kind of stuckness create a crisis.

It seems that the only way to re-establish full functioning is to manually assist by opening up the lens apertures or by re-programming the memory banks from the outside. This suggests that assistance from others is needed. More on how this can be accomplished is discussed in the next chapter on Intervention With Others.

---

2. CRISIS STATES-OF-BEING DIMENSION

The second major dimension of sizing up a crisis considers the degree to which those involved experience personal, and also interpersonal, disconnectedness. In other words, how fragmented are they in themselves and in relation to others in their environment? Proposed here are five crisis states of being, representing various gradations of integrity. Integrity is viewed here as a dynamic, always-in-flux human condition representing the degree to which we are, from moment to moment, whole and complete in our life-space. It is intended that the crisis integrity states be present-based, operating in the "here and now" rather than being developmental or time-bound. Yet they can also be used in a congruent manner with the developmental stages of life, aligning with these stages from time to time, according to the nature of ever-changing human wants and needs. These crisis integrity states can be directly observable, offering an operational viewpoint for various aspects of one's identity development.

Understanding these states leads to a "hands on" approach to sizing up a crisis and intervening effectively. The crisis integrity states offer to the crisis intervener a working framework which allow her to guage to what extent, different types of supportive actions are needed. Once the crisis intervener becomes comfortable using the crisis states of being, beginning interventions can be formulated quickly an spontaneously.

As illustrated in Figure 9, the first four crisis states move from a high level of responsibility in life to a very low level. The final state (separated from the others above) represents the condition of covered-up or no responsibility towards one's present life circumstances. The Beyond Content viewpoint suggests that we start by being in a natural state of integrity, and then we fall through fragmenting life experiences, from this natural state of grace. This falling happens both momentarily through immediate crisis and in a more chronic way as we lose our resiliency to repeated crises in our lives. Each state will now be discussed in greater detail.

State 1 - At Naturalness

This state of being is where we start in life and where we struggle to return throughout our lives. We are born into this state unless nature has been unkind to us in some physical way. Healthy young children best typify this state. They seem to "roll with life's punches" and do things effortlessly. They seem to unconditionally accept others and to be accepting of others as relationships seem more important to them than their identity. Of course, when a young person's caregivers are less than nurturing, which is increasingly a phenomenon in child-rearing today, the "fall from confidence" occurs.

FIGURE 9

CRISIS STATES OF BEING

CRISIS STATES INTEGRITY BASED	SPECTRUM OF FAILURE	SPECTRUM OF CONSCIOUSNESS	INTERPERSONAL BOUNDARIES
AT NATURALNESS	Living with error	Beginning Transpersonal	 Self with Self
AT LOSS * Emergency * Danger	Anticipated failure	Total Organism vs. Environment and Others	
AT NON ENTITY * Insignificant * Non Existence	Imminent failure	Ego\Body Separation	 Barrier
AT EFFECT * At Injury * Incomplete	Suppressed failure	Ego\Body Separation and Confusion	 Barrier
AT SURVIVAL * Confrontation * Manipulation	Supressed failure Causing others to fail	Persona\Shadow	 Barriers

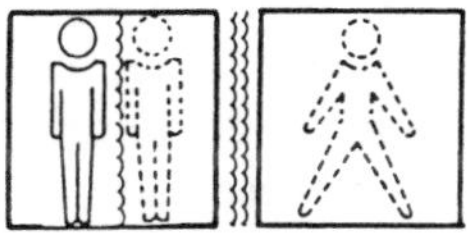

Sizing up a Crisis   87

Few people in our society are supported enough to stay in a state of naturalness. Those who do have an apparent abundance of enthusiasm and always seem to others to be satisfied, yet goal-oriented. Crises become an acceptable part of living--dealt with, flattened out, and forgotten. Generally, people operating at naturalness do not need the assistance of crisis interveners. On the other hand, they may use them in highly productive, self-initiated ways, because they recognize the power of support from others.

This state is often viewed with mistrust from any of the other states below it. How can anyone be so satisfied? Those below a higher state think that someone above is hiding something or that she may be lying about being happy or satisfied. In fact, most of us are envious of people who appear to be too happy. Some people actively oppose a happy person just to get them out of this state.

The good news is that this state actually exists and that when one assists people in crisis who predominantly live life at naturalness, their state can be contagiously rewarding and enlightening. The bad news is that very few people live in this state and that not many crisis interveners know how to effectively assist such people in a crisis situation. In summary, then, this crisis state is one in which upsets in life are naturally embraced as part of one's journey. Everyone becomes a resource in a crisis, and every crisis becomes an opportunity to discover more about one's aliveness. When in this state, the individual becomes responsible as the source of happiness, satisfaction, love, and freedom in their lives.

State 2 - At Loss

Paradoxically, it has been said that "nobody gets out of this world alive." In this regard, one of the main challenges in the melodrama of life ought to be to uncover, develop and fully experience our unique selves. In the process of so doing, we inevitably experience being "at loss" frequently throughout our lives. This state unfolds when our needs and wants are **temporarily** unmet. A degree of urgency prevails, usually accompanied by agitated behaviour. This state is commonly characterized by acute unhappiness. Such unhappiness may be exemplified by the prolonged crying of a young child when its mother has been detained in a car accident for an extended period of time. Or it may be seen in the situations created by the loss of one's wallet, one's automobile breaking down on a remote part of a highway, the loss of a romantic relationship. the loss of a job, the loss of a grandparent, and so on. Most often a person in this state finds it relatively easy to ask for support and assistance from a crisis intervener, surrogate parent, or significant adult. Consequently, intervention results are usually quite successful; and most crisis interveners experience these types of interventions as rewarding. The problems attendant on this state are perceived as outside of oneself, or as outside of one's skin barrier.

Problems are initially perceived as emergent concerns; and most of them are resolved by the person re-organizing the circumstances in her life, often with the immediate assistance of others.

However, if this state of "at loss" persists, individuals may revert to historical, entrenched coping behaviors.

State 3 - At Non-Entity

Barrier

When a crisis persists, anticipated failure turns into imminent or manifested failure. Failure is then perceived as a nullification of the person we think we are. The fear of being a nobody or of being insignificant begins to become indelibly imprinted on our ego or self. The mind responds to this fear by blanking out.

This state is remarkable by its indescribable nature; it is not experienced as being either in charge of one's life or being oppressed by life's circumstances. It is typified by a detached state in which one is alien to both one's self and to one's surroundings. A person in this state quickly learns to disconnect emotions or physical sensations from thinking or thoughts. Thus the ego-mind and the body split off, retaining only a tenuous connection. Quite often this is the state in which suicide becomes a fleeting thought, as non-existence through being insignificant becomes the prevailing tunnel-vision experience.

While this state is neither up nor down and might best be called the "grey zone", it is one with which most people have momentary encounters at several times throughout their lives. When we are in this state, our ability to perceive what is going on around us becomes discolored as we are unable to get a sense of our mind and body working together. This is a state in which feelings tend to be shut down or cut off. Confusion reigns, and seeing others as useful becomes difficult. Nonetheless, this is also a state in which individuals know intuitively that they are fragmenting themselves. While their feelings may be shut down, there are other perceptual modalities which can generate loophole experiences that allow them to escape from this state. One might experience this state after failing an exam, after a breakdown in marriage, after a debilitating sickness, or after injury or the loss of significant others.

State 4 - At Effect

Barrier

When we sink to this state, life on the surface appears not worth living. Nevertheless, glimpses of freedom occur as the person has not yet totally denied responsibility for her circumstances. This crisis state begins when one suppresses her losses because she feels powerless to do otherwise. One acts as if life were a tragedy and she were a victim. This crisis situation is initially characterized by the person's taking little or no responsibility for **action**, only for the outcome of the crisis. At this state, a person may recognize that within is an on-going struggle between wanting to rebel or become a tyrant and being a victim and wanting to be rescued. Most exemplary of this state is the attitude and expression of "I don't know." A person in this state is most reluctant to be rescued by others, as she instinctively knows she needs to rescue herself; yet she feels caught up in being controlled or run (at effect) by the events and experiences in her life. Hoping and wishing predominate and become excuses for not doing anything about her circumstances. When a person is in this state, she suffers from pronounced emotional confusion and is unable to get a clear sense of the resources available to her. This confusion tends to draw rescuers who also do not know how to take care of themselves. Consequently, crisis interveners who unconsciously fulfill their needs through rescuing others tend to be victimized by the person in the crisis state of at effect. It is interesting to note that a person stops being a victim when no one is left to rescue her, or when the pain of irresponsibility becomes too great.

When one is operating **at effect**, she is subject to repeated injury as her state of inaction renders her highly vulnerable to mishaps. This old adage, "If you don't stand for something, you fall for everything," seems to apply to a person in this crisis state. Or, as Joseph Brodsky (1987) suggests, "There are no causes in this world-effects alone. And people are victims of their own effects . . .".

An extreme variant of this state occurs when the individual allows herself to become a martyr, stuck at not knowing why. Or, at the other end of the continuum, she becomes a **hopeless** rescuer of others.

In summary, the first four states might be briefly characterized in the following ways:

Naturalness - a person makes things happen in their life,
At Loss - a person avoids things happening,
At Non-Entity - a person wonders what's happening, and
At Affect - it's happening to her again.

The final crisis state happens when one shifts gears and ceases to accept responsibility for the crisis situation. This state of At Survival is a backlash to feeling hopeless, insignificant and fearful of losing permanently in life.

State 5 - At Survival

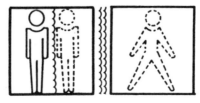

Barriers

Survival is a condition in which crisis are woven into the fabric of one's personality. After having experienced the states above, the person may make a decision to operate from the premise that, to avoid losing, she will do anything, even lie about losing when she has lost. Sinking into this realm produces two distinctive stages.

The first stage is identified by the highly confrontative style of the person in crisis. She confronts or opposes everything in life since basically, life is of questionable value. Emanating from her mind are rules about right and wrong, and ways to maintain these rules by continuously confronting others as well as her environment. This condition leaves no room for others to be right. Life for this person is not about happiness, as everything is confronted or opposed. For an individual who gets stuck here, life becomes misery-bound. The primary aim is to keep others away by creating boundaries between oneself and others. This state requires energy to sustain it, and the state draws power away from others and from the environment rather than allowing one's own natural power to emanate in a balanced way. Recovery from this stage is most difficult, once it has taken hold. After repeated efforts to psychologically survive by being confrontative, the individual perceives others, rather than one's self, as being confrontative. The problem feeds on itself: The more that a person projects her problems to others, the more she requires confrontation as a process for ensuring that she is alive.

Finally, the lowest condition of survival unfolding from confrontation takes hold when we make a pact with ourselves to manipulate others and our environment in calculated ways. When we wake up to discover that confrontation can be extremely energy-draining, we discover that by pretending to be all right we give off a sense of cooperation that can allow us to get what we want, at least temporarily through the manipulation of others. A person operating out of manipulation is essentially disloyal and prone to betraying others. This person may even enjoy getting energized by watching others be betrayed. She manipulates people and relationships; she is revengeful, resentful, jealous, and judgmental.

Very few of us have not touched base with this state of being, if only for brief moments in our lives. Consequently, most of us know how demeaning this condition can be and how a person in this condition actually hates what she is doing, yet is deathly afraid to face up to it. Most of us just wish that our anguish would go away and that we could ignore what we are actually doing. When we are actively manipulating, we have this internal sense that we cannot trust others, must less ourselves -- a sense that grows from losing touch with who we really are. Crises become a steady diet as we seek to maintain excitement in our life by manipulating rather than creating. Life, then, becomes exciting yet questionably not really worth living.

It may be obvious to the reader that, when one is manipulating either oneself or others, there are parts of oneself that we want to disown. As seen in the identity levels depicted in Figure 2, page , these parts are described as our shadow. The more that we disown our shadow, the more that we have to exercise effort to keep ourselves from failing by ensuring that others fail. Interpersonally, our mind splits off from itself as we develop ACTS in life. More often that not, we are not fully aware of our various ACTS, as they are created beneath our level of awareness.

---

3. ACTS OF SURVIVAL DIMENSION

The third dimension of sizing up involves discovering or uncovering what ACTS are taking place in a crisis. To detect ACTS, it is of value to be clear about how they develop. Therefore, an overview of the birth of the act will preface an exploration (through some exercises) of how ACTS might be revealed.

Birth of the ACT

Acts, or roles as some people like to call them, are subsets of ourself. Intent to survive and to avoid being **"at effect"** in the world, as well as to avoid the anguish of experiencing insignificance, we put together an ACT based on how things are presently perceived by us and what has actually happened to us in the past. More often than not, the ACT begins to take form by the time we reach school and life experiences begin to consolidate our embryonic view of life. As life progresses, our viewpoints become distorted and begin to reflect conditions which are outdated or maps of life that are inappropriate. To avoid the pain of being out of synchronicity with reality, we then tend to perceive life as if we were in an act in a play, rather than being the author of the play.

In a more explicit way, Figure 10 provides a Flow Chart of how our ACTS develop and how they are subsequently maintained. Now, in a step-by-step manner, let us examine how this occurs.

Personal History

It is commonly held by many theorists in the field of human development that our basic personality is determined by seven or eight years of age. Parental moulding and environmental supports become the background upon which ongoing life crises unfold. Our own unique skills and personal resources interact with ongoing life experiences to produce our personal history. What we inherited by way of a family and an environment along with our early development, provides the backdrop called our personal history. This backdrop manifests itself early in life in the form of "points of view."

Points of View

Because of our ability to store information and recall to past experiences, we tend to develop conscious maps regarding different aspects of our living. These conscious maps are actually tracers of past events. They become a point of view when something remains incomplete about our past. For example, a five-year-old boy is learning to play the piano upon his mother's insistence. His father walks in and makes the offhand comment that "playing the piano is for sissy's." The young boy then begins to develop a point of view about piano playing. However, not all our mental maps are conscious. Unconscious maps can develop as a result of extremely traumatic experiences. A young person may choose to suppress awareness of the trauma, yet retain a point of view which operates below his level of awareness. An example of this possibility might be a situation in which a young boy is forced by his mother to dress up as a girl. To avoid the excruciating pain of embarrassment, the young boy suppresses his male instincts and begins to increasingly develop a point of view that it is better to be female than male, despite his physical characteristics.

Significant Events

Once points of view are established, life produces significant events which then tend to consolidate one's point of view around certain life issues. In the example already mentioned of the young boy being dressed up as a girl, a significant event might be his having to dress up like a girl for his birthday party or for a family reunion. In the example of the young boy playing the piano, a significant event may be his father openly criticizing him in front of his friends for playing the piano.

After such significant events, our point of view becomes generalized and therefore susceptible to distortion. More often than not, these significant events represent failures rather than successes in our lives. Once the points of view which we hold become sufficiently well generalized, perhaps through repeated experiences, we then reach a point of making a fundamental decision about how life is for us.

Fundamental Decision

We arrive at the point of making a fundamental decision (which is more like an imprinted point of view of life) when we are faced with the realization that being one's self is not enough. This is a turning point when our perceptions become distorted in such a way that we begin to perceive present and future events inaccurately. When we make a fundamental decision, we lose sight of and touch with how our decisions perpetrate our unhappiness. In real-life terms, we may make the decision that we are a "stumblebum" and cannot play sports. Or, we may make the decision that relationships never work or that having friends always produces enemies, or that we will never do well enough in school to please our parents, and so on. Once we make a fundamental decision, we then tend to generate beliefs and attitudes around that decision.

Beliefs and Attitudes

Beliefs and attitudes are mind-generated positions in life. They serve to provide solutions for the decision made that who I am is not enough. Beliefs and attitudes reinforce our fundamental decision to the extent that more often than not we lose sight of how the fundamental decision was made and how it controls our life. Examples of beliefs that emanate from fundamental decisions are "Don't trust anybody," "Nobody really cares," "Everybody is out for themselves," and "All's fair in love and war." Some attitudes that develop from the fundamental decision might look like the following:

1. I'm going to do it my way.
2. The world is all screwed up.
3. I come first before anybody else does.
4. Don't let anybody know how dumb and afraid or stupid you are.
5. Act tough and be hard to get along with.

Coupled with our beliefs and attitudes, on-going melodramas or crises that we experience in life set the stage for us to create our own unique ACT.

FIGURE 10

DEVELOPMENT OF ACTS

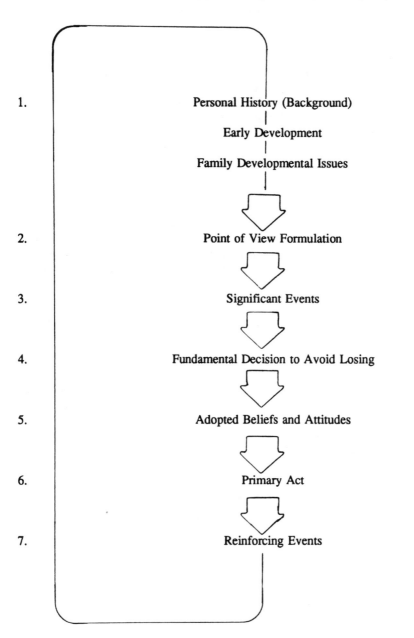

1. Personal History (Background)

   Early Development

   Family Developmental Issues

2. Point of View Formulation

3. Significant Events

4. Fundamental Decision to Avoid Losing

5. Adopted Beliefs and Attitudes

6. Primary Act

7. Reinforcing Events

Development of Acts

Most of us generate an Act after having adopted the position that, if we can't win around certain life issues such as making relationships work for us or making money or being successful in school, then to avoid losing we will solve the problem through acting in a number of unique ways. The Act is a manifestation of our fundamental decision and can either be conscious or unconscious. More often than not, after years of practice, it goes underground and we cease to recognize how it runs us. Though the Act which we develop is utilitarian, it loses its effectiveness and resilience after repeated use; and we then become a victim of our own Act. Acts are extremely challenging to detect as they are really designed by ourselves to be elusive and to protect us from further loss. It is often the case that our Act becomes so unconscious that we are the last person to know that we are Acting. More often that not, we perceive others as Acting and not ourselves.

There are some seemingly universal Acts that thread through most people's lives. As these Acts are born out of adversity, they are essentially survival-based, with the goal of avoiding further suffering. Some of the beliefs and attitudes mentioned above are really fledgling Acts. As these beliefs and opinions become solidified through reinforcement of our experiences, some undercurrent themes of acting begin to surface. For example, one of the most obvious ways of acting is to withhold. An extreme example of this is suicide. In this case, further loss is avoided by simply not playing in the game of life. Another primary act is to preclude others from winning, thereby ensuring that nobody wins. As long as the game is never over, then the experience of loss can be avoided. Rebels and tyrants are borne out of this position.

There are countless numbers of ACTS which we can develop to protect ourselves from ourselves. ACTS are not people coming together, they are people's stories or melodramas interplaying with one another. A melodrama, as the word might suggest, is akin to a soap opera, in which good and evil continuously intertwine in a web-like manner. In the melodrama, good never seems to triumph for long before some evil interrupts.

When we put our ACT into play, we become caught up in this web-like affair. The web catches us like automated robots or "mindless bugs" programmed to repeat our mistakes.

Our ACTS are utilitarian, as mentioned before, in that they serve as a type of armour which we use in order to avoid the possibility of painful experiences. Nevertheless, the resistance they create actually further impoverishes our life. ACTS are power-draining rather than power-generating. The most we can then get in life is temporary well-being. As we tend to be a condition species, our ACTS tend to be indelible and tend to resist change, unless a more serious turn of events occurs in our life.

Recognizing one's own ACT is an enormous challenge. It requires an extraordinary effort for the individual to probe into her resistance and to see herself as competent and fully responsible for her life experiences. When we look into how we resist our aliveness, we can potentially get glimpses of our ACT and how it drives us as if we were an actor in the play of life, rather than the author of the play as already mentioned.

Regardless of how predisposed to our ACT we may be (either consciously or unconsciously), it is possible to make good use of our ACT, in fact, to transform it so that it becomes congruent with our true self. When we begin to recognize our ACT, it gives us the opportunity to play with it and to modify it even to change it to reflect moment to moment changes in the upsets in our life.

Revealing Acts

The nature of ACTS is such that they become increasingly more revealing during crisis events. First of all, the interpretation that the mind makes of a crisis is most readily telecast through one's face. The face becomes the predominate stage or battlefield where the ACT or combination of ACTS carve out their melodrama. Character armour (Alexander Lowen, 1967) follows, and is developed in various parts of the body. This character armour builds over time, creating barriers to protect our perceived vulnerability and to reinforce our chosen way to ACT.

From a crisis-intervention viewpoint, the face can reveal telltale aspects of an ACT. This is often ? quite visible, although these telltales can also be subtly camouflaged in an attempt to avoid or divert unwanted attention. Nevertheless, despite attempts to deny or divert direct access to her face, the person in crisis more often than not ends up revealing to the perceptive crisis intervener many aspects of a crisis ACT, without really knowing it.

The sizing-up worksheet at the end of the chapter lists a few of the innumerable descriptions of face ACTS. You may find it useful to review them now and even to speculate on your own face ACT descriptors in preparation for the exercises which follow.

These exercises are offered to invite you to explore and perhaps have a glimpse of the nature of ACTS. Doing these exercises can serve to reveal unusual pathways enabling the crisis intervener to more accurately size-up the crisis. It is also important to note that by means of personal review of one's own ACTS the crisis intervener can become much clearer about how personal boundaries get in the way of her effectiveness in serving others. Therefore the first exercise is a personal review of ACTS.

Exercise No. 1

Seek out a quiet space where you can be undisturbed for half an hour or so. Let yourself get comfortable and begin to let your mind wander back through your early childhood. Allow yourself, if you will, to notice early events in your life. It is useful to refer back to the guidelines on "observational tuning in" on page 83. Continue now to recall times when you were experiencing not being acknowledged, being put down, or being unaccepted for who you were. Notice, as if you were a participant observer watching your history, how the events in your early life placed you in a "no win" situation. As you explore these significant events, look for underlying points of view that came up for you at that time. Now look for decisions which you might have made regarding these points of view. Take your time during this process. Now, ask yourself what plans you made to solve the problems you were facing in your life at that time. Did you come up with any decisions such as:

* I will show you who is boss!
* Nobody will ever control me again, I'll do it my way!
* I'll get sick and then they'll be sorry!
* Nobody else will do it, so neither will I!
* The world is mean and cruel, therefore I can be too!
* Nobody will know who I am, so then I can't be hurt.

As you uncover any one of these or any combination of these, or indeed any decisions which you made in the early part of your life, reflect on them for a moment. Notice if any of them are still in operation for you today. Notice if they serve you in ways that support you being fully alive and competent. Look to see if they support you life being joyful and full of satisfaction. See if they hinder your relationships or your desire to make a difference with your life.

If you have made any decisions like those mentioned above or any of your own unique decisions, give yourself permission to acknowledge how they **were** valuable for you at one point in time. Allow yourself now the opportunity to choose to employ your current awareness about these decisions in a way that lets you give up on this decision and start living in the present. You may wish to let the past be the past and your old memories simply be old memories. You may wish to use these decisions in conscious and very selective ways in the future. Now, thank yourself for doing the exercise, and acknowledge yourself as the source of any realizations that surface for you. Your simple willingness to explore in this manner indicates your willingness to let self-mastery be the gateway actualizing your competency as a crisis intervener.

Exercise No. 2

For this exercise, begin by reviewing, on your mind's screen, two people you have worked with over the past year who have experienced significant crisis that have not been resolved. You may wish to choose people who have had repeated experiences of suffering or failure with one kind of problem. Now, using the flow diagram as a guide and using the sizing-up worksheet at the end of this chapter, complete this exercise, taking as much time as you need. If you encounter difficulty in clarifying what an individual's act might be, you may wish to again review the previous section on Perceptual Lenses and Crisis States before continuing.

Describing an ACT is at very best a trial-and-error activity. Once one becomes store practiced in her perceptual exploration of ACTS, a "felt sense" of an ACT can be obtained within the very first few minutes of a crisis situation. However, a danger exists in identifying an ACT too rigidly, as this can lead to a tunnel-vision viewpoint of an individual and perhaps even to a self-fulfilling prophecy about the outcome of the crisis. Therefore, a word of caution is offered, inviting you to recall your "second naivety" as you use the first phase of the SOURCE formula, **SHARE, OBSERVE** and **UNCOVER**. Rather than trying to generate an ACT from you cognitive understanding of another person, let an ACT gradually reveal itself to you. In this way, the ACT becomes vibrant and ever-changing in its subtle forms. Finally, you may wish to review this exercise a number of times as your own perceptual lenses in life become more open at one time than another.

SUMMARY STATEMENT

It is important to recall the process of "soft sensing" with all of one's perceptual capacities. This process both with self and with others, either as a self-preparation task or an initial sizing-up guideline, is the essence of impactful observation.

Self-sensing is allowing the right brain to guide and use the left brain rather than the other way around. Digital processing of information is superceded by analogic, integrative, and intuitive awareness. It is not mind over body or right hemisphere over left, not one brain function over another; it is the synergy of mind, brain and body. It's a question of balance.

This transduction process (Rossi, 1986) is an intimate affair, so entangled that to break it apart is to end up with strands that have little meaning or value. Another way of expressing this balance is to speak of being in a groove or "peaking" in our awareness. This indescribable state is known to us all, if only for fleeting moments. When this delicate balance occurs, sizing up a crisis becomes an exploration of the overall pattern that guides the individual in a crisis.

Using the first phase of the SOURCE formula as a guide for uncovering the three dimensions of sizing up a crisis can serve to reveal a beginning sense of the overall pattern. The crisis intervener can then operate in an ecologically balanced way, poised to cut through the crisis "dis-ease" with her intuitive knife. The next chapter will begin to focus on intervention with others, using the Beyond Content Model in its complete form.

EXERCISES - CHAPTER FIVE

1. Write out on a 3 x 5 card key words related to the initial guidelines for entering a crisis. Condition these trigger or anchor words by allowing your body to posture them and your minds' eye to create empowering images around them. By respectively going over and over these key words you can inculcate them as a wellness interaction pattern that automatically triggers off when you enter into a crisis.

2. Identify your primary perceptual mode you operate from when assisting others in a crisis. Which perceptual mode do you use the least? What types of crises do you find most troublesome. Use Table 3 for reference and attempt to clarify your understanding of behavioural traits related to these perceptual modes.

3. Recall two recent crisis events you were involved in and using the crisis-states-of-being, Figure 9 as a guide, reflect on how these states were differentially operating for each scenario. Record any questions regarding your need for further clarity regarding each case scenario.

4. Using Figure 10, offering a flow chart on the development of ACTS and the descriptions of the steps that follow, trace the development of an ACT or persona of someone you know on an intimate basis. Next, as a self observation exercise trace the possible developments of an ACT or ACTS characteristic of your lifestyle or professional posture as a crisis intervener. Record this information in your Competency Journal for future reference.

SUGGESTED READINGS

1. Three books by Virginia Satir, **Making contact** (Ca: Celestial Arts, 1975), **Self esteem** (Ca: Celestial Arts, 1975), and **Your many faces** (Ca: Celestial Arts, 1978), offer some practical ways to size up some of the basic patterns of communication mentioned in this chapter. Her most recent book, **The new people making** (Ca: Science and Behaviour, 1988), expands on the behaviour classifications mentioned in this chapter.

2. An account of how Self Life Positions (ACTS) are relevant to the practice of child care is simply discussed with practical applications in **Professional child care practice**, (Can: University of Victoria, 1988). This manual will be of value to anyone working or studying in the field of child care.

3. The two volumes by John Grinder and Richard Bandler, **Structures of magic I and II** (Ca: Science and Behaviour, 1976), offer a thorough explanation of how the primary perceptual senses serve as a representational system. They also demonstrate how this system can be used to map how clients in turmoil make sense of their ongoing experiences.

NOTES

NOTES

_____

_____

_____

_____

_____

_____

_____

_____

_____

_____

_____

_____

_____

_____

_____

_____

_____

_____

_____

_____

_____

_____

_____

_____

_____

_____

CHAPTER SIX

APPLICATION OF

THE BEYOND CONTENT MODEL

In the experts' mind there are few possibilities. In the
beginners' mind there are many.

- Suzuki Roshi

MODEL OVERVIEW

Up to this point the Beyond Content model has gradually unfolded from the previous five
chapters offering an evolving yet dynamic framework for crisis intervention. The question now
becomes, how does one make use of this model as a whole? This chapter will summarize how the
various components of the model interconnect. As well, it will demonstrate, in a practical way, its
use in the re-building crisis dissolving process with crisis situations. It will conclude with suggestions
on how the crisis intervener might approach working the model.

THE PRIMARY COMPONENTS

Figure 11 offers a rather simplistic graphic overview of how the various components
interconnect and flow together to form a coherent framework. An outline of the component parts of
these building blocks is also presented on the following page. This outline, as a companion to Figure
11, can be used for consolidation of one's understanding as well as for quick reference and review.

Beginning with the Dynamics of Competency in Figure 11, the intent is for the crisis intervener to willingly and in progressively refining ways stimulate within themselves the four forces of competency. In so doing, the crisis intervener can, at the same time, gradually yet spontaneously activate these dynamics in those she is attempting to assist in crisis.

Further down in Figure 11, we see the Beyond Content Contextual Principles which the intervener can embrace as guidelines for working within crisis arenas. Conscious awareness of these principles serves to clarify crisis and to mobilize intervention competency.

Next, the SOURCE formula serves as a pathway for a step-by-step approach towards crisis dissolution. This formula provides a conduit for operationalizing the contextual principles and makes real the crisis intervener's competency as well as the competency of those she serves. In an interwoven and progressively accentuating manner, the first half of the SOURCE formula addresses the question of how the crisis intervener can "size-up" a crisis situation. Making a connection through interactive **Sharing; Observing** perceptual stuckness; and **Uncovering** ACTS as well as identifying the Crisis State: these are the first steps in the intervention process. In addition, sizing up is a continuous process occurring as an undercurrent or background activity during the second or intervention phase of the SOURCE approach. The second half of the SOURCE formula accentuates intervention strategies, capitalizes on client resistance, and actualizes client competency in a re-building block manner.

The step beyond basic crisis intervention invites the crisis intervener to always consider the possibility of transformation. This aspect of crisis intervention boldly supports exploration of crises that considers the well-being of not only of oneself but also of others and of one's community. However, rarely does the well being of everyone in a crisis become a conscientiously sought after outcome, as mentioned so many times already, since most crisis intervention services do not mandate themselves to go beyond simple stabilization or coping.

Inevitably it seems our conditioned and overpowering need to respond to the trauma of the moment cloaks our capacity to perceive crisis as opportunities for enhancing our overall wellbeing. Allowing our natural wisdom to seek harmony and balance from aspects of one's crisis experience has all too often been grossly overlooked or dismissed as possible. Therefore, assuming that this is at the extraordinary end of crisis intervention where opportunities for growth are realized, the SOURCE formula serves to guide the crisis intervener beyond simple crisis resolution. Ever ready to capture unique "turning points," the crisis intervener entertains **expansion** or the exploration of new territories. This is first done by allowing transformation of crises events through the completion of all unfinished business related to the crisis in question. Then, armed with one's "second naivete," one can explore unknown territories as the client dares to risk stepping beyond her previously established boundaries. This could simply mean that those in crises awaken to potential they never thought they had. When this happens, the task is to challenge them to use this uncovered potential to further melt down the boundaries between parts of themselves and their whole self, between themselves and others, and between themselves and the outside world. To transform one's circumstances is to go beyond our conditioning and become masters of our own reality.

FIGURE 11

BEYOND CONTENT MODEL

PRIMARY COMPONENTS

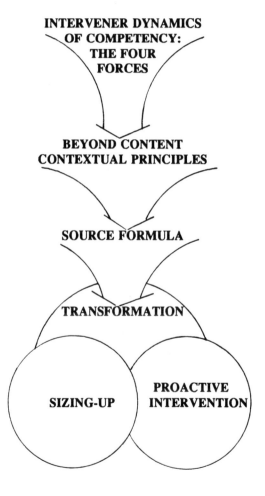

BEYOND CONTENT MODEL

BASIC BUILDING BLOCK COMPONENTS

1. PRIMARY PURPOSE

To **Assist** and **Serve** those in crisis to re-capture a state of balance by mobilizing their unused potential for restoring their natural competency, self sufficiency, and a continuously expanding sense of significance.

2. DYNAMICS OF COMPETENCY

* Integrity
* Purpose
* Creative Intention
* Self Mastery

3. GUIDING CONTEXTUAL PRINCIPLES

* On Client-Defined Crisis
* On Competency
* On Crisis and Opportunity
* On Immediacy
* On What Works
* On Neutrality
* On Augmenting
* On Blending
* On Inclusiveness
* On Self-Organizing

4. THE SOURCE FORMULA	TWO PHASES	OPERATIONAL COMPONENTS
S: SHARING	SIZING UP	PERCEPTUAL MODES
O: OBSERVING	PHASE	CRISIS INTEGRITY STATES
U: UNCOVERING		ACTS OR ROLES
R: RESOURCING	INTERVENTION	RESISTANCE AS RESOURCE
C: COMPLETING	PHASE	SELF EXPLORATION
E: EXPANDING		CREATIVE ORDEALS

STABILIZATION

TRANSFORMATION

THE RE-BUILDING PROCESS

In the last chapter, we described five crisis states of integrity, pointing out how they develop and flow from one to another. The next question becomes how one moves and facilitates movement towards competency, given the current integrity state of a crisis. Beginning with **"at survival,"** the most-bound up state of a crisis, and moving through to **"at naturalness,"** we will now explore ways and means of regaining competency. Figure 12 shows some of the most significant blocks that act as barriers to the various states of integrity.

The list of these blocks is by no means meant to be all-inclusive. Rather, the list at best offers a modest account of the primary issues that seem to surface at the various crisis states. You are invited to examine them and refine them in accordance with your own understanding.

1. UP FROM SURVIVAL

The survival state is the most common state encountered by crisis interveners. When people are operating at survival the odds are stacked against the crisis intervener making a significant difference. This is so because people in this state cannot see, feel, or hear any other way than their way at the moment. Trying to change them or alter their perceptions only draws the crisis intervener into their melodramatic web, where ACTS predominate and not one's true self. In this crisis state, those in crisis are actively working on being a master of survival. Therefore the crisis intervener is almost always perceived as an antagonist. Covertly, if not overtly, the crisis intervener is considered a threat to their ACT. The crisis intervener becomes "grist for their mill" as they discover how to manipulate her to be at survival state with them.

The survivalists who manipulate are going to resist the crisis intervener as they are unwitttingly resisting their own capacity for natural integrity. Resisting assistance from the crisis intervener is essential to affirming the survivalists' perceived need and to giving credibility to their crises. In almost all circumstances the greater the survivalists' resistance the greater the need.

In order for the crisis intervener to avoid being drawn into dead ending oppositional traps first and foremost she must recognize that resistance from the person "at survival" is necessary. Interestingly enough, the more the crisis intervener accommodates the survialist's resistance (without necessarily agreeing with the reasons for it) the more likely she will be perceived as valued and effective by the survialist. Acceptance and trust building with the crisis intervener is greatly aided when the survivalists experiences their resistance being legitimized and tolerated. The wisdom of this understanding nevertheless often gets clouded over by escalating resistance causing most crisis interveners to prematurely abandon this operating principle. Quite often the value of this approach not become apparent until after the conflict begins to subside. It is generally only at this point that does the resistance can begin to be capitalized on and used as a source of energy for re-establishing a "steady state of being." In this sense, resistance is to be perceived as a resource. Going with or aligning with resistance allows the crisis intervener to really be an ally of the clients' unconscious mind even though her conscious mind may vehemently continue to resist. Ironically, if there were no resistance, the crisis intervener would not be necessary. This is hard to swallow at times. Once realized though, it makes breakthroughs possible. The crisis intervener who stays consciously aware

---

FIGURE 12

COMPETENCY RE-BUILDING BLOCKS

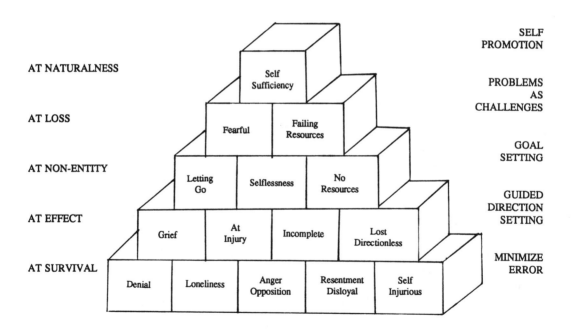

CRISIS STATES OF INTEGRITY	TRANSFORMATIONAL BLOCKS	SUGGESTED ACTIONS

AT NATURALNESS

Self Sufficiency

SELF PROMOTION

AT LOSS

Fearful — Failing Resources

PROBLEMS AS CHALLENGES

AT NON-ENTITY

Letting Go — Selflessness — No Resources

GOAL SETTING

AT EFFECT

Grief — At Injury — Incomplete — Lost Directionless

GUIDED DIRECTION SETTING

AT SURVIVAL

Denial — Loneliness — Anger Opposition — Resentment Disloyal — Self Injurious

MINIMIZE ERROR

that the **content** of a crisis or crisis story can be impoverished, inaccurate, over-generalized, or over-accentuated has the best chance of minimizing the shadow of resistance cast over her efforts to shed light on the crisis need. Highly effective crisis interveners are like magnates drawn to resistance recognizing that it as the gateway to aliveness. They plumb the depths of resistance, looking for the causes of avoiding being alive in the present. They endeavour to uncover the causes that are molding the resistance into its present form and to transform these causes.

As Figure 12 shows, the primary survival issues manifested by the person in crisis are denial, loneliness, opposition, disloyalty, and self- injury. The crisis intervener who instinctively senses this "boxed in affair" knows that you really cannot tamper with this self-contained, delicately balanced machine called the human being when it is operating out of a survival state. When the client is acting out of survival, your pre-eminent task becomes that of preventing any further destruction. This can be accomplished by carefully Sharing, Observing, and Uncovering the unique aspects of the client's current survival box. What is critically important here is to resist the tendency to take the box apart and fix it. You must also realize that probing by pushing buttons may cause further stuckness and rigidity or even a shift to another survival box, especially if you do the "hunt and peck" kind of button-pushing. Being a well programmed crisis machine, the human will become even more out of control and crazy-making if the information it gives out to the crisis intervener cannot be accepted. Therefore it is critically important that the crisis intervener seek only to minimize error and to reveal the boundaries of the crisis box. When the client is able to recognize the nature of her crisis box or boxes without being made to seem wrong or without having necessarily to do anything about it, she can free herself to see more clearly how her stance towards the crisis does not work.

A client operating out of a survival state is run by her ACT in life. While she may think she has become aware of her way of manipulating, she may be only partially awake to it. Other subtle forms of survival may cloud over current breakthroughs in awareness. This phenomenon is commonly experienced when someone appears to have realized her ACT, yet is seemingly unable to go beyond this awareness. In other words, someone gives the appearance of being stuck and frustrated with her awareness; and she is.

A Survival Encounter

Encountering someone at survival, the crisis intervener can begin by SHARING themselves as being someone who is curious and compassionately intrigued by the nature of the ongoing suffering. Care should be taken not to offer curative solutions to a crisis only a caring awareness. In this way, she shares herself as a possible resource when a turning-point opportunity arises.

Simultaneously, the crisis intervener observes in a sizing up manner, careful not to let her judging mind pick apart the individual. Through "soft sense" observing, the crisis intervener simply notices, allowing information to pass through her rather than becoming preoccupied with it. This way of holistic seeing and receiving integrates the flow of information continuously while remaining ever aware of whole patterns rather than partial ones. The experienced crisis intervener who "soft senses" remains alert to how past efforts by other interveners of examining and probing by disassembling have resulted in the inability to reassemble the parts into a whole again. The primary aim of the uncovering process is to become extraordinarily sensitive to the abilities of the client's self-correcting capacity, her capacity to regain a constructive posture. When a client recognizes her oppositional or manipulative survival efforts and can acknowledge them as not working, self-correcting becomes possible. Practically speaking, the crisis intervener connects with the individual's self-correcting and maintaining machinery by the process of inquiry. Part of the inquiry may go like this:

* The information you may be receiving could be causing the interference that you are experiencing. How accurate is the information you have? How does the problem you have get worse?

* Do you recall any previous experiences where similar breakdowns occurred? How did you self-correct then?

* How have you maintained effective functioning in the past?

* What do you get out of keeping yourself from self-correcting?

* What are you opposed to, and how do you oppose effectively?

* When you stop operating effectively, who or what is to blame?

* How specifically do you avoid losing, and when do your efforts to avoid losing not work for you?

* What clues have you been aware of that tell you that self-   correcting is possible?

Obviously, the questions that a crisis intervener generates will be phrased to fit the special nature of each survival state.

The process of clarifying and acknowledging one's ACT and survival state can be further aided through careful examination of one's perceptual stuckness. The movie camera analogy previously used will once again be interwoven as a metaphor for working with the malfunctioning of the primary perceptual modality lens. For survivalists, visual and auditory lens stuckness tend to predominate.

Visual Stuckness

Observing a person in crisis who is visually antagonistic, one can note that her visual lens is wide open. Her pupils may be dilated, giving the impression that she is blowing up inside or possibly that she is throwing daggers at those she encounters. At the beginning of the intervention process, there is wisdom in maintaining a comfortable distance to one side. The sharing process involves guiding in an indirect way, by noticing and acknowledging that the person in crisis needs to project her anguish onto something she can see. Acting as a reflection screen, the crisis intervener seeks to make this predominately visual energy bounce away towards less vulnerable targets in the immediate environment. In a sense, the crisis intervener acts like a movie producer, redirecting this highly sensitive visual camera towards targets that can produce a better resolution. Redirecting can also

---

simultaneously include a "reframing" and "editing" process. This is accomplished by presenting workable and unworkable viewpoints alongside of one another allowing for a synthesis of this information to produce a revised viewpoint for the person in crisis. Operating in this manner, the crisis intervener can stop the show periodically, so that a re-vision can be made. The crisis intervener gently prods the oversensitive actor or actors to look at as many different viewpoints as possible, including those of others involved in the crisis. The intent is to gradually reduce the visual rigidity of the person in crisis, permitting her to see how the coincidence of opposites can free her from a restrictive way of seeing.

The next step is for the person in crisis to recognize how to do her own self-correcting. This is generally a trial-and-error process in which the need to give up righteous positions is first of all acknowledged and then such positions are replaced by action. This action is based on what looks workable from moment to moment.

At this juncture, one often encounters apprehension which could again produce pronounced visual stuckness. When this happens, one should return to indirect guiding, giving the person in crisis an opportunity to project out again so that another attempt at fine-tuning is experienced. This recycling process may have to occur several times until the person in crisis can trust that you do not represent a tyrant in disguise.

When the person in crisis begins to gain confidence and become assured that self-observation will not make her overly vulnerable again, then she can be encouraged to comment on how others might perceive her when she is stuck. The client can now start to search for ways to be perceived as powerful, in control and yet not rigid or righteous. You can assist the client by asking questions such as the following: "What would it look like to be powerful and resource(ful)? What are some ways for you to now minimize the errors that have already been made? How can losses be avoided and kept to a minimum? How can you regain a foothold and redirect your energy to produce more workable outcomes?"

Auditory Stuckness

Another way in which a person in crisis can be stuck involves their auditory sending and receiving capabilities. Using the movie camera analogy again, we may say that it is as though the auditory apparatus is stuck in the wide-open mode. Turned up to maximum volume, the auditory channel gets distorted and also overloads the camera. Because this camera is a delicately balanced piece of equipment, the disruption of one function causes the other functions to over- or under-compensate. Similarly humans quite often compensate for auditory preoccupation by shuttering down their visual capabilities as well as their self-maintenance or kinesthetic (feeling) capabilities.

The auditorily predisposed person in crisis tends to be already overloaded with information. Therefore new crisis information is either re-directed outward, rejected, reduced in value, or screened by the intellectual brain. It seems that a highly activated internal voice is continuously operating in a judgmental manner on what it hears. Serving as a watchdog, it edits both incoming auditory information as well as thoughts arising from the person's memory banks. In short, the noise inside competes with and overlays the noise from the outside, resulting in confusion and in emotional and visual constriction. This state of being is sometimes revealed by the critical nature of responses to questions from the crisis intervener. One common tendency for the auditorily predisposed person in crisis is to repeat every question asked by the crisis intervener either aloud or in her head in order to screen it through the mind for editing and evaluation purposes.

The crisis intervener has a formidable task with this kind of perceptual preoccupation as verbal dialogue tends to increase resistance. It seems that the fewer the words used by the crisis intervener, the better. Therefore, in a benign, yet inquisitive manner, the crisis intervener is wise to simply observe how the this person manifests resistance throughout their body. Indicators that might be observed are poor posture, listlessness, body twitches, furrowed forehead with no apparent affect, shallow breathing, staring with somewhat critical eyes and head angulated to hear better. This type of person might complain of migraine headaches, tightness in the jaw, chronic muscle tightness, and tiredness after very little physical activity.

Through whole-body observation and through mirroring the clients physical behaviour, the crisis intervener can more readily stimulate this type of person to talk. As well as mirroring, the crisis intervener can offer fairly neutral statements of a visually stimulating kind. For example, the crisis intervener can point the design of a coffee cup and invite the client to judge the quality of it or to comment on the appropriate size of the room or any of the objects in it. This way of soliciting comments can draw the person in crisis out of her predominating auditory mode by having her make visual observations. Next, in an effort to move towards where the resistance is greatest, the crisis intervener might encourage this person to comment or speculate on what her crisis might look like from the intervener's point of view. When this encouragement is prefaced by a comment suggesting that the client probably has a better idea than most people of how their crisis is viewed by others this tends to acknowledge the value and importance she places on her assessing and evaluating skills is acknowledged. This nonconfrontational approach quite often gets the client to begin indirectly judging the content of her own critical thinking. This type of client has an inordinate need to judge; and, if little opportunity exists for them to judge the crisis intervener, she ends up judging herself.

As you continue, take care not to judge the client's viewpoints; and exercise patience in just hearing what she has to say, knowing that internally she is blockading any attempts to be evaluated. If you can, resonate with their inner judgmental voice without siding with it. As you resonate with it, she will increasingly sense that you hear her, even though she may not have directly said what is on her mind. Sufficiently heard, the client can become more receptive to allowing her visual perceptions to contribute to her understanding.

Connecting with the client's feelings is another matter. Usually such clients are extremely protective, choosing to cast a shadow over their emotions for fear of catastrophic rejection either by others or even by themselves. In the latter circumstance, emotional self-evaluation is often one of their worst fears.

The approach of encouraging the person in crisis to share her superiority of thinking prepares her for eventually seeing that it will not be devastating to experience her emotional self. The sense of assurance is further enhanced when the crisis intervener maintains a soft, receptive voice, a slower than normal speech pattern, and a non-judgmental, reflective stance. This way of being can be quite pleasurable for the crisis intervener compared to more adversarial interaction and also can indirectly serve to model how humility can work. The critical stance and somewhat laboured communication of this type of person makes it far too easy for a crisis intervener to become hooked into an adversarial dialogue characterized by harsh and stilted words. Staying psychologically neutral is essential to avoid confrontational traps.

Developing a trustful interaction with an auditorily predisposed person in crisis is rare since such a person has so much inbred distrust for aspects of herself. Nevertheless, crisis intervention can prepare the ground for ongoing counselling or therapy, simply by encouraging the client to continue to use her judgement capabilities.

Finally, as the opportunity arises, generate dialogue that allows for this person to reflect on other people's crises that are similar to her own and have her advise you of what are some intervention possibilities. Explore with her how these similar circumstances manifest physical symptoms that are observable as body armour in others. Get the client to evaluate and judge these comparable crisis scenarios of others. Further, ask this person to picture, if she can, a crisis scene in which the bound-up energy is far more extreme than in her situation. You can then invite her to comment on how others must feel when so restricted.

This bridging of thoughts with visions and feelings tends, contrary to what the client thinks, to enrich their intellectual reasoning capabilities. For the crisis intervener to be successful here, she almost always has to exercise a humble tolerance of being overly judged, misinterpreted, and discounted. The auditorily predisposed person in crisis tests the crisis intervener's willingness to go beyond these roadblocks, as this type of client is truly a master of manipulation.

2. UP TO AT EFFECT

Emotional Stuckness

If one looks cojointly at Figures 9 & 12 which picture the Crisis States of Being and the Re-Building Blocks respectively, it may be obvious that the arduous task of surfacing above the survival line does not offer much in the way of consolation. In fact, being AT EFFECT is like stepping back into our past where life was really terrible! Actually, Survival was the escape hatch out of the anguish of being at least partially responsible for our circumstances. To return to AT EFFECT is to once again allow ourselves to be a victim of life as opposed to a victimizer. Letting ourselves stay in this state is to allow grief, accidents, unfinishedness, and lostness to hang like a cloud over our existence. The absence of anguish becomes our only hope. While we have limited awareness of being responsible for our circumstances we take little or no responsibility for our actions during a crisis.

In this state, the tendency is to suffocate ourselves by suppressing our aliveness. We become a reaction machine "knee jerking through life." Most exemplary of this state is the attitude and expression of "I don't know." At this crisis state, ACTS are formulated although not yet fully cast. Being insufficient forms the basis for this stuckness. Therefore even one's evolving ACT is not yet sufficient. At this state of being, the individual becomes immobilized by her pseudo-feelings while her real feelings are bound up.

Preoccupied with minimizing self and avoiding further deterioration in the eyes of others, this person hides out in her own shadow. The shadow envelopes her like a fog, excluding the possibility of seeing or hearing what is really going on outside the shadow.

Encountering Someone At Effect

When encountering someone AT EFFECT, the crisis intervener will notice that this person appears to be in a trance-like confusion that keeps them split off from their surroundings. The person's body gives the impression of being heavily ladened and incapable of moving without extraordinary effort.

The crisis intervener, recognizing this state of affairs, cautiously watches for the subtle ways of being hooked into rescuing the client. Even though this client has some awareness of what may be the source of her problems she does not know what to do about them. What is more, she seldom trusts that anyone else knows what to do either. Advice from others is often shunned for fear of being conned and losing oneself at the expense of another. Yet, ironically, the client continues to search for answers from others, who may too readily want to rescue her. The crisis intervener will observe that not only has this client restricted or shuttered down her visual awareness, she has also overlayed opaque and obscuring filters on her auditory apparatus. It seems as though the client fears that her feelings will engulf her if she does not anethesize herself into not feeling. Consequently, her emotions get recycled within her mind/body, creating both physical and mental stuckness. What gets portrayed to the outside world are simulations of these genuine emotions, coming out in the form of pseudo-feelings such as guilt, depression, frustration, and confusion.

Great care needs to be taken not to let observation turn into a subtle form of judgement of the individual's pseudo- or even of her real feelings. Instead of saying "Your looking sad" the crisis intervener might say, "The chair you are sitting on is large and has a colorful pattern." Or, if the client is electively mute, you might comment on how silence leaves room for much to be said both inside ourselves and to others.

Guiding Intervention

The primary approach to a person stuck AT EFFECT is to directly guide her towards action. This can be started by focusing on background aspects of the crisis situation and by attempting to draw attention to these aspects in a neutral way. While the client may remain reluctant to see directly, she may begin to see with her mind's eye when the crisis intervener makes simple, neutrally phrased observations. Continued attention to the landscape surrounding the client can draw her out of her stuckness. Statements work better than open-ended questions. When the person in crisis begins to make eye contact, she is usually inviting you to involve her in the conversation. This can be best accomplished by making a statement and following it with a question requiring a minimal response such as **yes**, **no**, **good**, **bad**, **right**, or **wrong**. For example, a crisis intervener might say, "For some people, listening is more important than speaking. Is this true for you?"

Guiding is a gradual step-by-step UNCOVERING and RESOURCING process in which the guide must often stop and wait until the person in crisis is ready to move on.

Making Physical Contact.

Physically, the person stuck AT EFFECT often looks, as mentioned, as if she has a heavy load on top of her. Her eyes may appear heavy, unfocused, and even blurry. The person's affect is generally quite low, her body crumpled-looking. She may have a "dead pan"look carved on her face. More often than not, this person is wanting consolation in the form of contact. Sighs of relief or changing body positions can be openings for the crisis intervener to serve as a conduit for the release of bound-up energy to the environment. Such release can be effected done by carefully connecting one's hand to the client's left shoulder, upper back, forearm, or knee. Accompanying comments that draw this person towards making contact with her surroundings or with significant others can generate a sense of acceptance and caring. Here one is "caring with" rather than "caring for" the client. "Caring with" actively encourages the client to use you as a guide leading her to safely recover herself. Sharing yourself in this way demonstrates that, re-connection is possible without further loss.

Story Telling

Story-telling from your own experience can guide a person AT EFFECT towards re-viewing their own circumstances as perhaps not so devastating as other people's crises. The stories might reflect how someone else you know was in a crisis so overwhelming that no recovery seemed possible. Yet they came through it and actually learned something useful to them and to others associated with them. Stories have a way of allowing the person in crisis to take a holiday away from their own sadness. Occasionally they well up or re-kindle a desire to do something that they had decided to do some time ago but had forgotten about.

Story-telling is quite easy and a lost but easily found art in some cultures. Starting is the hard part. Anyone, regardless of their experiences, can tell stories. Witness the rich imagination of children in play, the gleam in their eyes as they let go of their inhibitions. Becoming childlike, yet adult-directed, spin a tale by starting in your own mind with the context, "Once beyond time..." With this as a starting point, let your story flow from your mind unrestricted by your internal censor, yet linked to the crisis state of being of the person in crisis. You will find that, the genuineness and the meaningfulness or relevance of the story will naturally unfold.

In summary, even though a client may be emotionally stuck and confused at this state and thus may resist support, the primary task is to connect with her by offering oneself as a guide or by pointing out others who can be effective guides for them. The challenge is to have this client establish a pathway that she can travel on and to have as many guides as possible offer her assurance that **action** will result in clarity and restoration of well-being. By offering oneself as a model or by uncovering others who can serve as inspiring models, can lead the AT EFFECT person to crisis-dissolving possibilities.

3. UP TO NON-ENTITY

If the person in crisis mobilizes herself sufficiently to follow the guidance of others, what quickly can loom up is a sense that she is insignificant while others, especially those guiding her, are significant. Most people have many momentary encounters with this state throughout their lives. This

---

state anticipates failure that occurs as the mind notices the body is cut off and actively at risk. Not trusting itself or its body to succeed, the mind tends to disown aspects of both mind and body as the mind feels it has sold out to significant others.

Clearly then, it makes sense for the crisis intervener to support this person to set mind goals congruent with her body's current capacity to achieve these goals. Starting from the body, as it is the path of least resistance, this person is encouraged to reconnect their body to their mind. Re-possessing the body or "host in life" can generate resources and remind the mind of how useful, resilient, and powerful the physical self can be. Sometimes the most impactful approach is to ensure that the client in this state entertains action-based externalizing experiences that "wake her up" to her physical self. Ordeals might be suggested, such as climbing a hill, deep-breathing exercises, building something, or making a special cultural meal. The intention would be to mobilize or trigger off affective core-feeling responses, such as anger, joy, sadness, and excitement. Such ordeals challenge the individual to step outside this grey zone by causing messages to be sent from the body to the mind about how the body feels. Other activities that can awaken the individual at this state are play therapy, art therapy, psychodrama or even drama, sports, bioenergetics, and the multitude of body work interventions. To introduce self-enhancing goals or targets for the mind to work on during these regenerative ordeals is to introduce the potential for melding the mind/body together, re-minding this person of the untapped reservoir of power that can well up from this reconnection.

Effectively, the person in this state has allowed imminent failure to replace anticipated success. Since it is not yet full fledged failure , movement can just as easily go up towards AT LOSS rather than down towards AT EFFECT. This state is clearly a transitional "way station." Consequently, it is highly responsive to crisis intervention, preventive counselling, and brief therapy. Unfortunately, as few crisis intervention resources exist, by the time counselling or therapy become available, the individual has fallen into a more entrenched crisis state.

In summary, an individual passing through this state learns to anaesthetize herself to their fear of loss by disconnecting emotions and feelings from thinking and thoughts. This is a transient state of integrity, in which momentarily the mind or ego splits off from the body so as to cut off or blank out the fear being generated by the crisis event. Reconnecting the body to the mind is actualized when the crisis intervener operates with confidence and assurance that the goals of intervention will unquestionably be achieved. Such assurance re-affirms to the person in crisis that she can recharge herself and that she ise "in charge" of her fear. Being in charge, she can make her fears work **for** her in achieving her renewed goals.

This renewed sense of mastery raises the person to the state typified by the question, "What if these efforts fail?" Movement up to AT LOSS causes the various faces of fear of failure to re-surface. It may now once again appear that the necessary resources are not going to be there or that the effort cannot be sustained.

4. UP TO AT LOSS

Returning to this state really suggests that ones crises are manageable and that they surface as situational episodes. Crisis intervention becomes a straight-forward affair of prompting the individual

---

to view anticipated setbacks or problems as challenges. In other words, the individual is encouraged to uncover the true source of resistance on her own and to shift towards the resistance rather than away from it . Instead of letting anticipated failure fester in a catastrophizing mind, anticipation can be reframed as excitement and adventure. Now it becomes the client's turn to discover ways of using the situational resistance as a resource for transformation. In this way the problem suddenly generates aliveness and adventure rather than draining our energy. When a client operates at this state of crisis, she becomes a joy to work with. Often the client will teach the crisis intervener more about self-exploration than the reverse. This becomes understandable in light of the possibility that this person is operating directly with her core feelings and is on the doorstep of her core self with a breakthrough possibility on the horizon.

5. UP TO NATURALNESS

As mentioned earlier, naturalness is where we start in life. Returning to this state is like coming home to your true magnificent self. To do so is to awaken the realization that all problems are opportunities even when they defy our logic to make them so. Crises at this stage are taken in stride with living itself. When others transgress in your life space, this is received as a natural part of life's journey. Crisis interveners are challenged beyond their own beliefs to assist a person at this stage. The issue is how the intervener can make a contribution with her life so that not just she but others benefit. This crisis state struggles with the question of how to promote oneself with others so that everyone wins. Self-promotion is far from easy as others are fearful or distrustful of one's motives. Consequently, many roadblocks are encountered that appear to be needless and territorial. On the rare occasions when a crisis intervener encounters this state of crisis with a client, extreme care must be taken to encourage self- promotion but not at the expense of others. To promote naturalness, the crisis intervener must operate from this state as well. Otherwise, likely as not, the crisis intervener will be a liability.

WORKING THE MODEL

The Yo Yo Experience

It is arguable that as many as three out of four people predominately ACT out of the state of survival, especially when encountering upsets in their lives. Nevertheless, it is possible for a person in crisis to fall into a survival state only momentarily and rebound on their own to any one of the states above the line of "no responsibility." Furthermore, moving back up the states can be a cyclical journey. Often an individual will bounce up and down the states as she re-discovers or encounters unfinished issues that become highlighted through the recovery process. The seasoned crisis intervener recognizes the necessity of this "ebb and flow" process and patiently supports a gradual evolution through the experience of upsets. In this way, setbacks (movement down the crisis states instead of up)are actually perceived as progress towards regaining one's wholeness. This is done by carefully tracking the individual's movement through the various crisis states and responding, guided by the many intervention suggestions mentioned at each state. For quick reference and review, these guidelines for the five crisis states are also briefly summarized at the end of this chapter.

Returning to the Primary State

What often happens is that a client will become stuck mainly at one of the states, and then, as a result of repeat crisis episodes, make forays into **AT SURVIVAL**. If this process continues and becomes chronic, the person will eventually formulate an **ACT** that protects her from returning to the state where she is most stuck. Working the model in these circumstances requires the crisis intervener to gently draw the client towards her primary stuckness. This is accomplished by allowing the intervention model to work strategically in a re-building manner.

Concluding Statement

The **SOURCE** approach can be an invaluable guide for a crisis intervener if used progressively and differentially throughout the crisis states. This model, by interweaving the operational phases of sizing up, proactive intervention, and transformation, opens up many access pathways for the crisis intervener. The model should be practised within the Beyond Content contextual framework and guided by the dynamic forces of competency.

Finally, it should be added, as a note of encouragement, that intervention with others, despite what it often feels like, is a privilege. The greater the struggle, the greater potential exists for truly making a difference. Allow yourself to be challenged and fortified by this highly resilient crisis-intervention framework.

BRIEF SUMMARY
OF
CRISIS STATES OF BEING

STATES AT NATURALNESS

- Social & Environmental Self-Sufficiency
- Natural/In Balance
- Supportive, Enthusiastic
- Enhancing
  Responsive, Interested, Unnoticeable

ACTION DESIRED

- Promote you and your goals
- Enlist others as supports
- Give away your achievements
- Harmonize opposites

AT LOSS: ACUTE CRISIS

- Emergency - Natural Conflict
- Beginning of Unhappiness
- Leads to Danger - Loss of Hope, Generation of Fear
- Development of Acts

- Perceive problem as challenging
- Consider failure as an opportunity

AT NON-ENTITY

- Permanent Loss
- Suicide State
- Grey Zone
- Loss of Significance/Hope
- Not concerned about self, others or environment

- Set a goal
- Come out of hiding
- Generate responsibility

AT EFFECT

- Threshold of Permanence in Disable Stance
- At Injury - Self-Destructive
- Accident Prone, Careless
- Generates a Sleepwalking State with the word being "I don't know."
- Everything Seems Incomplete

- Obtain a guide, teacher or someone to follow
- Complete tasks
- Set a direction to pursue

STATES AT SURVIVAL

- Characterized First by Opposition/Confrontation, then Disloyalty/Manipulation
- Nobody wins
- Cheat, Lie, Steal, Seek Revenge, Resent, Blame
- Boxed in/Unable to see one's own folly.

- Give up being right
- Acknowledge and share the truth to oneself and others

EXERCISES - CHAPTER SIX

1. Write out in your Competency Journal two experiences where you used the SOURCE formula outlining the results achieved both positive and negative. In both of these experiences identify the predominating intervention principles that were operating. Comment on how they worked and speculate on what could be done (if necessary) to have those principles not operating be mobilized.

2. Take three recent crisis interventions and state how you were able to use the resistance to change as a resource for transformation.

3. Make a list of 6 to 10 creative ordeals you have or would use to assist someone in crisis expand their awareness of opportunities or options that result in re-establishing a steady state of harmony.

4. Practice the model as a whole with at least one client a week until the framework becomes integrated into your behaviour. Keep notes on various short comings of this model for you. Discuss your observations with a colleague, trainer, or within a team or group.

5. Make a mental note of the traits of a competent crisis intervener you have encountered, then Self-Observe with the intent you allow yourself to emulate these desired traits in a potential crises. Visualize yourself assisting and serving others in crises with these traits in action. Identify competencies you have that make it possible for you to make a significant contribution to the troubled lives of others.

NOTES

SECTION II

CRISIS TOPICS
AND SPECIFIC STRATEGIES

This second section focuses upon several major crisis topics and attempts to re-frame the issues within a transpersonal or Beyond Content framework. Specific Beyond Content strategies are offered for each of the following five topics: suicide, self mutilation, violence, grief and mourning, and substance abuse.

Starting with suicide intervention in Chapter Seven, an effort is made to examine suicide as it might exist along a continuum of self- harming behaviour. An argument is made that suicide intervention is a rare and improbable experience for most crisis interveners. Furthermore, intervention is often unsuccessful, largely because of the confusion which crisis interveners experience when they broad-band the full range of self-harming behaviours into a suicidal framework and then attempt to formulate consequent life-saving intervention protocols. The intervention proposed in respect to the full range of self-harming behaviour reflect a differential approach, that vary in accordance with the different Acts, states of integrity, and forms of self-harming behaviour exhibited.

Chapter Eight contains a review of self-mutilation as a specific form of self-harming behaviour, one which is argued to be the polar opposite of suicidal intentions. Moreover, intervention strategies for self-mutilation are specifically based on contemporary yet pragmatic viewpoints of borderline characteristics.

Chapter Nine makes a shift from self-harming towards other-harming behaviours by examining violence both towards others and, in particular, towards the crisis intervener. A speculative schema for perceiving violence is postulated, so as to distinguish between genetic or biological triggered outbursts and social, cultural, and psychologically reactive life-experiences. Initial intervention guidelines are suggested for both kinds of violence as well as case examples using the Beyond Content model as an intervention framework.

Chapter Ten goes on to cover the crisis concerns related to critical loss, resulting in overwhelming grief and subsequent mourning. Five well-known stages related to death and loss are examined as they align with the crisis integrity states. An attempt is made to demonstrate how these stages of recovery can be stimulated, using the Beyond Content model.

Chapter Eleven completes this section with a review of crisis intervention with substance abusers, both with those actively under the influence and with those severely troubled by social-psychological dependency upon drugs or alcohol. As in the previous four chapters, a Beyond Content context is offered in ways which are meant to be symphonic or non-competitive with existing tried and true intervention wisdom. Overall, the intent is to "re-kindle" a practical and transpersonal vision that embraces the symptoms of substance abuse within a competency re-building framework.

CHAPTER SEVEN

SUICIDE CRISIS INTERVENTION

That suicide is best understood not so much as a movement toward death as it is a movement away from something and that something is always the same: intolerable emotion, unendurable pain or unacceptable anguish. Reduce the level of suffering and the individual will choose to live.

- Edwin Shneidman

SUICIDE AS SELF HARMING BEHAVIOUR

Suicide, what is it? Underlying our primary or well functioning self do we humans inherently possess a "suicidal subself" that is out to kill or be killed? Is suicide about dying or about surviving intolerable inner anguish? Do you have to be severely depressed or half crazed to commit or attempt suicide, or can you entertain it as a voluntary reasonable act, given one's impending death from an incurable disease? What about involuntary suicide, where self-sacrifice for others, for social belief systems, and for religious belief systems seems to have little to do with having a mental disorder? What about "focal suicides" or self-mutilating behaviour? Where does this much more prevalent behaviour fit into the realm of suicide? These and other questions challenge those encountering suicidal behavior to make sense of the phenomenon called suicide as it may fit into a continuum of self-harming behaviour.

Suicide is likely the most profound and most feared barometer representing the erosion and lack of resiliency of our social and cultural fabric. More and more professional attention is being paid to this and other self-harming phenomena. Unfortunately, while professional and paraprofessional preoccupation with self-harming behavior has its value, it is a far cry from being an effective replacement for personal, interpersonal, family and community responsivity to the needs of someone struggling with a pronounced sense of insignificance.

If the truth be told, suicide is an enigma to us all. Many explanations for its occurrence abound, yet few intervention approaches are effectively generated from these explanations. The reported causes or etiology of suicide undoubtedly have their value in revealing specific aspects of suicide. However, there appears to be no unified and universally applicable theory. Consequently, the crisis intervener is faced with overwhelming data related to symptoms, a multitude of risk formulas, numerous protocols for working with depression, and a seemingly unlimited number of "coping" techniques. If confusion is possible, then this scenario fairly boggles the crisis intervener's mind. Ironically, what is most needed is an operational framework that can embrace the entire spectrum of self-harming behaviour without excluding any of the valuable information alluded to above. In this respect, the Beyond Content model modestly attempts to honour "the state of the art" in respect to suicidal knowledge by supporting the crisis intervener's use of whatever strategies, explanations, and assessment tools that personally prove to be workable. Additionally, the model offers a competency-based framework within which chronic versus acute suicidal behavior can be examined as distinctive suicidal patterns. Having said this, a disclaimer is necessary. The competency-based framework (as outlined in Chapters Three and Four) do not offer definitive or comprehensive explanations for crises or more specificaly for suicide. What it does offer is simply a framework through which to view suicide and to strategically intervene so as to reduce the risk of terminal self-destruction.

For most crisis interveners, intervention with a high-risk suicidal person is a rare occurrence. More common is intervention with individuals whose self-harm or threats to harm others occur without the intent or outcome of immediate death. Differentiating or drawing a line between these two cases seems to be almost impossible. Yet the needs and the belief systems associated with these needs differ quite remarkably from one to the other. In many respects, suicide and self-mutilation exist at opposite ends of the continuum of self-harming behaviour. This chapter begins the exploration of self-harming behaviour by focusing on suicidal issues. The next chapter continues by addressing self-mutilation as a distinct phenomenon that is often confused with suicide even though it sometimes produces a suicidal outcome. Both forms of behaviour are further explored as they compare and contrast with one another, as well as how they profile along a continuum of self-harming behaviour.

A BEYOND CONTENT VIEW

In the context of the Identity Spectrum shown in Figure 2 (Chapter Two), a suicide state might be viewed as a state of pronounced mental constriction. In such a state a suicidal person casts a shadow (the unwanted emotional pain or anguish) over one's awareness. This shadow increasingly impoverishes the persona (personality) obliterating it in similar ways that a cancer would to a body. This can potentially occur to almost anyone when highly impactful overwhelmingly acute crises awaken and energize the shadow (or unwanted aspects of the self) when otherwise it remains an undercurrent, somewhat dormant force of one's identity. Circumstances such as a major career setback, loss of a significant other, incarceration, family breakdown, or loss of important psychological freedoms (e.g., freedom from pain, guilt, shame, rejection, or aloneness) could energize one's shadow creating an acute suicidal state of being. What can surface is a full blown crisis when one's shadow takes over and begins to envelope the persona. This can create a profound sense of insignificance characterized by a futile sense of helplessness and hopelessness. When this pervading state of **Non-Entity** generates levels of emotional anguish that are intolerable the individual makes a shift to the

Survival state of integrity. It is at this state that the individual rallys sufficient oppositional energy to engage in a suicidal act as a solution to being "boxed in" with their perceived intolerable pain and anguish.

This rare and episodic state of survival only occurs when the individual allows a state of dissociation and pronounced constriction of thinking and feeling to take over. Since the underlying integrity state is one of being a nobody, then taking one's life is perhaps a purposeful, need-fulfilling escape from the void of being a nobody, not necessarily a needless escape from all aspects of life. In the words of the well-known suicidologist, Edwin Shneidman (1984), "There are many pointless deaths, but never a needless suicide."

In other respects, often what is left to do, once the decision is made to kill oneself, is to ensure that this culminating act carves out an epitaph of profound distress on survivors. In some sense the contemplating suicidal person may be driven towards suicide knowing that their suffering can be passed on to others in compounding ways. Perhaps the image of many others suffering as a result of their suicide sufficiently alleviates their anguish so that suicide actually becomes unusually attractive. It may well be the case that the suicidal person can recapture a sense of their own significance, albeit in a negative perhaps infamous way by leaving behind indelible emotional scars on others.

ACUTE SUICIDE STATE

Figure 13 endeavours to make a rough contrast between acute and chronic suicidal states. Acute states seem to be characterized by the manner in which they surprise significant others, leaving them bewildered and confused about how suicide could have ever become an option. This surprise occurs even though quite often many subtle hints may have been made as last-ditch efforts to be rescued. In such cases, provided that the suicide attempt is unsuccessful, crisis intervention can be invaluable in reducing anguish, tension, and pain by uncovering other ways for the suicidal individual to minimize restrictive thinking and feeling. Figure 13 suggests that, when the acute condition occurs, the individual becomes shocked by some significant crisis and drops below the integrity level of sufficiency into the constricting grey zone of non-entity. Here the individual has first thoughts of suicide as an alternative to the intolerable anguish. If a decision is made to follow through with a suicidal plan, the impression of becoming stable may be given suggesting that the crisis may be passing. Actually, at this point as mentioned already, a suicidal plan can be generated with the suicidal person actively operating from a survival state driven by a consuming condition of disloyalty.

CHRONIC SUICIDAL STATE

In chronic suicidal circumstances, an underlying and longstanding insidious condition of Non-Entity may pervade a person's persona. An ACT based on well conditioned limiting beliefs is established, perhaps quite early in life, characterized by the idea that life is not worth living. Eventually, after repeated, episodic, up-and-down reinforcement of this continuously diminishing state of insignificance, the ACT goes underground and begins to fester, causing the shadow to rise and begin to cloud conscious awareness and common sense. When this happens, the body tends to automatically shut down, which reinforces mental and emotional restriction. In a mutually reinforcing way, the mind/body increasingly becomes more and more discounted. Survival then becomes focused on escaping the pain of intolerable, unacceptable perceived anguish of being insignificant. Again, Figure 13 is meant to depict, in some approximating way, how the depressive bouts of the chronically suicidal individual tend to be cyclical in a progressively worsening way. Suicide more and more becomes a preoccupation until finally a breaking point is reached. This person may then try out self-harming Acts as a survival tactic. Some of these survival tactics take the form of trial-and-error experiences designed to give this person a reinforced assurance that suicide is the only solution. Finally, convinced of one's plan, the individual lets go of control and gives into the shadowy state of Non- Entity. Then, an ACT of disloyalty arises out of their shadow. Similar to the acute suicidal scenario the unfolding act seems to generate the appearance of improved functioning when actually it is a pseudo flight into wellness. This appearance of getting better seems to be a consequence of the individual's ACT becoming committed to the final suicidal decision. Quite often this person will deny any suicidal plans and will be unusually compliant and peaceful-like. Therefore, the illusion of improvement can easily be mistaken for genuine recovery.

In both acute and chronic circumstances, the suicidal condition may well be generated by an overwhelming, intense, formless, nameless hatred of others or of one's life space that cannot be expressed. Rather than allowing oneself to go insane, the person gives in to an anesthetized-like state characterized by hopelessness, **haplessness** and **helplessness**; and this surrender results in a turning-point solution. Clouded and stuck by their seemingly overwhelming circumstances, the individual turns the anguish inward.

INDIRECT INTERVENTION

In circumstances in which a suicidally intent person writes to the crisis intervener, makes telephone contact, or passes messages through a third person, it is invaluable for the crisis intervener to have a framework from which to operate. The Beyond Content contextual principles (see Chapter Two), can serve as an intervention foundation setting the stage for the SOURCE intervention approach to be applied. A case scenario is now offered, along with some guiding statements for telephone crisis intervention, as an example of how the the SOURCE approach might be used.

THE CULTURAL MISFIT

Sharing

You receive a call from a girl who tells you she wants to asphyxiate herself. She begins by sharing how she feels trapped and cannot see any way out except to kill herself. To begin with, an initial contact like this is usually quite awkward. But generally, there is ample opportunity for you to set the stage for the sharing process to unfold. Since the call is made voluntarily in this situation, you ask for her first name and after receiving it you would do well to ensure that all interactive communication with her is prefaced by her name. In this way a revival of her fading identity is fostered. Additionally, at the earliest opportunity you acknowledge the girl for caring enough about some part of herself to make this call. As well, you acknowledge in some manner that it took an enormous effort of **self-control** just to make the call.

FIGURE 13

CRISIS STATES RELATIVE TO SUICIDE PATH

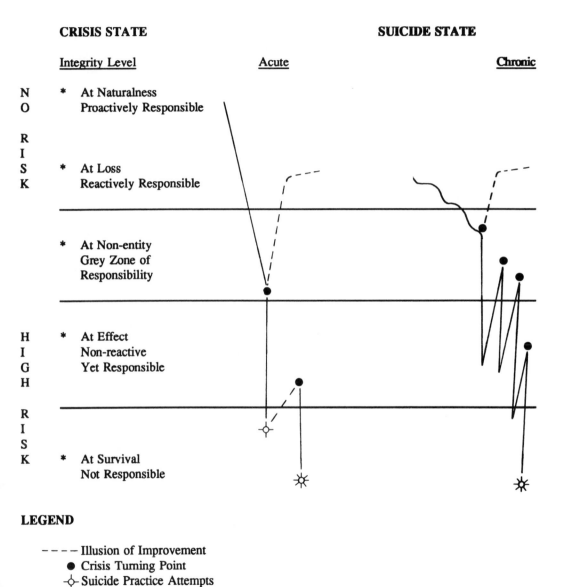

CRISIS STATE   **SUICIDE STATE**

Integrity Level   Acute   Chronic

N   *   At Naturalness
O   Proactively Responsible

R
I
S   *   At Loss
K   Reactively Responsible

     *   At Non-entity
         Grey Zone of
         Responsibility

H   *   At Effect
I   Non-reactive
G   Yet Responsible
H

R
I
S
K   *   At Survival
         Not Responsible

LEGEND

- - - - Illusion of Improvement
     ● Crisis Turning Point
    ○ Suicide Practice Attempts
    ☀ Suicide Completion

Suicide Crisis Intervention   129

Moreover you also share that it is a privilege to be of some value to her in whatever way you can. This simple yet impactful gesture is often overlooked, as a crisis intervener tends to become immediately preoccupied with the crisis event.

Having planted an initial seed of competency through sharing in the form of acknowledgements, you then allow the sharing experience to be underscored by a few key listening guidelines. These guidelines are as follows:

1.   Whenever possible, listen to her whole story with few if any interruptions. In so doing, you impress upon the girl that she is worthy of your undivided attention. Periodic brief affirmations can encourage her to continue without arresting her efforts for fear of being judged or rejected.

2.   Listen with "soft or porous ears". When you listen in this way, information passes through you rather than being absorbed by you. You listen as a witness rather than as a co-sufferer. As a witness you endeavour to be curiously humble.

Now primed to receive, you hear from this girl named Alisia that she is a 17-year-old grade 12 high-school student living in the inner city with her Greek parents. She tells you that her parents strictly adhere to their cultural values and associate only with the Greek community. Neither of her parents speaks English, and neither make any attempts to learn. She complains bitterly about having no freedom and no friends. Her father demands that she come home immediately after school and look after her mother, who is dying of cancer. Recently her father threatened to send her back to Greece, because she was associating with male youths from outside her culture. She also mentions to you that her grades at school are dropping and that her father is reacting to that fact by confining her to her room on the weekends.

Sharing at this stage is not about convincing her not to harm herself or about telling her that her suicidal thoughts will pass. It is about being with her in her current moment of pain. To do this at a distance requires the crisis intervener create a transpersonal space of concern that legitimizes, while not condoning, suicidal thoughts and desires. This might be communicated by saying something like, "I know that there are some moments in peoples' lives that the pain of day-to-day living seems so great that ending matters by killing oneself appears to be the only answer for the moment. This state sometimes seems like it will last forever yet it does go away for people who care enough to call as you have done." Also, thanking the girl for sharing this painful situation lets her know in some small way that you are privileged to be someone they can risk sharing with. Moreover, you let it be known to her that her willingness to make this call assures you in itself that buried deep down inside her is the wisdom that knows that relief of the present intolerable pain is possible through making contact with others. Her call is an indication of her struggle to move away from this intolerable pain and her desire to discover other ways to get what she really wants from living. Clearly, she values parts of herself enough to persist in wanting to get rid of this intolerable pain.

Observing

Obviously, observation is primarily restricted to what pictures you create from how she speaks and what she says to you on the telephone. It is crucial to listen for affect, particularly in how what she says generates pseudo-feelings. As you listen, share your appreciation for her reality, taking care to not suggest that her reality is one you support as the **only** possible reality. This form of observational listening searches for patterns in what is said and endeavors to get a picture of how what she is saying produces body responses, as well as those around her. In the process of listening, it is useful to formulate a picture of the individual's background as well as herself. You could also notice whether the primary "crisis state" is AT LOSS, AT NON-ENTITY OR AT EFFECT. Listen for clues indicating whether her predominate concern is that she has lost her freedom, or that she feels insignificant, or that she is always shortchanged in life. Once you arrive at a rough idea of the primary crisis state, listen further for perceptual stuckness and for indications that this crisis is either chronic or acute. Often acute crises can be distinguished from chronic crises by an absence of previous suicidal gestures and an absence of a well-practiced ACT of survival.

This process of sizing up the crisis can be done while you are listening, and it need not be done in any specified order. Finally, it important to notice whether there is any inappropriate laughter, as this is often a sign that the person's suicidal shadow is taking over.

Uncovering

In the explorative process with Alisia, you may next entertain asking her directly how seriously she thinks about dying right now. Invite her to tell you whether her circumstances could get worse and if so, in what way and when?

Alisia tells you she is afraid of her father, especially since he is drinking excessively and he frequently bursts into fits of rage. She also mentions that she sometimes wishes that she was dying instead of her mother. At this point, more fully exploring her catastrophizing fantasies may well lessen her fear of them and even reveal that someone other than herself should bear the suffering for these circumstances.

You now invite Alisia to become your advisor regarding her risk level, and you also support her by suggesting that she is capable of being in control of her suicidal thoughts. At this stage the loss of control is the paramount concern: for that reason any opportunity to reveal to her how she might exercise control over her life is invaluable.

You may now engage in further uncovering dialogue with the aim of simply highlighting her competencies without trying to prematurely use them as reasons for her not to kill herself. Share the evaluation task with her, beginning with her competency to assess her own lethality, since she is the one making the decision to kill herself. Specifically, she is encouraged to tell you how long, under what circumstances, and under what conditions she can continue to exercise control over her impulses. As well, ask what fantasies or magical solutions to her anguish she has thought of, such as being involved in a fatal accident, abuse of food or alcohol, or running away with nothing. Moving to background supports and competencies, inquire if she can identify what others have recognized or could recognize about her that is worthy. You may also suggest to her that you suspect from what she has shared with you that she is a **caring** daughter and that she really wants to honour her family if she can. Likely she respects her parents' culture, although does not agree with it entirely. Uncovering could also seek to reveal anyone she admires right now or appreciates or looks up to and what attributes does this person(s) possess. If no one is mentioned, suggest some possible adolescent idols and ask about their competencies from her point of view. Invite her to speculate how these attributes are also developing within herself. This line of questioning may serve to trigger off a shift in her perceptual stuckness. Assurance is of significant importance at this point as she may be prone to discount herself and what others say about her that is supportive.

Alternately, you may state that you suspect that in the background of her life she has made a contribution to others and to her community. While the primary goal of uncovering is to reduce the level of present anguish, the subgoal is to uncover alternative ways to become more socially congruent with her living circumstances. It may be worthwhile to explore ways in which she can assist her mother by discussing with her ethnic community the benefits to her mother of a cancer support group. Also, she might seek ways in which her community could help her father with the anguish of his pending loss. Uncovering by listening is a 30 - 70 proposition. Only about thirty percent of what she will say in a crisis accurately reflects what is really happening. Being aware of this fact can reduce your tendency to get caught up in the impoverished seventy percent discord in her life.

Resourcing

After uncovering and revealing her suicidal fantasies as well as her personal competencies, the challenge becomes one of supporting Alisia **consider**, as she is capable of being quite a considerate person, counteracting the devestating intent of her shadow. Her competencies now need to be **mobilized** to create alternative escape routes from her anguish so that suicide becomes her last choice rather than her first choice. To counteract the powerful effect of her negating shadow, it is recommended that at least five demonstrable competencies are identified. These competencies need to be carefully identified and highlighted. Her shadow can be gradually forced to one side and kept at arms length as her conpetencies are used to spearhead alternative courses of action leading to increased self mastery and of course, aliveness. Unconditional encouragement and assurance from the crisis intervener is essential to assist her make this commitment to discover other anguish-solving activities other than suicide.

Completing

In the process of Alisia being encouraged to take action, it is worthwhile to extract a commitment from her to give up suicide as an alternative for a specified period of time, to be determined by her. This self-controlled rather than crisis intervener controlled qualification is necessary since she would be giving up her present ways of resolving her anguish and her fantasy gratifications for something that is not yet of proven value. The important requirement here is to have her say she **will** not kill herself because.... The time of commitment can vary, but it is critically important that the commitment be strongly worded. Promising not to, trying not to, doing her best not to are insufficient levels of commitment. You need to persist until the commitment is solid, even if it is reduced to only a few hours. Any other commitment is prone to fall apart.

Completing also involves making doubly sure that Alisia hears her commitment restated several times in several ways and that she has active tasks to accomplish in order to re-connect to meaningful resources in her life.

Expanding

Beyond completing tasks, Alisia can be supported to further expand her support network to include formerly disregarded significant others. She can now be encouraged to expand her life-line of support, perhaps to include a counsellor from the school, extended family members, significant members of the Greek community, or some form of counselling or therapy. Linkages to bereavement programs, Cancer support groups, and substance-abuse support resources for youth can be considered. By supporting Alisia to open up again to her own self-sufficiency, she can be encouraged to generate creative ways to support her father's need to reconsider his disciplinarian stance toward her.

In review, this model supports more than anything else, the recapturing of significance and self-sufficiency. Rescuing is always the course of last resort undertaken only when the risk of harm is so great that it suggests that hospitalization or some other short-term form of intense supervision.

DIRECT INTERVENTION

An Anniversary Event

You encounter a young man named Bill who has just allegedly tried to hang himself in his prison cell. Bill has been charged with child molesting and is awaiting trial in protective custody. What you know about Bill is that he has dropped out of university in the his last year and that he has no prior criminal record. Bill was noticed by the passing volunteer prison librarian talking to himself and laughing at what he was apparently saying. You have been called to intervene shortly after he was caught tying two belts together over a ceiling pipe.

Sharing

Engaging Bill in a conversation is somewhat awkward, as he appears quite tranquil and somewhat lifeless. He is very compliant and somewhat apologetic for having caused anybody any concern. He states that he really was only bored and was just playing around and doesn't know what all the fuss is about. Since it is obvious to you that he is going to deny any suicidal desires, your first objective is to establish some beginning levels of rapport. Starting from the background, you begin by sharing your interest in his belts and how they were made. It is not uncommon for the instrument or the means used to entertain suicide to have some significant symbolic or historic value. In this case, one of the belts belonged to his father and was used to beat him when he was a young boy. Continue by showing interest in anything pertaining to his cell environment. In very neutral ways, you simply share your interest in the environment around him, encouraging him to comment as he wishes. As the sharing process progresses, you state, as naturally as possible, your role and your purpose in being there, allowing Bill an opportunity to be more open Sometimes it is invaluable to be upfront and direct about your views of voluntarily killing oneself. While you do not condone it, you suspect that very little can be done to stop someone if they truly want to commit suicide.

As in a telephone crisis intervention, it is useful to connect on a first-name basis. In this way you are continually reminding him that you know who he is and you are interested not so much in his relationship with you as in his relationship with himself. You may share with Bill your sense that most of us have a part of our selves that is, from time-to-time depending on life's upsets, out to destroy us. Fortunately, we are blessed with a deep core self that can quite masterfully turn this enemy self into an ally. This powerful core self when tapped into can allow us to **really** get what we want despite the overwhelming challenges we may encounter through our living. This dark shadowy side of us can sometimes trick us into giving in to it. Fortunately, most of us wake up in time, and recognize the error in judgement we are making. Sharing in this way lets Bill know that you recognize the legitimacy of his shadow and at the same time conveys your belief that he can gain from his shadow if he stays consciously aware of it and keeps it in check.

Observing

In the process of sharing, you watch for incongruencies in what he says and in how he is acting. In this situation, Bill may have a glazed look to his eyes, almost as though he is in a trance. Through continuous observation, you notice that he really is not seeing you or much else around him clearly. Facially he may portray sadness and a contorted anguish, yet he denies feeling anything except being allright. You further observe that he seems to not care what time it is or where he is. As well, he seems to only partially hear what you have said. This is a clue that you may need to share repeatedly in order to be even minimally understood. As you continue to observe, it becomes more and more apparent to you that he has largely shut down all his senses. His actions are avoidant and perhaps manipulative, yet he exudes an aura of hopelessness and haplessness. He does not appear to be concerned about others or his environment. So it may seem to you that he is primarily stuck at the NON-ENTITY crisis state of integrity. Consequently, he has mobilized his survival state in a pronounced disloyal way to cope with this unbearable state of NON-ENTITY.

Uncovering

The challenge now is to have him recognize that his disloyal tendencies may be directed not only toward himself but toward another or others as well. The primary task for the moment is to minimize any further error. Keeping that in mind, try to uncover the degree to which he thinks that he is in control and the degree to which he thinks that someone else ought to pay for the circumstances he is in. Bill may not deny at this point, yet he likely is wondering what he can share without giving himself away.

Next, you may acknowledge his judgmental ability and argue that, because of this judgement, he is the best person to assess his own lethality. Pointing out his ability (competency) to disconnect from his surroundings, his way of keeping tranquil, and his non-offensive manner may stimulate him to react, especially if you point to concrete examples of how these competencies are visible around him. Speaking more directly now, you ask about his future plans and what tasks or issues in his life he has to do something about yet. You continue by asking him about special dates in his life and how he celebrates them.

Coming from a non-judging and nonexhortatory yet naturally curious approach, you enquire about the life around him, gradually centring more and more on him until finally he mentions in an offhand manner that his father died on father's day three years ago. Enquiring further, you discover that his father actually committed suicide and that he and his father had been quite distant since his parents divorced when he was eleven years old.

Bill now begins to show some minimal signs of interest in sharing, as he senses that you are not about to change his mind about anything. You then ask him about his fantasies: What would he like to be doing with his father now? was he ever angry or sad about his family circumstances? and so on. Once again, Bill briefly mentions that he wouldn't want to do anything ever again with his father. Questioned further, he alludes to his father's taking advantage of him when he was quite young and didn't know any better. It is evident that the pathogenic nature of his behaviour requires therapeutic intervention. The task, then, is to pave the way for this possibility.

Resourcing

Resourcing begins by carefully counteracting Bill's preoccupation with denial of life and the need to avoid any further suffering. This can be accomplished by gradually revealing to him, despite the contaminating aspects of incarceration, that his significance to others can be demonstrated. Since doing "dead time" during incarceration can compound a sense of futility it is usually critical in this respect to activate both the mind and the body by entertaining activities that demonstrate his value to others and his community, activities such as writing letters, starting a journal, completing or starting projects that had previously been postponed or overlooked that reflect consideration for others and personal competency, physical exercise or involvement in recreation experiences that he has been know to be proficient in are some possibilities that can begin this mind-body awakening process. Taking out a pad and paper, you ask Bill about his family by drawing a family tree and placing his relatives along the branches. You then ask what activities or experiences he engaged in with each one of them, where they are now, how close he is to them, what he needs to do for them, if anything and so on. The aim here is to counter Bill's constriction in thought by attempting to widen his viewpoint about possible discounted resources. His present dismissal of these recounted resources is to be expected as part of his constriction and lethal intent. Nonetheless, creating a list that he can project his negative thoughts onto acts to reduce his lethality and to potentiate the possibility of his choosing something other than suicide, even though the something else may still be a lousy alternative.

Then with patience and perseverance, you begin to explore ways to have Bill's identified competencies become useful resources for him during his awaiting trial period. During this process, you continuously perception-check what he would do first before considering killing himself. You may find yourself still unsure about his sincerity, which warrants your making arrangements for his safety. Bill is then encouraged to make special qualifying statements such as "I will only stay alive if..." This allows him to retain the decision-making power to satisfy his need for self-control. Qualifying statements need to be based on a time period that he can commit to and that can fit the crisis intervention commitments that you can make. Of course, the aim would be to get the longest time commitment possible. In any event, you then base your seeking of safety conditions on the perceived genuineness of his commitment to the qualification. Needless to say, it is wise always to err on the side of caution when judging the commitment of a seriously suicidal person.

Completing

Calling upon his interest in creative writing and poetry, as demonstrated by some of his college interests, you then encourage Bill to write about his thwarted needs as if he were going to mail his thoughts to various members of his family. As well, he is encouraged to read some of his favorite poetry and to comment on it to you during the next crisis-intervention session.

In the course of completing with Bill, you attempt to have him establish a support group that he can call upon when he disconnects from himself. Completing is asking him to commit to be active and to entertain a therapeutic relationship with someone on his own accord, as opposed to having therapy ordered by the authorities.

Expanding

Given that Bill is a serious, ongoing suicidal risk, you end the crisis-intervention process after three sessions by establishing with him a step-by-step approach to increasing his mastery or control over his historical conditioning, his shadow, and the current events in his life. This is meant to be a practical game-plan that he generates from his competency base. As a precaution against the fading or drying up of the supports he has identified, it is useful to have Bill identify a back-up resource behind each support, thereby creating an interwoven support system. For Bill, just the possibility of a small change in his sense of hopelessness and his overwhelming disgust and guilt was enough to divert his suicidal intentions.

IN SUMMARY

When confronted with a potentially suicidal person consider doing the following:

1. Examine and confront their death fantasies compassionately.

2. Fully probe into their suicidal thoughts and methods of suicide considered.

3. Generate alternatives to suicide for the immediate future so that suicide ceases to be the individual's first and only perceived course of action.

4. Disrupt, distort, and disconnect the individual's suicidal restriction in thinking attaching more pain to having these thoughts than having alternative thoughts based on identified personal competencies.

5. Use the SOURCE formula as a guide and allow your "hunches" generate the strategies based on what works rather than what is right or wrong according to superficial intervention protocols.

Clearly, the case examples given are not meant to cover all the complex issues of treatment relating to the suicidal person. Rather, they serve to give a snapshot perspective of this crisis intervention model. In this respect, it would be foolish to take the suggestions made as a prescriptive protocol. Nothing offered so far precludes the crisis intervener from risk of failure. Yet even failure, in its truest form of integrity, is really an opportunity, even with those who test us beyond our beliefs with life-ending actions.

SUGGESTED READINGS

1.   The works of Edwin Shneidman on suicide are by far the most extensive done by anyone in the field today. His numerous books and over 100 articles on suicide and death stand out as leading-edge efforts to give mental heath practitioners both a conceptual as well as a practical understanding of the phenomenon of suicide. Anyone working with suicidal people would do well to review his major works, which include **The cry for help, Deaths of man, Voices of death, The psychology of suicide, Definitive suicide** and numerous edited books such as **Essays in self-destruction, On the nature of /suicide and death: Current perspectives.**

2.   Those interested in ongoing research and emerging approaches in theory and practice to life-threatening behavior may wish to read the multi-disciplinary journal **Suicide & Life Threatening Behavior**(New York: Guilford Press), the official publication of the American Association of Suicidology.

3.   An excellent book on childhood suicide by Isreal Orbach entitled **Children who don't want to live** (Jossey Bassey: San Francisco, 1988) offers indepth case histories illuminating suicide issues with children. Orbach has formulated a comprehensive phenomenolical framework that is simple to understand and easy to make use of with children and their families at risk.

NOTES

NOTES

_____

_____

_____

_____

_____

_____

_____

_____

_____

_____

_____

_____

_____

_____

_____

_____

_____

_____

_____

_____

_____

_____

_____

_____

_____

_____

_____

_____

_____

CHAPTER EIGHT

SELF-MUTILATION INTERVENTION

Mutilators have been cuddled, loved, slapped, shocked, counseled, drugged, stimulated, isolated, reprimanded and even lobotomized. In most instances we have very little convincing evidence that these interventions successfully prevent or ameliorate self-mutilation.

- McKay & Ross

IN RELATION TO SUICIDE

As mentioned in the previous chapter, self-mutilation is often erroneously viewed as suicidal behaviour when it is actually not. While a self-mutilator may progress to a suicidal state, such a person actually profiles quite differently in many ways from the suicidal person (see Table 4). To begin with, the suicidal person tends to let go of control in their life, whereas the mutilator is historically fearful of being excessively controlled by others or their environment. The suicidal person appears to have no options to relieve anguish, whereas the mulilator appears to have a wide repertoire of options. Suicide is an act to avoid the pain of living, whereas self-mutilation seems to be an act to release pain in order to accentuate living. The suicidal person does not generally perceive self-destruction as an act against the self, as the self is no longer of consequence; the self mutilator, on the other hand, tends to act against self to gain attention from others. Comparing further, the suicidal person seems not to value life at all, feeling already dead and quite insignificant. The mutilator seems to want to alleviate guilt; viewing life as cheap, the mutilator often feels victimized and incompetent. If the suicidal person retaliates against others for being insignificant, then the self-mutilator blackmails to gain notoriety. Both are reported to have contagious capabilities, and both often conduct their acts ritualistically.

Sizing-up these two conditions, using the Beyond Content model suggests the following:

SIZING-UP ISSUES	SUICIDAL PERSON	SELF MUTILATOR
Primary Crisis State	Non-Entity	At Effect
Perception State	Primary Modes Shut Down	Chaotic\Repressed
Acts or Roles	Somebody will know how much I have suffered	Anything goes to regain control

Table 5 offers a overview of these two conditions as they fit into a proposed continuum of self-harming behaviour. This continuum starts with suicide at one end, moves to suicide attempts then to self-mutilation and ends with the "catch all" general category of self-harming behaviour.

AS A BORDERLINE CONDITION

There is probably no part of the human body that has not been mutilated. Such behaviour has occurred in every major institution and every conceivable setting. It cuts across all age groups and has been practiced by persons as young as five months and as old as ninety. The literature on the subject is voluminous; yet, as in the case of suicide, no unified theory or treatment approach seems to have surfaced. Almost all explanations imply that the cause is a deficiency either from some form of hereditary malfunction or psychopathology.

The dominant motif underscoring self-mutilation appears to be captured best by the increasingly popular diagnostic category known as the borderline personality condition. Clinical features of the borderline personality reported in the literature are extremely varied and highly controversial. Consequently, there are many different viewpoints, offering different composite arrangements of this personality classification (Kroll, 1988). Nevertheless, it is interesting to note that self-mutilation appears consistently as a major symptom of persons with this personality type. Although not all self-mutilators can be classified as borderline personalities and not all borderlines are self mutilators.

In reviewing the varied and often contradictory borderline classifications, Kroll(1988) appears to offer not only a thorough review of the borderline issues but also a contextually based schema that can serve as a composite framework from which to view self-mutilation. As such, it endeavours to stay away from stigmatizing statements and causal references and diagnostic categories. In this way, it leans toward competency-based intervention and, by assumption, to the Beyond Content Crisis Intervention model proposed here.

TABLE 4

SOME COMPARATIVE REMARKS

SIMILARITIES AND DIFFERENCES

SUICIDE	SELF MUTILATION
A No Option State	Many Options Possible
An act to avoid living	An act to accentuate living
An act against survivors	An act against self
An act of transferring guilt to significant others	An act of alleviating guilt
Ironically life is precious enough to take it	Life is cheap
Completion based	Relief based
Generated at a state of non-entity and acted upon at disloyalty	Generated at a state of "at effect" and acted upon out of opposition
An act to end emotional pain	An act to relieve or react against emotional pain
Ritualistic possibilities and contagious	Ritualistic possibilities and contagious
Retaliatory	Emotional blackmail

TABLE 5

CONTINUUM OF SELF HARMING BEHAVIOUR

SUICIDE	ATTEMPTS AT SUICIDE	SELF MUTILATION	SELF HARMING BEHAVIOUR
1st Choice	Often Last Choice	One of many Options	Optional
Dying as an act of killing other(s)	Will they notice desperation	To be noticed shock, horror, and revulsion	To fulfill
Grief producing	Fear producing	Relief\tranquility producing	Rejection producing
No control of anguish	Seeking control of anguish	Being in control of anguish	Ignoring, covering up anguish
*14/100,000	*3 - 10 times suicide rate	** 53+ times suicide rate	Unquantifiable

FORMS

Hanging	Minor Overdoses	Cutting	Smoking
Shooting	Acute Alcohol Abuse	Biting	Drinking
Cutting	Vertical Wrist Carving	Abrading	Overeating
Drug Overdose	Drowning	Severing	Undereating
Auto Accident	Burning	Inserting	Accident
Self Immolation		Burning	Proneness
		Ingesting	Negligence
		Constricting	

*	Ross & McKay (1979)	
**	Favazza (1989)	
***	Categories are not mutually exclusive	

An overview of his core borderline features separated into cognitive and emotional categories are:

TABLE 6

CORE BORDERLINE FEATURES

COGNITIVE STYLE DISTURBANCES	EMOTIONAL INTENSITY
DISORGANIZATION UNDER STRESS	LONELINESS AND EMPTINESS
SELF-RUMINATION	VICTIMIZATION
IMPULSIVE ACTION	PROV0CATIVENESS
IDENTITY ISSUES	SELF-DESTRUCTION
SPLITTING WITH OTHERS	INCOMPETENCY
TRANSIENT DISSOCIATION	SUBMISSIVENESS

Consistent with these features, borderline self-mutilators present as volatile, unpredictable, highly reactive, and disturbingly "noisy" as clients. Referencing the Beyond Content model, they continuously vacillate between the crisis states of AT EFFECT and AT SURVIVAL. They generate and actively display their crises with hardly any provocation. They are also fully capable of being simultaneously enraged and outraged without seemingly much regard for others. In this respect, they stir up intense feelings in crisis interveners through their demanding nature and attention seeking self-harming behaviour. Their high profile nature, in comparison with the more pronounced state of suicide, often raises concern about progressive deterioration and potential for suicide. Figure 14 attempts to chart the lability cycles of self-mutilating borderlines and suggests that they can indeed be a risk for suicide. Given their propensity for risk-taking, they can suicide by accident, especially when their attempts to get others to rescue or respond to them fail despite their escalating antics. Finally, self-mutilators may feel such overwhelming frustration that they depersonalize to the extent that their self-abuse drives them over the edge of sanity and into the void of suicide.

When working with self-mutilators, it is extremely difficult for almost any crisis intervener to avoid their own conditioned behavior patterns. This type of client easily provokes crisis intervener rescuing behavior as well as the fear of being exploited. Because many crisis interveners wish at some level to be caretakers, they tend to get caught up in trying to do too much for these people. The ability of self-mutilators to get others to perceive them as long-suffering, unprotected victims of abandonment, oppression, and abuse is extraordinary. Their actions speak to a desperate and insatiable need for warmth and understanding, and they seem to easily evoke nurturing and caretaking sentiments from even the most seasoned therapist or counsellor.

This type of person precipitates many crises, because they tend to get their needs met through crises. In the process, they burn out many crisis interveners as well as anyone else who cares enough to want to help. Consequently, they are much talked about, in maligned or frustrated ways; and many professionals say they are too intractable to treat.

FIGURE 14

CRISIS STATES AND LABILITY CYCLE

CRISIS STATE   POSSIBLE LABILITY CYCLE

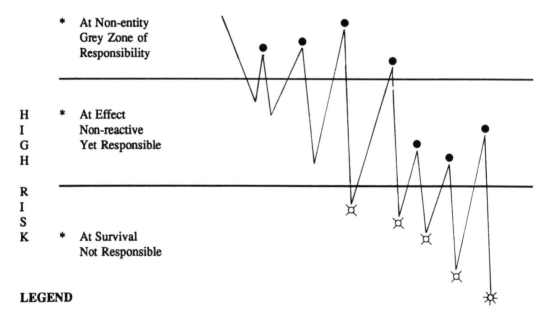

N   *   At Naturalness
O   Proactively Responsible

R
I
S   *   At Loss
K   Reactively Responsible

     *   At Non-entity
          Grey Zone of
          Responsibility

H   *   At Effect
I   Non-reactive
G   Yet Responsible
H

R
I
S
K   *   At Survival
          Not Responsible

LEGEND

● Crisis Turning Point
✗ Possible Relief From Self Mutilation
☀ Suicide by Apparent Accident or Overwhelming Frustration

Despite these issues, The BEYOND CONTENT perspective views them as an enormous and adventurous challenge worthy of our best effort. The following SOURCE intervention scenario illustrates in a prototypical and perhaps oversimplified way many of the issues which occur in the crisis intervention with a self-mutilating person.

BEYOND CONTENT MODEL APPLICATION

You are called to intervene with a young 16-year-old male "punk rocker" who has just slashed his wrist and received nine stitches. He has taken the bandages off and has made several attempts to remove the stitches earlier in the day. The overriding concern of the referral source is that he is potentially suicidal and may need hospitalization. Up to this point he has steadfastly and successfully resisted any attempts to be put into a hospital.

Sharing

Upon meeting you he glares at you and smirks as if disgusted by what he sees. Learning that his name is Michael, you begin sharing with him, acknowledging his wound and your emotional reaction to it. While you are emotionally peaked with curiosity, you nevertheless remain neutral.

Michael notices that you notice his stitches and asks why you do not turn away in disgust or do something as he begins to pick at the stitches. Turning your attention to his overall visual presentation, you ask him with an open curiosity about the large tears in his clothing, the carvings on his arms, the pierced nose, and the mohawk hair style. He mentions that they fit with how bad he feels inside. You continue by sharing that your purpose is to listen to him and learn from him, acknowledging that he is the only one really in control of himself and he can decide on what he wants from you or from anyone else. You share further that you wonder about what it's like to be in control of how other people respond to you. You imagine others will often turn away and not look at you or stare in a shocked manner. Michael shares back that he enjoys watching other people show disgust for him and says that he hates himself. At times he feels as if he is evil and as if he wants to destroy himself.

Michael now seems a little more at ease with you since you are not acting in a negatively predisposed way toward him nor are you showing any signs of wanting to control him, even when he begins to sabotage the intervention by picking at the stitches. You support his competency as a young man by acknowledging that you sense that he has a capacity for insight and that his way of being is extremely **creative** far beyond most people's understanding and reflects his **challenging** nature. After you have let him know this and that you see him as being in control, he stops his picking and seems to go into a trance-like state.

Observing

In your sharing experience with him, you observe him become more at ease and not so painful looking. Michael seems to be in a temporary lull, so you take the opportunity to continue to observe him. This state is not uncommon as a post-mutilation effect. Observing further, you notice that his fingernails are battered and raw and that he has what appears to be cigarette burns on the palms of his hands. Michael's neck also has small razor nicks, as do both sides of his head. It is a cold day; and he is woefully underdressed for being on the streets, which is where he was prior to his cutting episode. It is apparent that Michael is able, with little difficulty to effectively tolerate or even block out the experience of pain. At this moment, you may sense that he is somewhat AT LOSS and that the opportunity exists for you to gently begin to uncover what is going on inside of him.

Uncovering

In a neutral manner, yet curiously interested in knowing how he functions, you may ask Michael such questions as, "What is it like to go into a space where you don't feel anything very much? Is there anything you fear? If so, how do you control your fears, and what really works for you in getting your needs met?" Michael states that he goes into a void to stop his mind from experiencing being empty, yet sometimes he feels so much inner anguish that he has the desire to cut himself. When he does cut himself, he feels relief for a while. Michael further mentions that he does not ever want anyone to abuse him again. If anyone is going to abuse him, it will be himself. He then says that it is impossible but would be nice if someone else could ever know how lonely he is and how terribly overwhelming it is to be incessantly plagued by so many bad memories. Care at this stage needs to be taken to not get trapped by his oblique demands into giving rescuing assistance.

Continuing to explore, you may inquire by asking him which bad memories could he talk about and which ones does he prefer to avoid sharing about at this time. Encouraging him to list these memories in order of discomfort experienced gives Michael the opportunity to reflect on his emotional scars without a felt sense of having to reveal feelings of vulnerability.

In the process of sizing-up Michael's crisis you mentally note his personality exudes a natural **challenging** nature, albeit directed towards acheiving negative or destructive outcomes. He is also **colorful** in both his attire and mannerisms. His dialogue with others is mysteriously **captivating** as he seemingly draws the attention of others towards him in both a compassionate and a repulsive way. As well, his actions seem driven by a **compelling** and insatiable desire to find some way to stand out from the crowd and be noticed.

Resourcing

Michael has had numerous unsuccessful, often times parasitical encounters with therapy and counselling in the past. Consequently, he has learned to become quite sophisticated in his ability to set up traditionally trained helpers for rejection. He has done so by offering facile assurances of interest in order to draw crisis interveners into his own cycle of self abuse by accepting then rejecting them over and over again. Eventually these helpers have become so exasperated and exhausted they abandon their efforts to be a resource to Michael, leaving him once again, convinced not to trust others.

To **Resource** Michael is to firstly offer him alternative ways to gain control and be **challenged** by his relationships with others. Secondly, it is to alter his mental images related to his ruminations or preoccupations with old unsavory memories of rejection or loss. This can be done by letting him know that he can be in charge and can master his images of the past. In fact, he can be encouraged to restructure them by **compelling** them to reveal ways they can serve him rather than control his thinking. Micheal is assured that now that he has **captured** you as a resource you are obliged to assist him restructure the images that currently control him. Care is now taken to persistently punctuate the dialogue with Michael so as to affirm his **challenging, captivating** and **compelling** competencies over and over again. Michael can also be encouraged to channel both his **colorful** and **creative** attributes by having him advise you (and subsequently a chosen counsellor) on how to assist others who demonstrate self-mutilating behaviour. In asking him to do this, you might co-opt him to educate you about self-mutilation. This process can evolve further by having Michael be of direct assistance to others who are not as clear as he is about alternatives to self-mutilation. Essentially, you invite him to be useful and by contributing to others who may be embarking on a similar pathway.

In the Uncovering process, consistent with his **challenging** and **creative** nature, you discover that Michael is quite artistic as well as athletic. He knows how to play several musical instruments, and he has performed extremely well in cross-country races in the past. Obviously his current life-style does little to foster these competencies. To restructure his images of the past with respect to these talents, begin cautiously by having him recall only successful experiences. In the process, encourage him to uncover ways he can revitalize his current life-style through use of these talents. The crisis intervention process here is meant also to set the stage for Michael to consider entering into more in-depth counselling following the present intervention. The aim at the momemt is simply to outline possibilities for future exploration and possible incorporation.

Completing

It goes without saying that self-mutilators require persistent and congruent intervention over a long period of time. In completing, then, the most important aim should be to revitalize Michael's faith in the value of explorative counselling with someone he chooses. Ideally, Michael will come to want a counsellor who will equally **challenge** his outrageousness and support him to exercise his **creative** abilities in a variety of different activities that are not self-harming.

Given that the crisis intervener's primary purpose is to stabilize the current situation, the onerous task then becomes how to make the present intervention more than a band-aide. Though the mandate does not support exploration of root causes, completion of the presenting crisis can be achieved. To accomplish this, the crisis intervener should persistently focus on having Michael mobilize his competencies, gain some insight and self-mastery from this current episode of self-mutilation, and cease lumping together all past events into a reason for the past being more powerful than the future. Teasing out and operationalizing Michael's competencies is paramount to this goal.

Expanding

It is obvious that Michael knows how to capture other people's attention through self-destructive behaviour. His expertise in this area of drama and public display suggests that the performing arts or other forms of artistic expression besides "epidermal art" could be an alternate avenue of release for his self-expression. Actually, in Michael's case, he was sufficiently inspired by the crisis intervener's acknowledgement of his artistic capabilities to begin to "sketch out " his inner feelings. This eventually resulted in informal showings of his art work to the public. Michael also got connected to a small theatre group, at first working as a stage hand and later in small acting roles. Activated in these ways, Michael ceased practicing self-mutilation as one of the manifestations of his borderline condition.

Expanding this self-mutilator's crisis field in a way that allows him to exercise control over himself and his environment is a challenge that requires considerable networking supports. A crucial step is to have him commit to forming a competency support group (not a self-mutilation prevention group) with the assistance either of a primary counsellor or of an acceptable significant other. Such a commitment will allow the self-mutilator to be the centre of attraction in his life in even more provocative and powerful ways than before. Michael is gently guided to this possibility, with care taken to allow him to control how it happens, because he obviously knows many different ways of getting people to attend to him and his needs.

The risk here, of course, is that he will slip back into his outrageous ways in order to experience a sense of power over others, especially over a fledgling support group. For a support group to really be meaningful, it must be coached so that "rescuing traps" are avoided and so that the support is coordinated and networked together. This is essential if the potential splitting behaviour (divide and rule approach to others) is to be minimized. This form of group support requires either an experienced professional or a committed and knowledgeable networker backed up by consultation support and training.

Finally, you may request of Michael that he let you know about anybody with whom you might discuss this current incident. To ensure that he is really in control, after naming a person to contact, you ask him if he would be willing to make the introductions and then, in his own **colorful** manner, support an open and frank discussion about the self mutilating behavior. This step enables Michael to potentially expand his support resources beyond the crisis intervener

IN SUMMARY

Embedded within the SOURCE formula there are a number of steps that can be considered in mobilizing a self-mutilator from a survival state to a natural state of self-promotion. To summarize these steps are:

1. Begin by first minimizing the self-harming error and respond in a compassionate yet neutral way.

2. Align with the self-mutilator by being actively interested in knowing all about his self-mutilating efforts.

3. De-pathologize his behavior by acknowledging his actions are a genuine attempt to control an overly controlling environment.

4. Seek out a commitment to make a contribution to others whenever possible.

5. Establish some goals that are bold, highly stimulating, concrete, self controlled and easy to achieve given his natural competencies.

6. Activate his competencies within his chosen support networks.

7. Assist him in the process of restructuring his disabling past images.

This brief account of self-mutilation and the application of the Beyond Content model is offered as a snapshot of some intervention possibilities. The subject of self-mutilation has been thoroughly researched and theorized about, yet the intervention approaches remain impoverished. It is modestly suggested that the Beyond Content model can create treatment **openings** with this notoriously difficult-to-treat-and-prevent behaviour. The model's utility depends on continued refinement of the strategies as well as on the clarity of approach that the crisis intervener is able to develop. Clearly, the Beyond Content approach is far from a panacea, although it may foster breakthrough thinking.

SUGGESTED READINGS

1. One of the most comprehensive reviews of the phenomenon of self mutilation is authored by Robert Robinson and Hugh McKay and simply entitled **Self mutilation** (Toronto: Lexington Press, 1989). Arising out of both a research and a treatment initiative conducted in a Canadian Training School for girls, this account endeavors to demonstrate through the offering of practical examples how the many theories on self mutilation are conflictual, lacking heuristic clinical value, and even counter productive in terms of desired treatment outcome. Through trial and error effort the authors claim to have stumbled on to an intervention approach, while not readily accepted by traditional treatment institutions, nevertheless produced remarkable results. In this respect, their well documented case reviews are is worthy of special consideration by those who are regularly confronted with clients who self mutilate.

2. Although the issue of self mutilation is not specifically addressed in J. Haley's **Uncommon therapy** (New York: Norton Co., 1973) the book offers many intriguing and unusual interventions that could, with thoughtful examination, be extrapolated for use with some self harming clients. Equally, the book **Provocative therapy** by Frank Farrelly and Jeff Brandsma (California: Meta Publications, 1974) could also stimulate creative ideas for intervening with the self-mutilator or otherwise classified border line personality client in crisis.

NOTES

NOTES

_____

_____

_____

_____

_____

_____

_____

_____

_____

_____

_____

_____

_____

_____

_____

_____

_____

_____

_____

_____

_____

_____

_____

_____

_____

_____

_____

CHAPTER NINE

CRISIS INTERVENTION AND VIOLENCE

One must be humble when he approaches this subject, for there are still many unknowns. It has become more apparent to us that there are no quick and easy solutions to the problem of violence. Violent patients must be viewed with compassion and understanding as individuals with their own needs and qualities.

- Denis Madden & John Lion

ENCOUNTERING VIOLENCE

Those who act out aggressively in crisis situations often do so in order to ward off feelings of vunerability and helplessness. In the process they nevertheless invariably draw others into an aggressive survival struggle with them, for violence attracts and feeds off of more violence. This contagious aspect of violence can even draw the most trained and wary crisis intervener into their own survival state as they desperately search for ways to avoid losing control. Therefore, effective non-violent intervention within a violent or assaultive situation requires extraordinary skills.

It seems that most of the training available for crisis interveners strongly emphasizes self-and other protection by prescriptive and physically oriented intervention of a defensive nature. As a consequence, there are countless do's and don't's protocols offered in the literature(Hafen & Peterson, 1982; Madden & Lion, 1976; Mitchell & Resnick, 1981; Wicks, et al, 1982). While useful, these protocols do not adequately attend to the crisis intervener's own personal responses to aggression or to any underlying beliefs and values. Hence, crisis interveners oftentimes get mindlessly caught up in their own unique responses and struggle to remain balanced and psychologically neutral.

Application of the Beyond Content principle known as psychological neutrality is of paramount importance in order to avoid being rendered helpless by violent and aggressive behaviour. Psychological neutrality, when successfully manifested, becomes a cornerstone for intervention in violent situations. This Beyond Content contextual principle, when accompanied by the other nine principles outlined in Chapter Two as well as by the self-preparation exercises covered in Chapter Four, create a powerful platform for those who dare to intervene in violent situations.

Often violence happens in such a way that crisis intervention rarely occurs until after the fact. Nevertheless, the intent of this section is to specifically focus on Beyond Content crisis intervention during actual episodes of aggressive and assaultive behaviour. Violence to the self has been covered in the preceding two sections (on suicide and self mutilation); now an overview of violence to others (including the intervener) will be presented.

A SCHEMA FOR VIOLENCE

There are so many different causes of violence that we cannot even begin to discuss them all here. Moreover, though it is important to understand causes, what is needed most is a schema that can conceptually guide the crisis intervener towards practical crisis management of violence. A suggested schema for crisis interveners, presented here in Figure 15, flows out of the crisis integrity states (Figure 9, Chapter 5) , while also echoing aspects of the identity spectrum (Figure 2, Chapter 2).

This schema presented in Figure 15, is really an oversimplification of an immensely complex interhuman and intrahuman process. It is meant to be no more than a beinning level guide for the practicing crisis intervener.

Organism Based Crises

The first of the two scenarios presented in Figure 15 is meant to reflect circumstances in which disease or physiological imbalances of a primary, often unconscious nature, short circuit the natural flow of emotions causing them to erupt out of the body in seemingly uncontrollable ways. Like an active volcano, this predisposed human being can erupt at any time depending on the degree to which it is physiologically "state bound (Rossi, 1986). In other words, human emotions can erupt in unusual and unpredictable ways, seemingly without any mental restraint, because of unstable or idiosyncratic physiological undercurrents that surface from time to time. Often there is a trance-like quality to these outbursts, such that the person, when questioned afterwards about the behaviour, report being vague or unclear about their actions. Normally the body tends to absorb and deflect these emotions when they arise, either allowing the mind to reframe and subsequently channel them towards body expression as pseudo-feelings (part 2 of Figure 15) or they filter through and dissipate through general activity over time.

If one's adaptation capability, as Hans Selye (1955) discovered, is short-circuited by internal physiological factors, state-bound emotions can unpredicitably explode as free-floating anguish. When displayed as aggression, this anguish is often sprayed all over the place, onto self, others, and the environment. It is also possible, that any of the other basic emotions such as fear, joy, sadness and agitation may be released in raw unsanctioned form as well. For example, uncontrollable excitement

FIGURE 15

A SCHEMA FOR VIOLENCE PATTERNS

1.ORGANICALLY BASED CRISIS

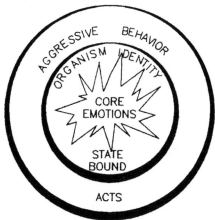

2.MIND BODY CRISIS

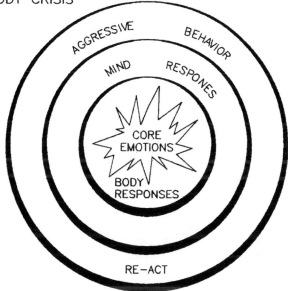

sometimes labelled hyperactivity can occur; or panic attacks can erupt out of the blue, suggesting some form of histrionic behaviour.

The crisis integrity state that seems most fitting to this scenario is AT LOSS. A person stuck at this integrity state feels mystified and definitely confused about just how both their mind and their body have seemingly lost control over their environment. Over time, repeated outbursts take on a conditioning flavour, depending on history-making trauma; and therefore they can also reflect the more adaptive mind/body response pattern outlined in part 2 of Figure 15.

Compounding this situation, when social trauma gets generated as a result of organism based outbursts, the fear of being AT EFFECT of these prevailing circumstances tends to surface. In these circumstances it becomes even more complicated and consequently it is extremely challenging to know how best to intervene.

Mind/Body Crises

As depicted once again in Figure 14, the second scenario suggests that the mind part of the body acts as an early warning system filtering the upwelling of primary feelings through the mind's memory and body banks. In so doing, it endeavours to recall any previous learning experiences that served to control these emotions. Pseudo-feelings, such as frustration, depression, guilt, boredom, and oppression, can create a buffer zone that prevents the primary emotions from getting out of control. Yet this method of containment, while it produces short-term control, tends to reinforce a boundary between the mind and the body. This boundary gets more restrictive as crisis events pile up in one's life, until eventually the mind begins to project or spill over primary emotions beyond the body and assume that these emotions are actually coming from others.

What then transpires is a vicious circle, where one's own emotions, erroneously perceived as coming from others, are reflected back onto oneself. The mind may then send a message to the body to aggressively "act in" versus "acting out". Sometimes the body does so by simply getting sick, getting injured, or breaking down. This outcome reinforces this person getting stuck at the crisis state of AT EFFECT. When this form of inadequate and unsatisfying relief persists, becoming more and more pronounced, the person may then choose to RE-ACT. The mind then instructs the body to react by striking out aggressively to relieve the internal pressure. It seems that, in order to survive what it has cast outside of itself as a shadow, it attacks anything, including its own body. The Act that gets played out becomes one of aggression, designed to remove the sources of frustration perceived as having caused the loss.

The losses reacted to can be either potential or real, tangible or intangible. Examples are failure to win at sports, loss of a relationship, failure to get a job promotion, failure to do well at school, rejection; being threatened physically, divorce, business failure, and so on.

This is not to say that others in our environment are not responsible for creating some anguish in our lives. However, it is what we do that keeps our anguish energized, when the impulse to live fully suggests that we should let them go and move on to other experiences. Table 7 contrasts just a few of the indicators that these two scenarios tend to present:

TABLE 7

VIOLENCE INDICATORS

Organism Based Crises	Mind/Body Crises
* Child-like actions	* Adolescent-like action
* Plugged mind-state	* Plugged-up mind state
* No apparent precipitating cause	* Identifiable feeling
* Random "scatter gun" action	* Target practice
* State of shock appearance	* Seething rage
* Eyes bulging	* Eyes narrowing
* Pronounced body agitation	* Body compression
* Ghost-like appearance	* Flushed or mottled face
* Excessive sweating	* Little or no sweating
* Impulsive speech	* Quivering, raised voice
* Full body agitation	* Fists clenched

Although the warning signs listed in Table 7 are valuable indicators, the very best predictor of violence is a history of previous violence. Knowing whether or not a person has committed violent acts in the past allows the crisis intervener to become more sensitized to how these scenarios can and do overlap. Furthermore, if alcohol or drugs, either prescribed, or illicit, are present in a person who has a history of violence, the risk of violence significantly increases.

INITIAL INTERVENTION GUIDELINES

In light of the distinctions made between mind/body and predominantly organism based violence states, separate intervention guidelines are offered for each. These guidelines are not in any order of importance, nor should they be used in a rigidly prescriptive fashion. First let us consider the organism-malfunctioning scenario, in which someone is profiling as out of control in an unpredictable and random fashion:

Organism Based Crises

1. Usually, one of the first actions to be taken is to clear away the most vulnerable or high-risk targets from the crisis territory. All people not needed as part of the intervention ought to be cautiously directed away from the crisis scene. All too often in crisis intervention we try to remove the person out of control to a more controlling environment, only to inadvertently compound the crisis and increase the possibility that others will become victims.

2. Next, whenever possible, carefully solicit the assistance of several aides who are unconditionally willing to work as a team with one person appointed as a coordinator. Violent crisis situations almost always result in widely differing points of view on what should be

done. In a cautious yet expeditious manner, the leader must take charge, being advised by his or her cohorts yet fully empowered to network the manpower and environmental supports with clear authority. In this way, even if mistakes are made, recovery is easier, because one approach is being taken rather than many potentially conflicting approaches.

3. First and foremost, ensure protection of life and limb. Intervene with calmness, assurance, and a clear purpose of preventing any further harm.

4. Use environmental, non living supports as alternate targets for aggression. In fact, try to create as many of these diverting targets as possible, to allow the aggressive energy to dissipate quickly with minimal physical restraint.

    Interact with the violent person by persistently inviting them to voluntarily channel their aggression in ways that are less and less destructive. Do not try to reason with them, as they will be unable to understand what they are she is doing at that very moment.

5. Re-direct the person in crisis towards a crisis territory in which you can establish perimeter controls. You may be required to verbally guide or physically assist the person in getting there. If so, act slowly and purposively, with the intent of simply relocating. This can often be done by strategically corralling the person towards the safer area or by introducing the safer area as an attractive place for the person to be.

6. In choosing an alternate crisis arena, be guided by a general rule of thumb that it should be big enough to allow a minimum of 8 to 10 feet of distance between the person in crisis and all the support personnel involved.

7. Direct attention towards attractive distractions, such as food, a blanket, a sweater for warmth, or the chance to make a telephone call to a significant other.

8. If at all possible, keep the person in crisis continually moving through out the crisis arena. Attempt to match the intervention activity with her level of agitation, until her energy gradually dissipates and she awakens enough to reconnect with her mind.

9. Once the persons mind begins to willingly interact with you, quickly offer several alternative ways or patterns (at least three) in which she can become consciously in control of her prevailing emotions and behaviour. In this manner the fears of judgement or punishment as well as face saving anger can be used as resources as opposed to eventually being masked over by pseudo-feelings such as guilt, depression and resentment. This approach can create the room for her to travel with more confidence abeit still vulnerable, down the pathway of self-mastery.

The violence malfunctioning pattern for mind/body crises suggests both a qualitatively and practically different intervention process. Some suggested considerations for intervention are as follows:

Mind/ Body Crises

1. If there is more than one person in conflict, separate them from one another by guiding them apart. Allow each person to regain composure by being at least 6 feet away from anyone else. A good rule of thumb is to give the persons in conflict space enough to permit full view of each other and of you.

2. Rather than have a head-on confrontation with the violent person, maintain an angulated position, preferably off to her left side. Give the person sufficient space to be able to see all of you; otherwise you may quickly become the replacement target. Rarely is it advisable to touch a violent person. She most often reacts to touch as though it were a threat to her ability to be in control.

3. Acknowledge the person by quickly finding out her first name and prefacing all communication by that name.

4. Consciously slow down the interaction process in whatever way that you can. The longer the process, the greater the likelihood that the principle of "self organization" will do the stabilizing work for you.

5. Have all parties sit down if at all possible. Keep your voice low, and speak slowly and supportively. Make sure that you acknowledge the person who is most volatile by giving her the first opportunity to share or vent. Re-direct such venting towards a legitimized (acceptable) inanimate object. Let this person know that she can get more of what she wants in ways other than violence.

6. When the crisis is extremely volatile, ensure that there is an easy way for her to escape from the conflict. This allows the agitated person to feel less trapped.

7. Watch with "soft eyes" for physical indicators, such as excessive sweating, teeth-gritting, fist-making, breath- holding, hair-bristling, face-reddening, and voice-raising. Encourage the person to alter such behaviour by mirroring and modelling it, letting go of the tension away from others.

8. Appeal to the violent person's competency characteristics, guiding her towards self-acknowledgement of her competencies. For example, you might say," Sharon, from what I can see around you, it looks like you enjoy cooking. My guess is that you know a lot about different ways to please others with your cooking skills."

9. Violent people are enormously frightened by loss of control. At the peak of their frustration, look for ways to give them control over something that is neutral. To short circuit their anguish and quickly re-direct their pent-up energy to some competency aspect of themselves requires trial and error effort. Fortunately, when intervention is based on "what works" rather than on what is right or wrong, stabilization tends to occur eventually.

10.   In rare circumstances, physical restraint is necessary. Unless the crisis intervener is well trained in nonviolent restrainment approaches and the person in crisis is risking serious harm to self or others, physically restraining or disarming someone is not recommended. Even then, the police should be called upon first and foremost.

11.   When the violence is directed towards you, protect yourself by ensuring that adequate distance is maintained. Do not threaten with consequences, and do not make this person wrong. Keep uppermost in your mind ways this person can escape from their threats of violence through face-saving alternatives.

In the interests of demonstrating, in some rough way, how various aspects of the Beyond Content model might be used in crisis situations reflecting the two violence scenarios, an example for each is now offered. These examples are modifications of real occurrences and are presented in the form of dialogue interspersed with intervention guidelines drawn from previous chapters.

BEYOND CONTENT MODEL APPLICATION

1.   Hyperactive Violence

This first example is of an organism based crisis involving a 14 year-old male youth named Danny. This young boy has been placed in a residential treatment centre because he is prone to extremely violent outbursts of unknown origin. He has been labelled hyperactive and has had countless treatment specialists work with him, with no apparent success.

Very shortly after Danny is placed in residence, he spontaneously, without any noticeable provocation, goes on rampages lasting for several hours at a time. During these periods he spits at anyone who gets in his way, digs up flowers, breaks windows, kicks holes in plaster walls, shouts out random obscenities, throws food around, and punches anyone who tries to restrain him. Reasoning with him has no effect, as he does not appear to hear or see what he is doing. Limit-setting is quickly circumvented by his chaotic nature: He goes from one environment to another, leaving behind a path of destruction. Knowing that he is prone to long bouts of outrage and that restraint alone only prolongs these bouts, you recognize that his behaviour profiles like that of someone whose emotional circuits are malfunctioning.

Given the responsibility to intervene, you quickly form a crisis team with four others who can be available for a minimum of two or preferably three hours. As the crisis coordinator, you guide the team to act instrumentally with instructions only from you and not to try talking to Danny about his behaviour or getting him to settle down. The strategy will be to establish a safe environment for Danny to experience an ordeal that acknowledges his need to erupt before he can regain control.

Next, a gym-like space is quarantined off as the crisis intervention arena, ensuring that no spectators or interfering objects are present. The task is now to draw Danny to this area, using his resistance to being in control as a resource. You decide to let him see you take some of his belongings from his room to the gym without any attempt to explain what you are doing. As it turns out, he curiously follows you and your team into the gym, where you then secure the perimeter with the crisis team.

Now for the source approach...

Sharing

Keeping as far away as possible, you share with Danny that this is a place where he can safely work out what's going on with him. You say this slowly, repeatedly, and with confidence. You further state that the team is here to support him to regain control over his behaviour and that this will most certainly happen. Danny, in a hyperactive trance-like fashion, seemingly ignores what you have said and tries to leave. As he gets more aggressive, you guide two or three team members to hold him in the middle of the gym for short periods of time. These holdings continue repetitively, in synchrony with his fluxuating acting-out behaviour. The holdings vary in length from a few minutes to a maximum of 10 minutes. While he is held, no communication with him is tried by the crisis team. All questions from team members are directed to you as the crisis coordinator. Again you slowly and repeatedly assure him that he will regain control sometime soon.

When he is released, several large, soft play balls are left as devices for him to release energy: He can throw the balls against the walls, kick them, or play basketball with them. Danny makes several attempts to hit crisis team members with the balls and at times tries to break out of the gym by pounding the doors as well as the crisis team members. As you guide the process, every effort is made to avoid confrontation and to give plenty of distance between him and the crisis team members. The primary task is to maintain a safe crisis boundary. Sharing of reasons for what you are doing is not offered during this highly volatile phase.

Observing

You are aware that you must observe from a distance and that as the crisis coordinator you must not get involved in the holdings. Psychological neutrality is key to the success of this ordeal. As you maintain a perimeter vigilance, you guide the process and draw in resources as they are needed.

When you observe Danny kicking the wall, you instruct one of the team members to throw him the balls; then you invite him to kick the balls. After he kicks the balls as hard as he can, you acknowledge his effort in a neutral manner. He then starts to run around the gym shouting obscenities; and you ask the crisis team one by one to run around with him, keeping a safe distance and as well to talk loudly about running wild and what it is like to run free.

Throughout the crisis process, you continuously watch for changing body signs. As energy whirls through his organism, erupting as anger, sadness, excitement, and pleasure, you track it from moment to moment, watching for physical blockage points.

Uncovering

Danny starts clenching his teeth, and forming fists, stating that he is getting out of here. This time he is given a towel and challenged to tear it apart with either his hands or his teeth. He obliges, only to find it is difficult though not impossible. Following this, there is a period of exhaustion during which you may decide, in an impromptu manner, to hold him again. Since this not a restraining hold, Danny goes limp and remains passive. After two minutes he is released and goes to one of the gym corners. Passively he remains quiet for a while, yet you observe that he is still seething inside and mumbling to himself. Talking with him in a soft, very low voice, you once again throw him a ball. Again Danny loses control and throws the balls as hard as he can at the crisis team members. This time he is held for five minutes, and a blanket is used to prevent him from striking the interveners.

Several more outbursts and holdings occur over the next hour. Then, two hours after the ordeal started, Danny crumbles into a ball and begins to weep, saying almost inaudibly that he is thirsty. At this point, Danny is offered a cup of water and left alone for about ten minutes. Meanwhile the team members take turns walking around the perimeter of the gym in a slow, deliberate, and rhythmic fashion. In this way, the solidarity of the boundary is reinforced. Slowly and in a low and peaceful voice, you invite Danny to join with one of the team members in shooting the basketball for a while. Now, a first attempt to uncover his self-mastery capability is made. When you ask him what would help him to control his behaviour, he says that he doesn't know, it just seems to happen. Further explorative dialogue, while shooting baskets with him, reveals that when he gets upset he likes to ride a bike and lift weights.

Resourcing

Continuing with this intervention ordeal, you as coordinator instruct one of the team members to respond to Danny's outbursts by offering him three or more alternatives: riding a bicycle or doing weights; repeating this gym experience; getting sedated at a hospital; being admitted to a crisis residence; or asking for assistance from the crisis service. Danny is left to think about these possibilities for a while, in order to avoid pressuring him and at the same time re-affirm that the "gym" experience will continue as long as necessary.

Completing

Danny shoots baskets with himself for a while, then declares he is bored. A table is then set up in the middle of the gym, with two chairs, paper, and a pencil. Danny is encouraged to sit down with one of the team members and to do two things: write out his experience point by point, and write out an agreement on his options for controlling his outbursts. This somewhat formal process shows the importance of being thorough and complete. Care is taken that the agreement is not construed as punitive or judgmental. Once again, it is impressed upon Danny that he has to be in a state of harmony before this gym experience can end. Because the entire process has been quite intensive and emotionally draining, it is extremely difficult for Danny to fake or mask cooperation. The manner, in

---

which the team shows concern, plus acceptance of Danny's outbursts as important to him in some way, can leave an indelible and imprint on him. In Danny's case, it ultimately serves to countercondition or short circuit his "bound-up" emotional state, allowing him to re-establish mind control over his body.

Expanding

To really capitalize on this intervention and expand Danny's ability to be in charge of his emotions, clinical exploration is needed. Crisis intervention goes beyond stabilization when it expands Danny's view of himself and prepares him for being increasingly curious about how to refine his self-mastery capabilities. Before Danny leaves this experience, his ability to make his own decisions is carefully acknowledged. As well, he is reminded of the expanded options that he now has and of his capability to develop even more options.

This crisis intervention ordeal is meant to be an intrusive short circuiting process, uniquely tailored to Danny. Its utility in other, perhaps similar, situations is determined primarily by consideration of what to avoid, how to travel the path of least intrusiveness, and how to use resistance as a resource.

Danny's type of hostility is most likely to be encountered in institutions such as correctional centres, special school settings,treatment resources, and hospitals. Unfortunately, some of these settings, because of competing priorities, lack the capacity to focus intensively as was done by means of this ordeal. It is unlikely for hospitals to consider such an intervention, the choice here is usually to sedate the person with medication or to use mechanical restraints, especially if the person is psychotic. This is not to say that creative and out-of-the-ordinary intervention is inappropriate in such a setting. What works is looking beyond prescriptive intervention protocols and infusing vitality into them by taking each unique crisis and allowing the violence encountered in it to be used to guide the intervention. In this way, resistance becomes resourceful and invaluable to crisis resolution.

In circumstances in which a safe crisis field cannot be established in the immediate area, consideration should be given to using the outdoor environment to diffuse the crisis. When using the outdoors, the key contextual principle to activate is Self-Organization. The person in crisis should be actively encouraged to be or become in harmony with the environment by being challenged with ordeals in the community. Care needs to be taken that others in the community are protected from any unexpected outbursts of violence that require supervised intervention. In this regard, the crisis intervener needs to be guided by common sense.

2.   Interpersonal Entanglements-A Domestic Dispute

This next example attempts to demonstrate how aspects of the Beyond Content model might be applied to a domestic dispute. Before doing so, it may be worth commenting more specifically on the nature of entanglements.

Intervening in a violent confrontation between two people requires extraordinary sensitivity to both parties as well as to oneself. This dual awareness is essential in order to neutralize one's own experiences with violence, one's prejudices, goals, beliefs, and opinions so as not to confound the crisis task.

Short-term explosive entanglements are not the occasion for contemplative or exploratory intervention. An active posture is almost always warranted, and it suggests to those in conflict that their anguish is important enough to demand immediate attention. These situations are usually preceded by prolonged periods of frustration. They are driven by any number of escalating, well-developed fears, such as fear of identity humiliation, abandonment, loneliness, physical threats, and any potential loss of significance. The participants almost always are perceptually cross-wired with one another. One may be operating predominantly by how they feel while the other may be going by just what they see going on or what they have heard from others as well as the person they are in conflict with. Eruptions of violence can occur in a moments notice, taking the form of aggression towards others, behaviour that draws aggression from others, or aggression towards oneself. More often than not, the two participants desperately want to be heard and understood, yet they inevitably interpret each other's needs in dramatically conflictual ways. Each person, overwhelmingly aware of his or her own stuckness, tends to lose sight of the other's viewpoint. Eventually the persistent lack of resolution can trigger physically confrontative re-actions towards self as well as towards others.

A Domestic Dispute

John and Margaret, a married couple in their late thirties, are involved in a shouting and pushing match with one another, causing the neighbour in the next-door apartment to call the police. The police are familiar with this couple, having made two previous calls to their home over the past two months. This time the police call you in as a crisis intervener to assist them with this crisis. Arriving at the home, you are met by the neighbour, who asks you to come in quickly. John and Margaret are in the kitchen, Margaret sitting down with her hands over her ears and John standing over her, loudly trying to get her to hear what he is saying. Broken dinnerware plates and glass litter the floor, and two of the four kitchen chairs are upturned. Once, again the source approach...

Sharing

In a low, soft voice you state that you are from the crisis service, and in a controlled, sharing way, you gently move between Margaret and John, sensing that John is extremely frustrated and ready to blow at any moment. You tell John that there is something important he should know, and you guide him out of the kitchen into the living room. At the same time you also ask the neighbour to simply sit with Margaret, not saying anything, while you talk with John. Ensuring that you acknowledge John by saying his name at the beginning of every statement, you tell John that you know how he could make use of your services. First, though, you need to hear what resources are missing that are essential for this conflict to stabilize and for matters to get back to normal.

Observing

While listening, you observe with soft eyes and tune in with receiving ears to notice Margaret crying in the background, empty beer cans in several places, a marked-up job resume on the coffee table, and a family photo showing the both of them plus a young boy, all smartly dressed and vibrant-looking. Over on a shelf is this same boy playing hockey. Turning to John, you sense in John's voice a desperate need to be heard and recognized, as though he somehow had lost something. John wrings his hands and furrows his brow as he tells you his concerns, several times saying "There is no use." He is unshaven and looks like he has not slept for some time.

He complains bitterly about his wife's spending all her time at the church and at her volunteer work with the Cancer Society. John, in his late thirties, is an engineer who has not worked for the past six months. He mentions how hard it is to get back into the employment market after his bowel resection operation because of Crohn's disease. After John has talked without interruption for about ten minutes, he is less agitated than before; and he now asks, in a confused and somewhat paranoic way, why you are here.

Uncovering

By now you have, partially at least, sized-up the situation, surmising that John's ACT is to make somebody pay for his pain. John begins to profile as someone who has progressively allowed his self-image to deteriorate to the extent he now reactively disowns the way in which he is defeating himself both physically and emotionally. In order to avoid any further loss, he casts his shadow of inadequacy and dispair onto Margaret. More and more, his persona struggles to survive by making others wrong.

At this point, Margaret is asked to come into the living room and sit at an angle to John so as not to set her up to be a direct target for any possible blame. Thanking John for enquiring about your purpose, you then share that this could be an opportunity for them both to avoid any further trouble and to discover some new possibilities for getting what they both want. Your purpose is simply to assist them like a good neighbour, so that they can avoid having to go to more drastic and perhaps unacceptable measures. You are not there to treat them or to interfere with their lives in any way. With assurance, you comment that their willingness to listen at this point is and indication that favourable results are possible.
Speaking to John, you suggest that it is important to have Margaret share what she is experiencing right now and to find out what she wants. In that way, you will have heard from them both.

As Margaret slowly and apprehensively speaks, you gently advise John to save his comments for later, saying that this always works better. Margaret begins to profile as a victim who withholds support, allowing fate to take its course, and her religion to be her real salvation. She has stopped looking outward and restricts her listening to her religious belief systems. Margaret mentions that for the past three years she hasn't felt good about living. Recalling the family portrait, you ask about other family members; and John says that their son

William died from leukaemia three years ago, at age ten. It is obvious now that Margaret has not finished grieving the loss of her son and in a way has absented herself from the marital relationship. Nonetheless, both state that they want to stay together, even though the bitterness and violence is getting worse.

Resourcing

The intervention now shifts towards identifying the resources that are necessary for re-patterning the resistance between them. Individually, each is asked to state which competencies of the other they want, can support, or can acknowledge. Additionally, they are asked to identify environmental supports, such as extended-family members, who can assist them by providing time out support from one another. Even though those immediately around these people in crisis are often too close to the problem or are entertwined with it, they have value when employed in certain specific ways. The challenge here is to persevere, using the couple's resistance as a resource until you uncover the competencies that exist right around them.

At this point, both John and Margaret are experiencing a vacuum between them and are prone to get into conflict again. John leans forward and confronts Margaret by saying that she sabotages support from their friends and relatives. Margaret starts to get up to leave. Quickly you approach Margaret and guide her towards where John is sitting. While doing so, you ask John to move over to where Margaret was sitting. Continuing the repatterning approach, you ask each of them in turn to comment, as though they were the other, on what they are missing and how they might get it from the other. This role reversal gives them an opportunity to shift their perceptions away from their past stuckness towards what is happening in the moment. Care is taken to keep them present-and future-focused and to acknowledge any resistance they share by supporting them to move out of survival by means of a competency re-building process (Chapter Six). This process takes patience: Just when progress seems to have been made, one or both of them retract back into survival. To work with them from the crisis integrity state they are at in the moment, you must shift your intervention approach many times. The risk in trying to press ahead is that you, the crisis intervener, often become the target of their unresolved resentment and frustration.

Completing

Even though progress may be experienced in acknowledging one another's needs, this is only the beginning. Before they can turn the corner on their crisis, one or both of them needs to be willing to let go of their survival tactics, even though that may make either one of them more more vulnerable again.

Over two to four sessions, the task is to awaken at least one of them to resources that they have overlooked and to ways to activate their competencies in supporting them to let go of their opposition. Completing often requires that they verbally agree to forgive one another so that the past does not persist in disrupting them move towards a recapturing of their commitment to each other. So, at this point they are instructed to simply practice saying they forgive each other and then to comment on how realistic or genuine this feels to them both as senders and receivers. Encouragement to persist in this activity by stating their forgiveness many times and in many different ways is often necessary until a gradual growing willingness to "let go" of their resentment occurs.

To complete the crisis intervention is to get both John and Margaret to agree to be willing to try some alternative ways of living with one another that used to work for them in the past. Sensing that John needs to also find ways to re-establish self-sufficiency and that Margaret needs to complete her grieving, marital counselling is introduced as a desired intervention that is essential if they are to avoid entrenching themselves into survival with one another again. Their agreement to co-operate or explore this possibility is essential to completing the intervention.

Expanding

The extended aim of this crisis intervention is to have the integrity state of NATURALNESS be re-established with John and Margaret. From time to time during the crisis intervention process, they connected with one another at this state for brief moments, or else one of them regained this state while the other was still struggling. Whenever this happens, it becomes an opportunity for the crisis intervener to shift from directing to guiding. In this way it allows the person operating from a state of naturalness the opportunity to be reinforced in their episodic ability to make a significant unforced contribution to their living partner. Margaret, for example, might mention that she recently has been thinking about how she could iron some shirts for John, to support his efforts to become employed again. John suggests at a different time that he has been meaning to take their son's belongings and pack them away instead of leaving them still scattered around the house. In the process of completing the intervention, you recall these contributions and clarify ways in which they can be expanded, regardless of how impoverished they may be from circumstance to circumstance.

To travel an expanding pathway rather than a contracting one takes the same amount of energy, has relatively equivalent difficulties, and is not about getting better. It is about what works.

SUGGESTED READINGS

1. Everstine & Everstine in their book **People in crisis** (New York: Brunner Mazel, 1983) offer a comprehensive review of the many faces of violence. Worthy of note is the considerable attention they pay to practical guidelines and specific intervention strategies for domestic violence, rape, battered women and children, and sexual assault.

2. Regarding the nature of violence, an excellent article, "Does violence breed violence?" by Silver & Dublin in the American Journal of Psychiatry (126:404-407, 1969), presents a cogent argument for the contagious aspects of violence.

3. An excellent account of resistances produced by helping systems when they encounter aggressive or highly resistive clients is presented in Anderson & Stewart's book **Mastering resistance** (New York:Guilford Press, 1983). They offer rich case material about highly resistant families; and in particular they demonstrate how resistance can be effectively used to reduce anguish and foster better therapeutic connection.

4. Mitchell & Resnick, in **Emergency response to crisis** (London: Prenctice-Hall, 1981), present a practical handbook for those working in emergency medical services. In particular, the chapter covering violence in field situations offers a concise overview of major issues important to the crisis intervener working with violence and aggression.

NOTES

NOTES

CHAPTER TEN

GRIEF & MOURNING INTERVENTION

There are many levels on which to explore the grief we hold in our aching body and painfully separate mind. Indeed, it may well be that not until a traumatic incident has occurred will we start to pay attention to life at the level where healing is to be discovered and the subtle injuries are to be released.

...In open body, in open mind, in open heart, the possibilities are endless. Healing is to be found everywhere. Each step so precious. Each step is a new healing.

- Stephen Levine

A BEYOND CONTENT VIEW

It goes without saying that almost every facet of our lives is affected by loss, through death, dying and, increasingly through divorce or separation from others. Loss begins at birth; and, depending on how our losses are experienced, they cause varying degrees of trauma. Attachment and separation are lifelong issues, each in their own way producing the experience of suffering (Wilber,1979; Levine,1987). To be too attached or controlled is to lose one's sense of freedom. To be too separated is to experience fears of abandonment, rejection, or aloneness. It seems that we continuously struggle with both, seeking a balance by keeping separation and attachment somewhat disconnected and conflictual.

When the crisis experiences of dying, death, or separation repeatedly confront us throughout our lives, we tend to filter the experience through our current developmentally predisposed identity state. This state evolves or remains incomplete or stuck, depending on how we dissolve past crisis events. When crises leave behind unfinished business, we feel incomplete and increasingly become fearful of losing our sense of self-mastery over the events in our lives. Consequently, our evolving identity attempts to react to life by attempting to avoid, ignore, or deny loss of whatever we invest ourselves in. Fortunately, we nevertheless stumble forward by discovering that letting go and attaching happen naturally and that attendant trauma eventually dissipates. The form that this trauma of letting go and attaching takes is mourning and grieving. In this respect, grief and mourning become integral to our recovery from loss.

From a transpersonal perspective, loss becomes revealed as an illusion when one is functioning from a state of unity consciousness and transcendence. In this state, living and dying are natural aspects of the miracle of our existence. When not connected to this state, we find more often that not that our dread of death and loss and our reaction to them cause premature deadness as we mentally operate in a culturally conditioned way to restrict our aliveness. It seems that our tendency to be preoccupied with the parts of life causes us to fear that those parts, when lost, will take away from our wholeness. Actually, when one allows reality to sink in, it is really only the parts of our lives that reflect suffering, not our self as whole. Therefore, one can always transmute the impact of suffering by ironically embracing and re-incorporating it as an integral, indivisible aspect of the wholeness of life. Thus grief and mourning do not have to be as painful as we make them out to be. Practically speaking, grief and mourning can actually be celebrated as a process of completion. While this experience is rare in Western world cultures, it is not entirely alien to the human race. Several cultures around the world have for centuries treated the process of living and dying as two facets of the same coin. The traditions underlying Theravadan Buddhism, Taoism, and other forms of esoteric belief systems have honored death and loss not by ignoring or avoiding it. Instead they embrace it, celebrating completions rather than mourning endings (Kubler-Ross, 1975).

By allowing our emotions to flow through the grieving and mourning process and to witness with choiceless awareness in the midst of our distress without attaching to our grief, incredible breakthroughs can occur. In other words, instead of piling up our losses in our mind/body and letting them contaminate, drain, and bury parts of us alive until an overwhelming emptiness pervades us, we can actually have the opposite occur. By actively seeking to complete the mourning and grieving process in the context of being free from suffering, we observe how we are not "less than" because of the loss, but rather are now enriched and free to move with what has actually been a contributing experience to us. Significant losses can, if we allow them to, permit us to recover lost aspects of ourselves that have been buried by our own unfinished historical crises.

So, our challenge is to remove the blockages that prevent us from evolving our capacity to be at one with our surroundings. In a sense, we look upon this process as one of putting the finishing touches on living and life experiences so as to prevent us from carrying forward the baggage of our past.

Catastrophically, our Western world view acts predominately to deny death and terminal loss as though by so doing we can somehow control them. Just as we really have no control over the attachment or birth process, we also have no control over the separation or dying process, although we would like to think we do (Simonton et al., 1979). Transpersonally, our option is to gain mastery over our living and evolving. When we do so, dying reflects what happens in everyday life. The issues we face in dying can become naturally embraced as aspects of our way of living fully and completely for the moment. Every moment counts as one moment dies to the next. Even our pain can be our teacher. When we stop denying this possibility in our daily lives, we continuously wake up to the unexpected rather than being shocked into reality by crises.

Acceptance of dying as an ongoing every-moment process means that we can naturally allow ourselves to be at peace with living and to free ourselves from mind-created pain of loss. Shocking our senses can be a daily occurrence rather than an overwhelming crisis that causes us to retreat from ourselves in order to find ourselves again.

STAGES OF RECOVERY FROM LOSS

Much has been written about the emotional process of dying, (Kubler-Ross, 1969 ;Levine, 1987;and Gorman, 1983). In particular, Elizabeth Kubler-Ross has shed considerable light on the process of dying outlining five major stages.

These stages are:

DENIAL
ANGER
BARGAINING
DEPRESSION AND,
ACCEPTANCE.

They reflect what tends to universally happen when operating from a life-view that avoids dying by holding onto, attaching to, or identifying with our distress in life, until we eventually give it up. In a sense, we cover up our fear, anger, sadness and excitement of loss by an indelibly imprinted survival process. When death confronts us, we are shocked as the doors to the root cellar of all the pain of our existence are unlocked, revealing for the moment the underlying sources of our suffering. We counteract this painful awareness by initially raising to the forefront, our survival tactic of denial. This blanketing impact of denial is the first stage of dying. It is important to note that the stages of dying are similar to those manifested by anyone who faces any kind of extreme loss. As such, they are aligned with the crisis integrity states, as can be seen by referring to the Competency Re-Building blocks in Figure 12 (Chapter Six).

In the interests of viewing these emotional adjustment stages of dying within the framework of the crisis states of integrity and the respective competency re-building blocks, each stage will be discussed in turn. Furthermore, the stages will be described in an extrapolated or generic manner in order to reflect terminal loss as it manifests itself within ourselves, with others and as well with our environment. In other words, loss is treated as death in many forms; physical, social, interpersonal, cultural as well as psychological.

DENIAL

Being startled by pending terminal loss is somewhat like being thrust into an emotional tornado. The upwelling emotions become fearfully overwhelming; and the first reaction is to shut down, go numb, so as not to lose control. This first line of grief defense allows us to disconnect from

---

our emotions and our thoughts. Denial manifests itself in ignoring raw emotions in favour of manipulating our mind to disbelieve what is happening. This is a state of **At Survival,** where we first of all want to survive the onslaught of our own emotions. Initially, unwilling to face up to the reality, we may go about our life as if nothing had happened. This pseudo-state of wellness usually lasts as long as it takes for day-to-day events to confront us about what is really happening.

Assisting a person in this state of crisis requires that the crisis intervener listen without trying to get the person to give up her denial. Rather, through consistent and persevering availability, you support the person by acknowledging the need to deny. If you let the person totally define the nature of the crisis, they can quickly bounce up against the reality of their circumstances. The grief reactions of others, the funeral, or the need to begin adjusting to an altered way of living with the loss, wear away the numbness and erode this stunned state of denial. The role of the crisis intervener is merely to let the truth surface naturally. The person may then move within the **Survival** state from manipulation to opposition with their life-space.

ANGER

Acknowledging the truth of the loss can now thrust this person up against their fears, causing them to react by projecting their emotions away from themselves. Reality is confronted but not accepted fully. Somebody else must be blamed or made wrong for one's anguish. Grief is now characterized by bitterness, resentfulness, and opposition to even those who are supportive. At this stage, relief from this anger is essential; otherwise the person risks turning it inward onto themselves by acts such as pulling their hair out, getting into an accident, or beating on something or someone. As the loss begins to sink in, the real emotions begin to leak out, even pour out. These emotions, in raw form, leave one feeling overwhelmed and out of control. What inevitably happens is that the mind generates any number of compensatory feelings and actions as a way of dampening down and controlling the emotional upwellings. For example, guilt, depression, frustration, remorse, repression, as well as psychosomatic illnesses can mask the true emotions.

During this stage it is better to have the person fully share rather than to encourage, in well-meaning ways, cessation of thinking about the death, dying, or loss. The challenge becomes one of patiently guiding the person away from further debilitating, self-defeating behaviour. Alternatively it is to assist them take responsibility for their anger and sadness and for expressing themselves fully. By full expression, they can be supported in ways to re-direct their energy of anguish towards doing something that serves their current aliveness. For example, these bound-up emotions can be released in the form of excitation rather than tension. You can guide them towards transforming tension into productive excitement by such means as embarking on a rigorous exercise program, writing letters to others who may benefit from knowing what has happened, offering support to others who would be appreciative, and engaging in nostalgic experiences acknowledging gains as opposed to losses.

This tactic often leads the person into the bargaining stage. When they give up being right or righteous about the loss and entertain doing something productive with their raw emotional energy, an overriding need for assurance and support will pervade them. Moving out of survival, they reluctantly stumble into the crisis state of being **At Effect.**

BARGAINING

As one's vulnerability gradually takes over, moment by moment, leaving little room for avoidance of our natural state of fragility, so much seems incomplete. Allowing oneself to know that there is no real escape, no real control over death, or some losses thrusts us into a state of **At Effect**. Not knowing what to do, we bargain either unconsciously in our own mind or even overtly with ourselves and with our caregivers, to change our ways or do something to extend our life or to prevent the pending loss. At this stage, as we are at the effect of our grief, our anxiety rises as we frantically and desperately try to work out a better deal with life. Flights into health-promoting activities, such as becoming more religious or doing things now that one always felt were right and yet had postponed, might free us from the grips of death or loss at least for the time being. Bargaining may also occur just so that we can experience a family or personal goal, such as seeing a daughter graduate from college, complete the writing of a book, take a trip to DisneyLand, or hold a christmas family reunion. Unfortunately, even when a bargain is struck, it is often not enough, and the sense of being **At Effect** and short-changed by life persists.

The crisis intervener can best assist the person who is desperately trying to bargain by patiently guiding them set some direction instead of being scattered. This guidance is given over and over again until aspects of this person's life become complete. Care is taken to celebrate these completions, so that the person may move on without trying to re-attach when it no longer is useful for her to do so.

The bargaining may go on in search of yet one more loophole back into existence as it was, until, in most cases, the stark reality of not having control over death and loss eventually takes over. Depression of emotions can then ensue, causing a crisis state of **Non-Entity** to surface.

DEPRESSION

This grey and deadening zone is predominantly characterized by withdrawal from the external world. Choosing to shut down for fear of being overwhelmed or overly preoccupied with pending loss, they may create a vacuum around themselves. The challenge then is to awaken them to goals they may have in life that are immediate and demanding. Teasing them out of hiding is no mean feat. It is essential to be patient and to persevere in just being with the person's deadening space, carefully directing them to open up to neutral environmental influences that support their significance for the moment. In a non-attached way, exuding confidence and assurance, you would guide them toward non-threatening initiatives such as cooking, bathing, fixing something simple, and taking responsibility for telephoning others who view them as important. Since just **being** is intolerable, **doing** can become the pathway to recovery of their natural competence. What flows naturally, when the person successfully activates their sense of responsibility, is that problems start unfolding as challenges; and a growing acceptance of failure or loss offers breakthrough self-awareness opportunities. A state of **At Naturalness** can then be recaptured, and a growing acceptance of existence as it exists can take place.

ACCEPTANCE

Mourning and grieving come to an end when a shift in awareness occurs. For persons whose loss is external to themselves, an awakening to what they have been left with, how they have been indelibly affected by their attachments, emerges in the form of privileged acceptance. This recovered state of **Naturalness** surfaces in the form of tranquillity and peaceful action. A recognition of how we have been enriched by our losses surfaces, clarifying our growing desire to be whole and complete just the way we are. Acceptance harmonizes what we have with what we do not have. It opens a pathway for them to use the essence they are left with to carry them forward on the journey towards self-fulfillment.

This somewhat tranquil state that we are calling Naturalness is the recovery and reclamation of an inner experience of wisdom. It is characterized by an integration of the organic, psychological, and social traits and tendencies of one's personality into a harmonious whole. The person moves beyond victimization. They become less a stranger to themselves and begin to generate an aura of realness and congruence. Intervening with a person who has arrived or "come home" to naturalness and acceptance is unquestionably a privilege. The appropriate crisis response is to support this person to stay in the "here and now," to self promote, and to make a contribution to others. It goes without saying that if the client is at a higher state of integrity than the crisis intervener, the best that we can do is to learn from them and be mindful of how we might be inhibiting rather than contributing to their present state of aliveness. Ironically this occurs more often than most crisis interveners are aware of especially when the loss involves one's own impending death.

A person who has accepted a significant loss, for example, death of others and loss through injury or their own impending death, generally experiences themselves as an observer of their emotions and of the emotions of those around them. Feelings become messages and are no longer treacherous undercurrents of life. The person's feelings, thoughts, and experiences flow together in a congruent way as they now realize a desire to experience their environment as richer because of what they have contributed to it. This state is not an end of effort but an acceptance of one's current path of travel and a the creation of a space for peaceful connection to the whole. At this stage the person is recognized by their calmness and self-acceptance.

What such a person wants from a crisis intervener is an acceptance of their current state, rather than ambitious and unrelenting statements of hope and false encouragement. Too often a crisis intervener's expectations unwittingly clash with this dying person's desire to let go of expectations. The wise crisis intervener offers presence, an unattached beingness, along with a receptive ear to attend to messages conveying how to support completion and fulfillment. Sitting with this person for short periods, holding their hand if requested, simply listening to or being quiet with them - such things are what they often want from significant others and yet rarely get. Allow the person to direct your involvement, and only make your self available in accordance with their wishes. The most agonizing issue for those who are experiencing significant loss or the possibility of loss is the unfinished and unrealistic expectations of those close to them. The crisis intervener can be an ally here in quietly encouraging significant others to attend not so much to their own loss but rather more to the need for completion and self acceptance. Becoming connected to this person's essence (rather than to her form) allows a celebration of life's meaningfulness. The end is never without new beginnings.

SUGGESTED READINGS

1. An excellent book by Paul Gorman and Ram Dass, entitled **How can I help?** (New York: A. Knopf, 1988), can serve as an invaluable guide to just about anyone wanting to assist others through mourning and grief for a significant loss. Its simple approach offers a glimpse of how a transpersonal perspective can make a difference with those immensely distressed by their losses.

2. A book ostensibly for those confronted with cancer is in fact useful for any crisis intervener who encounters death in her practice. This book, **Healing into life and death** (New York: Double Day Press, 1987) by Stephen Levine, offers numerous helpful hints on how to relieve tension through simple yet powerfully cathartic meditations. It is strongly recommended for anyone interested in developing contemplative ways of working with grief and mourning.

NOTES

CHAPTER ELEVEN

SUBSTANCE ABUSE CRISIS INTERVENTION

There is no short cut to nirvana, no elixir, no amount of avoidance of pain and suffering, no major solution will allow our body/mind to be at peace with one another. When pain becomes an acceptable aspect of pleasure and pleasure an acceptable aspect of pain, escaping our body/mind will be unnecessary.

- Virginia Satir

A BEYOND CONTENT PERSPECTIVE

The decision to engage in substance abuse rather than in other compensating behaviors has been investigated, researched, and theorized about for decades. As with cancer, these research efforts have spun complicated probable causes but precious few solutions. One might say that the symptoms of substance abuse (which really have no energy of their own) have been probed, dissected, manipulated, and mutated to the extent they have at times been artificially elevated in importance and energized, overshadowing the need to develop meaningful intervention possibilities.

Substance abuse is much easier to define than to do anything about. It involves just about anything that one can ingest or inhale. It seems that we live in a culture preoccupied with oral ways to produce a sense of fulfillment. So prevalent is this apparent increasing need for oral gratification that our bench-marks of abuse and effective use have been largely obscured, permitting hedonism or self-fulfillment of immediate needs to be the prevailing wisdom. In this regard, denial of abuse is widespread and is justified as a semi-viable way to relieve the tension of being less than satisfied with our existence. Substance abuse, in some respects, is a short cut to (temporary) self-assurance and self-acceptance. Unfortunately, it is an elusive shortcut, because continued and gradually escalating misuse or abuse is needed to counteract the slippage back to self-doubt and a felt sense of being unfulfilled.

The Beyond Content perspective tends to view a crisis of substance abuse as a survival tactic that masks other underlying crises. Thus there are crises behind the crisis. It is viewed that substance abuse can be insidiously maintained by a complex array of personal and intrapersonal reasons which are intricately interwoven into a well conditioned "avoidance of loss" pattern of behavior. Substance abuse alters our state by dampening or suppressing experiences of loss, inadequacy and ultimately our aliveness. According to Sidney Cohen (1969), some suggested reasons why people take a drug holiday from life are the following:

1.   Severely inadequate, immature, depressed, psychotic, or borderline personalities, which seek a quick and magical solution to their character defects.

2.   Curious people with the opportunity and the money to afford drugs.

3.   "Joy riders" or people who feel bored with their everyday lives.

4.   Compliant persons with a strong need to belong to a control oriented social group.

5.   Artists who seek to alternative ways to become more inspired with their work.

6.   People with a real or imagined need to escape a certain situation.

7.   Accidental addicts who become hooked at an age or in circumstances in which they are unable to discriminate or to object.

8.   Those strongly persuaded by a "significant other," such as a lover or a family member.

9.   People suffering real stress from overwork or other negative life circumstances.

10.   Impulsive and poorly controlled people who "try anything" because they have little realistic regard for their lives.

11.   Those who have had a previous history of abuse and who seem to have quit.

12.   Those seeking personal insights or some variety of religious experience.

Threading through all these reasons is a felt sense of the insufficiency of life or of the self just being. Drugs allow an escape from this sense of insufficiency and emptiness by altering the mind's capacity for control and lessening its preoccupation with deficiency.

It is evident from a Beyond Content perspective, that these reasons form the basis for the development of Acts - the significant decisions we make about how we are going to run our lives in order to avoid losing. The reader may wish to review the section on the "Birth of the Act" in Chapter Five to refresh their understanding of how to make use of this information in sizing up a substance-abuse crisis.

Given Cohen's list of justifications, and a Beyond Content perspective, how might one respond directly and indirectly when substance abuse is suspected or identified as a major problem? Both possibilities will now be discussed individually.

DIRECT CRISIS INTERVENTION

When encountering someone under the influence of an unknown mind-altering substance, it is critical to watch for life- threatening medical danger signs. The primary danger signs are the following:

Danger Signs

1. **Unconsciousness**
2. **Breathing Difficulty**
3. **Feverishness or profuse sweating**
4. **Vomiting while not fully conscious**
5. **Convulsions**

It is beyond the scope of this book to offer instruction in first-aid responses to these danger signs. For those who are untrained in medical first-aid measures, for substance abuse, the best action is to immediately seek medical assistance and advice. In the process of doing so, endeavour to remain calm and confident of your ability to assist despite limited medical knowledge. Staying centred and competency focused even when you are unskilled in the pertinent first-aid emergency procedures, reduces the chances of you making any serious errors. Maintaining such a state can stimulate your natural intuitive wisdom to surface as an ally enabling you to reduce the risks of possible serious errors and increase your chances of making a significant difference.

Such a wide range of "in vivo" substance-abuse scenarios can occur that it is next to impossible to offer a generic protocol for crisis intervention. Depending on your professional training, you may already be obliged to follow well defined intervention protocols that are likely symptom based. Nevertheless, what seems lacking is a perspective that treats the individual in holistic ways. Developing a holistic approach is indeed challenging and rarely considered. It requires a shift away from the realm of opposites towards the realm of wholes. It is exemplified by a focus on finding sufficiency within and around insufficiency. Those people tempted to look for a holistic approach may wish to consider the suggestions that follow.

Some Suggestions

1.   Without question, the generalist crisis intervener who is directly confronted by an overdose situation should immediately seek medical assistance and obtain back-up ambulance or police support. These "most intrusive" interventions are designed to accomplish the task of minimizing the crisis error. Because the degree of risk is largely unknown, the most intrusive intervention is warranted for reasons of safety.

2.   Stay available to this person, - and whenever possible, direct others to get support and

---

resources. Leave only if risk of self-harm is high. It is important to note that violence is easily precipitated when the crisis intervener tries to single-handedly control, lecture, criticize, or threaten the person in crisis. Drugs generally reduce or inhibit the internal control normally exercised by an individual to reduce the potential for aggression. Consequently they represent a greater risk of unexpectedly harming others than when not under the influence of a mind-altering drug. If leaving the crisis scene is necessary, leave as slowly as possible, taking care not to react too quickly unless imminent risk suggests otherwise.

3.   The key competency attributes a crisis intervener can call upon when confronted with a substance abuser in crisis are:

> **Calmness**
> **Confidence**
> **Cooperativeness**
> **Concreteness**
> **Compassion**
> **Commitment**
> **Consistency**
> **Centeredness**

Mobilizing these traits requires the discipline of practice: as there is no substitute for regular or even daily practice (as mentioned in Chapter three, on Self-Preparation). One effective way to stay on track would be to keep a cue card in your wallet that you could refer to before , during and after a crisis with a substance abuser. This cue card would have each competency attribute written into your own personalized statement about what it means for you. For example, one personalized statement on **confidence** might read, " The more confrontative a substance abuser gets the more **confidence** it gives me to assist this person regain a sense of balance and control." Since the mind is a creature of habit that thrives on dominating emotions fed to it, adopt the habit of conditioning your mind to be dominated by emotionally charged competency based statements. Often it works even more powerfully when you create images of these competency attributes with yourself exemplifying the attribute at an extraordinary level. Using a cue card, even in the heat of a crisis, can be invaluable. Not using it for fear of being disrespectful or of revealing professional incompetence are the shadow aspects of the ego's way of preventing you from using what competence you do have. Being humble enough to call upon such external supports as cue cards actually is a sign of mature wisdom in a crisis, especially when coupled with confidence.

4.   The foreground in any crisis is always in a state of flux, always chaotic. The background tends to be more stable. Therfore, shift the focus of attention away from you as well as from those in crisis. Instead, attend to the background, and search for and begin to make use of the available resources. Often overlooked resources include significant others, clothing, food, music, cigarettes, hobbies, and other life style supporting props. Such resources can be invaluable in relieving the tension of the moment. In fact, anything that attaches the person in crisis to the supportive aspects of their immediate and extended environment can reduce the strain of the crisis moment.

---

5. Confidently and with assurance, encourage concrete yet simple task involvement between those in crisis and aspects of their background environment. The tasks ought to be related to their declared, known, perceived, or intuited competencies and capable of being done in their current state. The intent is to divert them away from catastrophizing their situation and to provide acceptable boundaries around their continuously distorting awareness.

6. Acknowledge the person's labile state, and describe it to them in non-attached, simple, observational ways. For example, let the person know that they look or sound sleepy, that their voice is quite loud, that their tears might want a tissue, that sitting down seems easier for them then standing up, and so on. These statements need to be factual, concrete, and offered as though you were a guide observing someone else's trip.

7. Talk with the client and not about him or her in the presence of others. By talking about the client behind the client's back, you most often disempower them and inadvertently support them to remain irresponsible. Frequently the person's limited contact with reality predisposes them to react to fragments of your behavior without fully understanding your intentions. In such circumstances, it is usually true that the less said the better.

8. Although it is essential to get information about the abuse whenever possible, centre your dialogue on the person and not on the substance abused. Communicate as concretely as possible that you are much more intrigued by how they are attempting to survive their life crises than in why they are abusing drugs. This is generally the opposite of what often happens, especially in hospital emergency rooms where a drug abuser is frequently treated as a problem patient. When treated as a problem, the abuser responds almost instinctively with further oppositional behaviour. Having the wisdom to recognize how our opposition most often triggers a flood of more opposition can allow the holistically focused crisis intervener to minimize the conflict and move the crisis more effectively towards resolution.

9. Make your statements slowly, and avoid asking questions that require more than a yes or no answer. This can be best done by first making a statement, then asking a question about that statement. For example, "The chair you would likely be most comfortable in would be this one. Can I assist you to get there?" Another example might be, " This warm clothing will help stop the shivering. Do you want it now?"

INDIRECT CRISIS INTERVENTION

Someone who isn't presently under the influence of drugs yet has a problem with substance abuse will almost always have a vested interest in distorting the truth. The first allegiance is to the substance being abused. The cardinal defense is for them to say that there is nothing wrong and that others do not know or understand what they need. Their life, full of inconsistency, unpredictability, and chaos, in some diffuse way side-tracks them and recycles them through one surfacing problem after another. Quite often those connected to the abuser are preoccupied with the abuse as a symptom that ought to be eradicated and have much more invested in this outcome than in anything else.

The crisis intervener - and, for that matter, any counsellor or therapist - can easily get trapped into competing with the drug in terms of being valued by the client. If this happens, the intervention often becomes a cat-and-mouse game with the crisis intervener endeavouring to corner the client into compliance or to manipulate the client into agreements that are inevitably grounded on quick sand. More often than not, the client eventually escapes from therapeutic agreements and interpersonal accountability by abusing simply drugs again.

Some Suggestions

1. In circumstances in which the primary initiators of the request for crisis assistance are other than the alleged abuser, the crisis intervener would do well to attend first the anxiety of those who requested assistance. Using the **SOURCE** approach, the crisis intervener would seek ways to diminish the catastrophizing of those around the substance abuser. Initially the crisis intervener might divert attention away from the abuser by sharing information about their mandate and by getting the others to share their worst fears. Because escaping from the conflict produced by the substance abuse is likely everyone's goal, it is of valuable to get everyone involved to explore viewing the drug abuse as something that attacks them all and it is currently beyond their control. The crisis intervener can then more objectively clarify how the drug abuse is interfering with everyone's well-being and causing trouble.

2. Confronting the abuse almost always reinforces the abuser's need to use it as an escape route from the their mounting sense of personal inadequacy. The crisis intervener who discovers ways to become intrigued by the client's struggle with powerlessness and lack of control without getting into a power or control struggle with them, bypasses confrontation with their well conditioned Act of survival. Since this substance abuse Act needs drama to survive, allowing the client to watch their own drama without having to change can open them up to examining alternative ways to manage their mental and emotional state.

3. Another important task of the crisis intervener is to examine with the client how useful their resistance is and, in as many ways as possible, how this resistance ironically can be channelled into more constructive forms of competency. By acknowledging the person's resistance and becoming intrigued by how much of their power is used up by being resistant, we can possibly awaken them to ways out of their own stuckness.

4. For a drug abuser to give up being right about their position on drugs and to acknowledge their disloyalty is a tall task. It is really only achievable if they can transform the state of surplus powerlessness (Learner, 1986) into surplus powerfulness. Alternative competency driven escape hatches to drugs must be offered, along with community based support groups, if personal competence or power is to begin being restored.

The Beyond Content approach will now be demonstrated offering a snapshot view of some of the issues regarding substance abuse intervention. The intent is to demonstrate heuristic aspects of the model and not to pretend that the model gaurantees a curative outcome with substance abuse.

THE BEYOND CONTENT MODEL APPLIED

Sharing

Edward is a 15-year-old living with his working mother and step-father of four years. His mother requests crisis intervention after she discovers several empty tubes of airplane glue and some used plastic bags in his room. After her initial concerns are presented to you she blurts out that her former husband died of alcohol poisoning five years ago. She is now deathly afraid that Edward is going to permenantly harm or kill himself. Allowing the mother to speak without interruption and share her full story, you learn that Edward often plays truant with school and often disregards curfews at home. Edward is offered the opportunity to share his story but he declines. Your acknowledgment of Edward for being concerned enough about his mother to be here at this moment acts to reduce his opposition somewhat. You also mention to him that very seldom do young people of his age recognize that they can participate in resolving abuse problems that attack families such as his. This recognition makes him unusual, possibly wiser than others of his age.

Edward starts to become more curious and a little less less resistant, experiencing more supported than he expected. He now begins to share by responding to questions as if he were only part of the problem and not all of it. The challenge now is to get him to see himself as part of the solution.

Observing

Observing in the process of sharing reveals that the mother sits close to Edward, touches him often, and connects with him in more of a sexual that a maternal way. Edward is agitated and somewhat immobilized by her overtures. Taking the opportunity to separate them, you invite the mother to have a coffee while you and Edward talk separately for a few minutes. It is often effective to separate those in crisis when the agitation mounts; it can give the person in the "hot spot" some relief from being stuck as the problem target or being caught in a double bind. This separate contact is to offer him an opportunity to share privately anything that he feels comfortable with.

Again Edward is acknowledged for the competencies he has demonstrated so far and also for those that you suspect he has. No attempt is made to tease anything out of him. Making statements followed by questions allows him the privilege of sharing as much as he wants without being cornered.

Uncovering

When the mother returns you unobtrusively ensure that you sit between them and guide them to sit facing each other. This repositioning shifts the nature of their interaction, allowing you to Uncover aspects of their relationship that may be underlying the substance-abuse problem. Edward becomes more relaxed and begins to talk openly with his mother about how he experiences problems affecting everyone in the family. You encourage him to continue as you briefly inform his mother of the nature of your private contact with him and say that he can tell her directly what they taked about if he wishes. Acting as a referee for them they are encouraged now to be frank in their sharing with one another. You re-assure them that having you as a referee ensures that the process can work for them both.

Resourcing

Edward refers to wanting to spend more quality time with his mother than he does now - she is always working; and she and his stepfather often go away on weekend ski trips, leaving him behind. At this point, you encourage both of them to consider suggestions you make for them making contact with one another that fit both his developmental and her maternal needs. They are invited to add or subtract to these suggestions and to discuss how the stepfather might be involved. Care is taken to ensure that the types of activities do not risk infantilizing or precipitating possible incestous fantasies. The resources needed for the mother to nurture Edward in age appropriate ways are carefully outlined., Both are then encouraged to comment on how workable these possibilities are. Even though glue-sniffing is the primary symptom, with truancy at school and non-compliance at home the secondary symptoms, these issues are not directly focused on until the underlying core relationship needs are addressed.

Careful examination and review of the family competencies reveal that the mother knits very well, does abstract art, and enjoys listening to rock music and to stories told by others. Edward likes sweaters, he likes to paint, and he wants someone to talk with about his school fears. He has some budding competency in rock song writing and playing the guitar; and he has an interest in cooking. The stepfather is a competent provider, a funny story-teller, a skier, and an occasional cook.

You then move to the foreground issues of glue-sniffing, truancy, and disobedience, encouraging the mother and Edward to share ways they can use the family's identified resources to keep them out of trouble. The effects of glue-sniffing on everyone in the family are now discussed and counteracting competency resources are clarified. Edward announces his willingness to discuss his substance abuse with the Ala-Teen group, and mother agrees to drive him to the weekly meetings. School and curfew are also discussed, once again, externalized as problems effecting everyone. The resources agreed upon are assignment to a different school (one with a music program) and a meeting with a family counsellor with the step father also involved.

Completing

The intervention becomes complete as both Edward and mother place time lines on action statements they have proposed. To determine how and when they will mobilize their competencies requires diligence and persevering commitment. Neglect of the mechanics here would allow room for confusion and misinterpretation. The challenge for the crisis intervener is to encourage and inspire them both to go beyond the self-organizing state they are currently experiencing and to solicit completing statements by all family members. This may well require a follow-up telephone call or even another meeting.

Completing can be experienced as a process blending everyones' competencies as well as environmental resources. The intent is to restore a balance of control and power by getting each family member to willingly activate some of his or her competencies towards the recapturing of family harmony.

Expanding

Finally it is important to adopt the position that completing is an ongoing developmental process. In this regard you might state that other troubles will loom on the horizon and that escape from them involves turning them into opportunities. They can short circuit old patterns by using any future tension that arises to activate or revitalize the competencies they may have temporarily overlooked. You offer suggestions of supports to call upon when they are stuck or even when they wish to merely enhance their desire to experience increased levels of personal and interpersonal harmony within their family. You complete with them by confirming that they do indeed have the capacity to expand. It often helps to view themselves as if they were a "rubber band" able to stretch instead of contracting when they perceive being "at the end of their rope" with one another. Their resiliency and ability to make use of any tightening up in their life space can result in new perhaps even breakthrough understandings of the family's changing needs.

IN SUMMARY

The **SOURCE** approach can offer a "structure of confidence" that does not restrict the crisis intervener by pushing them into rigid intervention protocols. It can allow the crisis intervener to use their current state of knowledge about substance abuse with confidence they can make a difference with their intervention. Combining the **SOURCE** approach with the Beyond Content intervention principles and the crisis integrity states makes for a powerful intervention platform regardless of the level of knowledge a crisis intervener possesses about substance abuse. Consequently, anyone who is willing to intervene and is mindful of her own limitations can offer invaluable assistance to those presently under the influence of a deleterious substance.

SUGGESTED READINGS

1.   Worth examining for its transpersonal view of substance abuse is the manual entitled **Stress management and serenity during recovery: A transpersonal approach** by C.L. Whitfield (Baltimore, MD: The Resource Group, 1984).

2.   With respect to how aspects of the self are disowned because of life crises and consequent abusive experiences, the book **The disowned self** by N. Brandon (New York: Bantam Books, 1973) offers insightful viewpoints that are consistent with the Beyond Content perspective.

NOTES

NOTES

SECTION III

PEOPLE IN CRISIS

It goes without saying that many human crises are the result of interpersonal conflict. The visible signs of anger, hostility, body lability (agitation), shock, fear, and sadness of people in crises are easily recognized as we have all struggled with others in relationships. How these more immediate and overt responses to crises generate covert or secondary symptoms such as sleeplessness, upset stomachs, headaches, poor concentration, resentfulness, hopelessness, haplessness, and other forms of depression has become the enigma of most crisis interveners. Since the visible signs usually quickly disappear as people in crisis seek to protect themselves from further loss, the challenge becomes that of using the protective symptoms as resources allowing people in crises to regain a sense of self-mastery over their primary emotions with others. This is easier said than done, as the symptoms often lead the crisis intervener astray. More often than not this dilemma is further complicated and compounded by established behaviour patterns which are generated from historically unresolved crises.

The Beyond Content Model of crisis intervention offers a transpersonal view of interpersonal crises that in a contextual way addresses the effects of history, as well as the role symptoms can play as resources in crisis recovery. The primary approach of this model is to view interpersonal crises as opportunities enabling those in crisis to become clear on how to have their personal relationships continuously revitalized and freed from the contamination of unfinished historical issues. Similar to the approach taken in the previous section on specific crisis issues, the aim of the Beyond Content approach is to recontextualize the crisis event so that a breakthrough towards competency and interpersonal re-alignment can be achieved.

This section includes two chapters which highlight transpersonal issues in man/woman relationship crises and youth and family developmental crises. Chapter Twelve, on relationship crises, rather boldly speaks of the illusions created by society around relationships and how relationships almost invariably deteriorate as the spiritual essence between people becomes more and more buried. This chapter starts with a discussion on how everyday relationships might be viewed as "recreationships" and on how they fall from grace. An example of how the Beyond Content Model might be applied to a domestic dispute is then offered. Completing this chapter is a brief statement of what can shift an ordinary relationship towards becoming one that continues to be vibrantly workable.

Chapter Thirteen on youth and family crises begins with a discussion of the characteristics of families that are perceived as well-functioning. These wellness characteristics are described as they relate to the family unit as a whole, to parents, and to young people. The chapter continues with a discussion of transpersonal ways to mobilize the competencies of family members. Next, a background scenario is offered, suggesting some contributing factors that underlie youth crises.

Following this are suggestions on how a crisis intervener might consider taming the outrageousness of adventurous crisis-bound youth.

The concluding section of this chapter shifts back to addressing issues related to family crises by speculatively offering a frame of reference for perceiving the origin of family suffering. Finally there is a step-by-step approach demonstrating, in a prototypical way, how the Beyond Content Model of crisis intervention might be used with families.

CHAPTER TWELVE

RELATIONSHIP CRISES

Having a relationship with another person that truly works is a great adventure. To be a great adventurer requires great courage. People who love life, themselves, and each other do have the courage and the passion to make the game worth playing.

- Stewart Emery

TRANSPERSONAL RELATIONSHIPS

The views presented here are somewhat radical in relation to how relationships are traditionally practiced. Traditional or ordinary relationships tend to be addicted to an external object-focus: it seems we attempt to escape the narrow confines of our self-interest (primary narcissism) by attaching to those who we think will enrich us and fulfill our need to feel complete.

Transpersonal relationships, on the other hand, are extraordinary because they actually start from a base of being sufficient and acceptable. From this posture, they go beyond the narrow confines of our self-interest as our sense of self in essence (or spirit) extends beyond two individuals towards a common purpose. Generating a transpersonal relationship is unquestionably an enlightening experience. Since such a relationship originates out of a natural state of integrity, this enlightenment is not something to laboriously work toward; rather it is a state we can come from, simply by exercising our intention that it be present (Emery, 1977). Coming from this space rather than having to get to it lightens up living considerably, as upsets are incorporated as part of life's journey and not to be taken too personally.

Because crises are really the natural course of living, even transpersonal relationships do not escape them. It is how crises are dealt with in transpersonal relationships that makes the difference. Otherwise, transpersonal relationships are nothing special.

Contrary to ordinary views, relationships are not outside us. They are inside, - and all those whom we relate with are mirrors for us and reflect our relationships with ourselves. Yet it is our intimate relationships that offer the opportunity to awaken us to the experience that all of life is relationship and that "we are all in a perfect relationship with everything that makes up our lives at this very moment" (Field, et al, 1984, p.36). Relationships are the natural state of affairs. We already are related, even though we cannot often see it or stay in touch with it. This viewpoint of relationship is spiritually supported by the notion that our essences are inextricably linked to an infinite source of intelligence. We all take a common journey, albeit a journey uniquely experienced in life. Even though we are linked and relationship is a pathway rather than an entity, we also are whole and complete just the way we are. This paradox reflects the non-duality of relationships that is so hard for many to understand, much less to experience. Erich Fromm (1956) comments on this paradox by suggesting that erotic love is highly individualistic and reflects our differences, whereas brotherly or natural love reflects our oneness. Nevertheless, the challenge of intimate relationships is to embrace this paradox by taking a journey through the veil or illusion of separation to an awareness of our ultimate oneness. This "interpersonal fusion process" he referred to as being the most powerful and fundamental striving in the human being.

A HOLOSYSTEMIC PERSPECTIVE

From a left-brain or cognitive understanding, a new-world unifying view of relationship would likely embrace some aspects of a holosystemic perspective (Bohm, 1985). From this viewpoint, the various personal, social, cultural, and environmental aspects of a relationship are understood as parts of an interwoven, patterned whole. Holism suggests that within the part exists the whole. Arising from the realm of Psychophysics, this concept endeavours to include the valuable aspects of systems thinking into the context of transpersonal knowing.

In specific yet simplified ways, David Bohm, a reknown physicist and philosopher, perceived that the ordinary or the explicate reality that we experience actually **unfolds** from an implicate reality. The implicate reality is where everything is coherently and harmoniously interwoven into an undivided whole. This senior reality is largely unseeable or non-manifest; yet it contains the manifest or explicate reality of inherently separate things in our world. He perceived that everything we see, hear, and feel is **enfolded** back into this senior or encompassing reality. In this respect, relationships are not really parts before they are wholes. This perspective is eloquently captured in the words of William Blake's famous vision, we may "see the world in a grain of sand, And a heaven in a wild flower." Alternately, a Buddhist image suggests that within one pearl of a string of ordered pearls exists a reflection of all the pearls; or "One moon shows in every pool; in every pool, the one moon."

RELATIONSHIPS AS RECREATIONSHIPS

Perhaps what we mistakenly call relationships are more likely "imageships" we create in an attempt to have a "recreationship". This is to say, we form an image of what we want from others and

---

correspondingly they with us. Then when our images connect we feel related. These images develop from our mind, which seeks to make itself satisfied by getting something from outside ourselves. These images tend to resist change, even though everything changes around them. The rigidity of our mental images inevitably results in disappointment, resentment, and frustration. Despite the emotional insecurity that our imageships produce, we cling to them anyway. Unfortunately, we become too attached to our images to be able to fully recreate them.

The way out of this dilemma chosen by most people is to hunt around for others to fit our restricting mental pictures. Our search for the "perfect other" is never-ending, and we become convinced (although seldom deterred) that the perfect relationship is not to be had. Recreation becomes a fragmented, semi-satisfying experience.

"Re-create-ion" in its fullest sense happens when we respond from a reality of oneness and abundance rather than from an illusion of scarcity. Operating from the realm of non-manifest wholeness or the state of natural integrity, we can actually do something about being related that makes a difference. On encountering another, we can recreate with them in ways that manifest a natural vibrant sense of unity. Recreation is to play in ways allowing each to enjoy the full experience of one's essence around another; to actually re-create, even pro-create with, one another. Most attempt to hold traditional relationships constant. But recreationships are not time bound. They are ever changing, continuously flowing experiences in which being with and letting go of experiences allow for new experiences to be unfettered by fragments from the past. In this way, boundaries between one and another are transparent (Gerard, 1978); and they are not perceived as barriers. Our individuality is enhanced as a position within the unity. It's somewhat akin to us and others being like pillars of the same temple. In this context the recreationship is the expression of our essence, and the pillars are our unique form, and the temple is the relationship. When re-creation has a purpose bigger than itself or beyond self-serving interests, it has, like the temple, a unifying meaning.

To be one with another is not to lose one's identity or individuality, for we can actually manifest our individuality from our oneness. In this sense, we are both implicate and explicate. When we allow ourselves to recognize that our recreationships are not outside of us but rather they are inside us, then others become mirrors of our natural desire to re-create with and alongside of them.

From another viewpoint, a recreationship is a triangular affair of sorts. Its components are you, me, and the truth (integrity). When natural integrity operates through you and me, the triangle dissolves into oneness.

ORDINARY RELATIONSHIPS

Most recreationships start out more or less in a state of natural integrity. This transitory state of unity soon slips away as life crises arise, causing a recreationship to lose its playfulness. Individuality slowly begins to take precedence, because the recreating is not fulfilling. Driven by the need to have ownership over the form of a recreationship, the participants exercise manipulation and control. When sufficient frustration and disappointment occur and our images of one another become sufficiently distorted, we no longer recreate and then leave.

Leaving is such a built-in unconscious process (Smothermon, 1985) that we leave both ourselves, our senses, and the other without fully being aware of it. In the process of leaving, we act to avoid any further loss of control by making sacrifices and compromising our natural integrity. The recreationship that unfolds seems to be one of a repetitive, never-ending cycle in which only instrumental living is handled. Our Acts of sacrifice or compromise then vacillate between holding a position or being in opposition with one another. We become either tyrants or rebels, victims or rescuers, entrappees or entrappers. We change in and out of these positions often, although we tend to adopt one form as a predominant stance when in a chronic crisis state.

Another way to view the mechanics of a recreationship is to see the individuals as analogous to a wheel. In this analogy, the hub represents the primary purpose in having a relationship. This primary purpose could be for sex, for my pleasure, for your pleasure, to raise a family, for higher reasons, and so on. Threading out from the hub are the spokes, which represent the things we want out of a relationship that are secondary to the primary purpose. Some of these might be a travelling companion, a good cook, a colleague, a sports partner, a provider, a nurturer, and so on. These are the mechanics that make life go around. Connecting these spokes is the rim or casing, which might represent our personality.

When our primary purpose is repressed, obscured, distorted, or out of alignment with the other person's primary purpose, our wheels seem not to connect by a common axle. Eventually, they wobble off in their own direction, because nothing sustaining is connecting them. In the meantime, both parties struggle to find a way to have the mechanics of their movement in a relationship handled by each other. From time to time our personalities resonate together, as our needs align for the moment and temporary wellbeing pervades. Too often this is short lived, and the dance goes on as we look for ways to be in step with one another. Our recreationship crises are almost always generated out of misaligned purposes. Any recreation that we stimulate eventually gets mucked up by the mechanics of day-to-day living.

BEYOND CONTENT MODEL APPLIED

A Domestic Dispute

Mindful of the true nature of relationships and using the **SOURCE** formula, let us review an example of a relationship crisis and walk through some Beyond Content intervention possibilities. Receiving a call from the police domestic-response team to assist with a marital crisis, you rush to the home; and, after the police officers at the home brief you regarding a dispute between Margaret and John, they leave. Margaret and John are in their early thirties. Both are employed, and they live in an apartment. The crisis results from John's reaction when Margaret returns home at 6:00 a.m., having been out all night. She refuses to tell John where she has been, and they start arguing. This goes on for two hours, causing the neighbor to be concerned enough to call the police for fear they may be hurting one another. You start the intervention process using the **SOURCE** approach ...

Sharing

Knowing that they have discussed their concerns with one another ad nauseam and that they are at a stalemate, you know that getting them to tell their "stories" again in this circumstance will more than likely be counterproductive. At this point, they are both exhausted and somewhat victimized by this crisis. In a personalized way, you invite them individually to share what they want for **themselves** at the moment. Believing that he has already been doing this for hours, John, with overtones of resentment and frustration, starts talking about Margaret's nocturnal transgression. Margaret responds by turning away as if to ignore him. Before continuing, John and Margaret are asked if they are willing to work with you and focus on whatever comes up, regardless of their past unsatisfactory experiences with it. After some hesitation, they both agree. They are both obviously at a turning point with the pain of their conflict. The challenge now becomes one of discovering ways to disrupt their destructive relationship patterns, then replace them with constructive, harmony-producing patterns.

You guide them to focus on what they now want aside from the crisis issue, and John says that he wants to go for a walk, while Margaret states that she wants to sleep. Acknowledging their sharing, you further invite them to state what they want out of the relationship right now. John wants an apology and a renewed commitment. Margaret, on the other hand, wants to forget about what has happened and get marital counselling later. Acknowledging them once again, you encourage them to comment on the primary purpose of their being together and how it has changed from the beginning when they first got together. They reveal that they are still quite committed to each other, although Margaret has become more desirous of having children and John has become somewhat addicted to mountain climbing, which takes him away on extended trips with others.

Observing

By maintaining a "patterned scan" of the crisis field, you keep the immediate environment in an even wash of awareness. A soft-eyed attention reveals that both are misaligned in their core purpose and that each is rebelling against being the victim of the tyrant nature of the other. John appears to be the immediate crisis victim, and Margaret the undercurrent or enduring victim. It is evident this difference or misalignment pattern needs to be disrupted before exploring ways to turn the crisis into an opportunity.

In the crisis of the moment, Margaret's survival needs are acted out as an integrity state of disloyalty, whereas John's survival needs are acted out as opposition. In this regard, John predominantly portrays as a tyrant wanting control over a rebellious Margaret. Their relationship--or, more appropriately, their imageship--is an entanglement of mis-aligned purposes.

The entanglement is further complicated because the mechanics of living together are also out of alignment. They are both attached to the form that they want the relationship or recreationship to take and have lost sight of or have moved away from a common purpose.

The challenge now is to uncover what values they still have in common and to stimulate interest in examining how their original common purpose in being together might be revitalized.

Uncovering

Through scanning their immediate environment, you discover that many books are scattered around, braced open or with book markers sticking out. It is apparent that reading is an avid interest of one of them. As well, religion plays a part, because there are numerous religious references, including several bibles. In an exploratory way, you enquire about what they do together right now and what they did when they first got together. They mention that in the last two years of their five-year relationship, they seem to have gone their own ways. In the past, they had been quite involved in outdoor pursuits. However, Margaret's recurrent back injury has caused her to discontinue her involvement in joint ventures. Casually you ask about their religious affiliations and their reading interests. They mention that when they lived in the East they were quite involved with a book club and with the board of a church organization. Exploring further you enquire about how they got together as a couple, what they like about each other and what common vision they had about their partnership in life. By so doing you attempt to resurrect old feelings, statements and images of alignment of purpose in their partnership. Having then become tuned into these past highly emotionally-charged memorable states and anchoring them to something in their present experience or environment, you then invite them to comment on who they admire as demonstrating the values about relationships and life they both can support. Mentioning these models can come from one's immediate or extended family, from community associations or from stories they have read or seen in the media or even in their own readings of the bible, they both recall biblical tales eschewing the virtues of commitment under the most adverse circumstances as tests of faith. They also both agree that Margaret's uncle inspires them because of his persuasive, spirited nature, despite his blindness. This person seems to thoroughly enjoy his living on all accounts. In particular, they admire his remarkable success with writing children's story books. They mention when they think of this uncle they often get an image of him being like the famous singer, Stevie Wonder, who they also admire and appreciate. With carefully stimulated positive emotions and two models of how others they know have made their relationships with living empowering, you now move to Resourcing.

Resourcing

John and Margaret are carefully reassured that out of their stuckness will come clarity and opportunity. This is reinforced by mentioning to them their commitment to one another still must be strong for them to stick it out with one another. This seems to be the case despite their enormously frustrating struggle with their current life experiences which seem to be driving a wedge between them. Now you begin to recount the resources that have been uncovered, perception checking as you proceed that these resources trigger off past memories of interpersonal alignment and success. This action is designed to neutralize the present emotional state and prepare it for possible replacement of a re-awakened constructive communication pattern. In exploring the options uncovered, you gently dissuade them from

---

directly attempting to resolve the immediate issues of conflict. It is essential to reframe with some constructive supports being available before re-creating an aligned purpose with new agreements; otherwise confusion and continued disagreement of purpose will cloud any attempt at reconciliation.

At this point, the suggestions that you offer to the couple are based on your perception of their willingness to step aside from their positions with one another and to activate whatever residual amounts of well-being they have for one another. Despite their stalemated position, John and Margaret exude a thread of mutual respect for each other. Sensing a rejuvenated interest in patching up their differences for the time being (Self-Organizing Principle), you invite them to use their surfacing mutual respect to imagine what they could do to support each other over the next few days. Their mutual interest in books and religious affiliations is recalled, and it becomes evident that they have let these interests take a back seat to the conflictual issues in their recreationship. Patiently, they are asked to reach some concrete agreements on what they can do together in harmony. Your careful monitoring of their energy level and of how it serves to fuel their intention indicates that John is more committed than Margaret. She nevertheless agrees to read some books together and to join a book club with him. As well, they both agree to visit the pastors' of the two churches that represent their common faith within the next three days. With a sigh of relief and a tentative air of enthusiasm, Margaret agrees to make the arrangements.

Still, Margaret seems somewhat overcast and hesitant about her commitments. So you ask her what would cause these commitments not to work. She blurts out that what she really wants more than anything else is to go away on a holiday together. John is surprised, because Margaret has not wanted to spend much time with him over the past two years, and they have not taken any holidays together during that time. They both begin to be more curious about what they can do and where they can go. Gradually, they begin to harmonize with one another, although with overtones of vulnerability on both sides, springing from fear that they will argue over what each needs from the other.

Completing

Now comes the delicate task of confronting both John and Margaret to become willing to vacate their survival positions and to discover what they can do to leave the crisis of the moment behind. John and Margaret are now encouraged to disrupt the destructive pattern of communication and consequent behaviors by reviewing how they negatively trigger each other off by what they say, do and portray as feelings.

Since we all tend to have "sayings" that we use to comfort ourselves around our traumas, they both are asked to recall favorite "self-sayings," commonly known as metaphors. John is reminded by Margaret of how he is fond of stating "There is always a bigger mountain to climb"; and Margaret remembers that she always felt better "after taking out the garbage." These visually rich self-sayings can be invaluable tools for breaking through our stuckness of the moment and for leaving it behind for the time being. Using these self sayings over and over again, along with any others they come up with from their religious teachings while they recall their crisis event, tends to break the conditioned negative pattern they have developed.

Completing requires that the couple activate their creative intention forces and act on plans for today and tomorrow. One cannot create against or in spite of what one opposes. Therefore, letting go of resentment, frustration, and sadness happens only when forgiveness has been given. It is initially a struggle for John and Margaret to let go and grant forgiveness, because they both fear losing what they want from each other. Practicing forgiveness by just saying it many times and in different ways draws them closer to experiencing the relief that it generates once it is done without reservation. Re-affirming their individual competencies and clarifying how these competencies are presently being manifested serves as the fuel to ignite connective interest in one another.

Suggesting that they let their good side teach and guide their not so good side supports them to recognize how self-mastery is available to them. When both are experiencing "aha" awarenesses about their crisis, they become primed for animation of their recreationship. Recalling their good sides to the crisis battlefield opens up their consciousness to the primary strengths of their relationship.

The process up to this point can tend to create an illusion of crisis resolution. This is a well-known effect, often referred to as the Hawthorne phenomenon by researchers in psychology, the field of human behavior. Our natural predisposition towards self-organizing can also heighten the sense that the crisis is over with. But full completion requires the effort of expanding, the final step in the crisis intervention.

Expanding

Now is the time to come full circle, given that both John and Margaret are in the space to examine their mis-alignment of primary purposes. Not everyone having crises like John and Margaret's are willing to step into this arena, because it could mean the dissolution of the relationship (imageship). Nevertheless, as already indicated, not addressing the underlying issue predisposes the couple to recycling the mechanics of the recreationship through the crisis mill. Eventually, the mechanics (agreements) will go out of syncronicity and "muck" things up again.

One should not confuse crisis intervention aims with marital therapy. It is not being suggested that an in-depth review of the underlying purposes be undertaken. Rather, this final step is most often one of simply revealing the discordance. You suggest that careful attention to the underlying tension can, with the assistance of a guide or therapist, turn it into the excitement produced by exercising self-mastery and discovering a vision that works for both of them. When you let them know that to make their relationship work beyond the ordinary requires an alignment of purpose, you plant the seed of transpersonal possibilities. In this case, John and Margaret agree that the risks are high; yet they affirm that they can trust their rekindled spiritual selves with each other and seek clarity from church support. You complete the expanding step by anchoring the sustaining values they have uncovered to the bible in their home. Encouraging them to put on a Stevie Wonder tape, you draw their attention to the bible by placing your hand on top of it and recount the values they both acknowledge such as commitment, forgiveness, giving pleasure to others despite adversity, and faith in one another. Mentioning the uncle, you ask them to recall his virtues and how they stimulate their own competencies of caring, commitment, cooperation and consideration. Stacking these competencies reinforces the possibility they can move beyond their present crisis with a renewed and expanded sense of vigor of being able to gain mastery over their relationship and living experiences.

ON WORKABLE RELATIONSHIPS

This next section is really optional reading. It is added for those who are curious about how transformative relationships can come to be despite the crises in our lives. To begin with, relationships (or recreationships) work when the Dynamic Forces of Competency (Chapter Three) flow through you and through another person, fusing together essences rather than form. These forces intertwine within a transpersonally working relationship in the following way:

Integrity

The unfettered truth, not beliefs or opinions, guides a relationship, keeping it free from the scourges of the image prisons that we stick ourselves into. The truth is naturalness personified. Knowing that you are always related is the first truth. Knowing that we operate in the realm of opposites (male/female, right/wrong, good/bad) and that these states are constantly changing in form is to be open to the context of a boundary-less or non-attached state of being with another. As George Leonard (1972) suggests, relationships work when withholding is eliminated as a practice designed to protect yourself from fear of less of the relationship.

Telling the truth is different from allowing the truth to naturally flow through you. The rails of a railroad track are always the same distance apart; but, being on them, you can see that the journey causes them to converge, even though the journey is never ending. Paying too much attention to the substance or form of the rail (integrity) can cause you to become too preoccupied with the gap between the two persons.

Purpose

Sustained workable relationships do not get better because of anything like more money, more sex, more drugs, a new job, more friends, more pleasure trips, or even more coca cola. These features are the mechanics of a relationship. Manipulating them and focusing on the form of the relationship and how it serves you gets you temporary well-being. Sustaining well-being becomes possible only when the relationship has a purpose above and beyond itself. Alignment of purpose comes from being truthful with what you want, even if it means leaving the other person. To create and recreate a relationship requires a willingness to explore and uncover what we want our positions to be with one another and to surrender to a common purpose. In this regard, to surrender is to give up control, so that your mutual power can create and re-create aliveness in your recreationship. Stewart Emery (1977) says:

If a relationship is ever going to work in terms of life, in terms of supporting each other's well being, we must surrender to each other. If you look up **surrender** in Webster's you will find that the first definition says: "to give up possession of or power over." Thus surrender in a relationship would mean to give up possession of the power over the other. "Wait a minute! Are you kidding?! That is a horrendous notion to think about. If I don't have possession of you and I don't have power over you, what's going to keep me around?"

Well, we really can't have a joyful relationship until we have removed all the reasons to stick around--all the reasons of need, and of form, and of living. We should only stick around if the value is there--if together we enjoy the adventure of life, if we joyfully support and acknowledge each other's process (p. 126).

Workable relationships play a challenging game in search of clarity of purpose. Beyond that, powerful relationships focus on manifesting aliveness through a unifying, clearly known purpose. As Antoine De Saint-Exupery states, "Love does not consist in gazing at each other, but in looking outward together in the same direction."

Creative Intention

Intention is another way of describing commitment, although the commitment is to your integrity and not to the other person as that person presently exists. Commitment to another almost always attempts to control or keep the form of the relationship from naturally changing. When committed to your integrity, your intention can guide you to fulfilment in a relationship. A transpersonal relationship is driven by the intention to support the other person's well-being in a companionship through the large adventure of life. This involves first recognizing that one's own well-being does not depend on another. With self-initiated inspiration (as opposed to expiration) and self-determination, create being supportable and lovable for no other reason than your significance as a person is really unquestionable. Without a preoccupation with getting better by needing a relationship you can begin the process of continuously re-creating a truly vibrant relationship. The emphasis can then be on supporting your partner's experience of wholeness with himself or herself over and above the form of your relationship with your partner. In short, non-attachment is to give; giving occurs when we are unattached to what we are. Creation comes from the unobservable implicate realm, and intention manifests it in the explicate or observable realm.

Creative intention, like commitment, though it requires a declaration and willingness, is not something that can happen just because you say so. You cannot produce it by wilfulness or determination to have it happen. It evolves out of the ground of genuine resonance, passion, and communication. According to John Welwood in his forthcoming book **Passion and Surrender**, it happens in three distinct stages. To begin with, there is an intention to work with whatever comes up regardless of the crises that surface. Doing so means staying focused on the present moment, participating fully and turning the tension of a crisis into the

---

excitement of a challenge. The second stage involves going beyond allegiance to our own personal pleasure and actively dissolving the barriers that restrict you from giving yourself fully to SUPPORTING or clarifying the primary purpose of your relationship. The final stage is to creatively explore ways to stay on track with your purpose over the long haul. Your intention at this point is to manifest a vision together that goes beyond the mechanics of day-to-day living. In this sense, you can become co-creators as your images of the other drop away and you naturally act to foster your partner's uniqueness as an integral aspect of your wholeness.

Self Mastery

In simple terms, self-mastery is to be whole and complete, with or without the form of the relationship. Self-mastery is to allow yourself to respond to your core felt sense of how to make your relationships significant. This is in contrast to responding to your survival-oriented mind that is fearful of losing control over what it thinks it wants from another in order to survive. Self-mastery involves using others to assist you on your journey, since we still carry baggage from our past. Those mundane issues that prevent us from growing up can best be dealt with within a relationship when you, as Sondra Ray (1980) suggests, allow your partner to be your guru.

SUGGESTED READINGS

1. A highly readable book by Stewart Emery (**Actualizations: You Don't have to Rehearse To Be Yourself,** New York: Doubleday, 1977) is based on workshops he has conducted throughout North America having a strong focus on communications in relationships. This provocative account of relationships strips away our illusions about human functioning offering a solid contextual base from which to explore how to transform one's relationships.

2. Scott Peck's milestone effort to integrate spiritual insights with the practical realities of day-to-day living is powerfully presented as "a book for our times" entitled **The Road Less Travelled** (New York: Simon & Schuster, 1978). Peck offers examples of how one might confront and dissolve interpersonal problems as well as insightful ways to achieve wholeness in relationships.

3. A thoroughly stimulating little handbook by Sondra Ray (**Loving Relationships,** Los Angeles: Celestial Arts, 1980) suggests ways to use affirmations visualizations and rebirthing experiences to confront the crisis of relationship deterioration.

4. An extraordinary self help workbook has been written by Ron Smothermon appropriately titled **The Man Woman Book** (Rohnert Park Ca.: Context Publications, 1985). Smothermon guides the reader through on interconnected experience after another towards revitalizing their understanding of relationships. His overriding goal is to have everyone awaken to the transformative power of love and how to manifest it in all relationships.

NOTES

NOTES

_____

_____

_____

_____

_____

_____

_____

_____

_____

_____

_____

_____

_____

_____

_____

_____

_____

_____

_____

_____

_____

_____

_____

_____

_____

_____

_____

_____

_____

CHAPTER THIRTEEN

YOUTH & FAMILY CRISIS INTERVENTION

Nothing has a stronger influence psychologically on their environment, and especially on their children, than the unlived life of the parents.

- C.G. Jung

A TRANSPERSONAL VIEW

A crisis to one family may be nothing more than a temporary annoyance, or even an adventure to another. It seems some families are able to perceive unexpected upsets as catastrophies to be learned from while others become seduced by the crisis symptoms. Transpersonally, or from a "holosystemic" perspective, the symptoms are seen as bait capable of drawing those in crisis into mind traps. These mind traps are largely based on unfinished crisis business from the past. It is difficult break out of these traps and operate wholistically in the present when we have been conditioned to think in bits and parts and to operate from a historical base of insufficiency. Tinkering with the symptoms is like correcting from the periphery inward, jury-rigging or propping up beams when the foundation is unstable. It's like putting a book of matches under a wobbly table leg, an act that produces temporary stability at best. The correction does not get rid of the issue, it merely chases it elsewhere. One symptom eventually turns into another, as "symptom tinkering" spirals through a family.

The "seat of the pants" Beyond Content approach to youth and family crisis intervention attempts to bypass obvious symptoms to attend to the core essence of energy emanating from each family member. It does this by focusing on the overall conflictual, as well as confluent, pattern of energy generated. In more practical terms the crisis intervener differentially attends to the flow of energy arising from each family member in accordance with their current integrity state. This first order intervention, simplified in Figure 16 as a triangular affair between integrity, the person in crisis, and the crisis intervener seeks to use the crisis energy as a resource revealing ways natural integrity can be achieved . When this occurs the triangle collapses such that natural integrity and the person in crisis become one. When a family member connects with, or awakens to, his or her capability to be restored to a natural state of integrity, then the truth flows through that member and creates a sense of harmony, balance, and oneness, even though chaos may still disrupt the family scene. This occurrence often produces a momentary yet extraordinary state of clarity, naturally revealing actions that have the potential to help each family member to dissolve the crisis. This process will be covered in more detail later when family intervention issues are discussed.

FIGURE 16

FIRST ORDER CRISIS

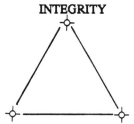

INTEGRITY

PERSON IN CRISIS   CRISIS INTERVENER

Figure 17 attempts to depict the pathways through the "eye of the crisis storm." It suggests by implication that the resources exist within each family member's core self to de-stigmatize or reconnect more clearly with the outside world. Armed with a clear purpose as well as the integrity of abundance and empowerment, the crisis intervener can cut through the inhibitive crisis symptom barriers to reach the essence or core self of the family member in crisis. In doing so, the crisis intervener becomes more than simply a benign catalyst. When the core self or essence of an individual family member is actually awakened, the crisis intervener's own integrity can then be used synergistically to activate some of the dormant or latent competencies of this family member. This then creates the possibility of achieving a more balanced natural state of integrity.

The intent with every family member is similarly to mobilize first the force of integrity so that natural competencies can become activated. Then, using the surfacing competency attributes as catalysts, the other forces of personal competency, namely purpose self mastery and creative intention can collectively create a breakthrough in the crisis space of the family. In this way the crisis intervener simply guides each family member, one at a time, member towards achieving a natural state of integrity. They can then each in turn, focus their energy towards the family unit to re-create family harmony, vibrancy, and well-being.

FIGURE 17

MOBILIZING FAMILY COMPETENCY

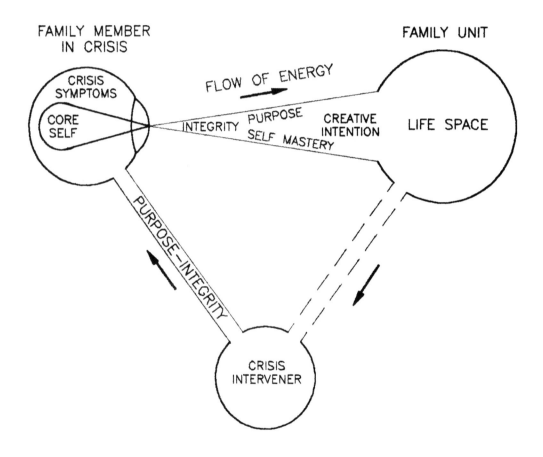

THE WELL OF WELLNESS

Tapping into our natural storehouse of competency requires almost of necessity that the crisis intervener enter into the seemingly incomprehensible realm of spiritualism. After entering, spiritualism becomes nothing other than essence or "spirited" and spontaneous energy. What seems to hold most crisis interveners back is the dogma attached to spiritualism and the lack of concreteness of the term essence. Nevertheless, manifestations of essence as family wellness attributes have taken form, at least contextually, through exhaustive exploration by bold self-actualizing researchers, (Ardell, 1977; Houston, 1982; Satire, 1982; and Tubesing, 1984; to name a few). As David Spangler, an early leader of the Findhorn community, puts it, "Manifestation is not magic. It is a process of working with natural principles and laws in order to translate energy from one level of reality to another".

To appease our left-brain need for data, I offer a list of characteristics of a well family, as extracted from countless sources. These characteristics are listed below, not in any order of importance.

Well Family Characteristics

1. **Humour**

   Levity awakens us to the present and allows us to momentarily escape the clutches of our past conditioning and preoccupations of deficiency. This "jogging of the innards" as a daily supplement diminishes the impact that crisis events have on well families. Humour allows us to give to our family environment rather than take from it. It is the tie that connects us spontaneously to others, especially to our family. Hugh Prather (1981) suggests that humour arises out of peace and is held in innocence. Manifesting humour is to know that we live in a funny world, where most often things don't go right.

2. **Story Telling**

   When families entertain themselves with stories, they thread their past to their present, enriching the present with images of interpersonal significance. Stories are a way of highlighting our lives and connecting us to one another. Story-telling can expand our understanding of how we make a difference with one another and with our core selves. Healthy rituals are sustained through story-telling. As well, peak experiences, when recalled, tend to inspire us to come from rather than have to go to the well of wellness.

3. **Ritual Practicing**

   Families who spend time together tend to stay together. When conscious effort is made to experience regular happenings (such as watching a television program together) as a ritual, these happenings affirm each family member's importance to the others. Most well functioning families have a time together each day that is sanctified and respected without the need to justify or defend its' value.

Since families also fight over rituals, well functioning families find it necessary to allow their rituals to change in accordance with changing family need. In other words, flexibility, accommodation, and freedom to participate underscore all such rituals.

4. Outwardly Serving

A common characteristic of a well functioning family is that it focuses on making a contribution to the community. Self-fulfilment is experienced through giving of oneself to some common good. Well functioning families tend to exude an aura of acceptance, abundance, and excitement. It seems that they have more than enough energy to go around. Even crises are opportunities to learn and discover what to do next with their family's aliveness. Satisfaction, rather than credit, is the aim of their serving.

5. Unconditional Gift Giving

Many well functioning families have discovered that gift-giving generates gift-giving and creates an atmosphere of abundance around the family. They secretly know that giving a gift at the most unlikely times, (not birthdays or ritualized dates) and without the need or desire for credit, washes away life's traumas and allows the family to ride on the crest of a wave of excitement. Gifts of affirmations are a steady daily diet of well functioning families. They acknowledge one another, not fearing that there isn't enough significance to go around. Living becomes a celebration and affirmation, gift-giving an invitation to play. From a "holistic" perspective, to give is to be unattached, and to be unattached is to give.

6. Self-Correcting

Within a well functioning family, waywardness is intuitively accepted as part of the journey towards self-fulfilment. Similarly, waywardness is known to be counterbalanced by one's Self-Organizing tendency, which naturally supports getting on track again. Members of well functioning families recognize, with a sense of assurance, that the self-correcting journey is common to all, even though the crisis evidence of the moment suggests otherwise. They intuitively know that the family, like an airplane heading for a holiday destination, is off course as much as ninety-five percent of the time; yet, because it is continuously self-correcting, it gets to where it is going ninety-nine percent of the time.

Moreover, allowing the crisis of one family member to unfold without taking it personally is to know that self correcting will naturally take place. When a family can allow self-correcting to go on continuously without taking it personally, the family gets to where it wants to go. Even though at times one family member may be operating in the survival mode, other family members do not tend to get embroiled in personality conflict. They know enough to stay connected with their core self and their family purpose as they watch their family experience episodic upsets.

Self-correcting also implies that we take full responsibility for our experience of our family life. When all family members take 100% responsibility for their experience of family crises, they can continue to rally around a sense of oneness. Anything less, such as being half responsible, means as Stewart Emery (1977) points out, that you end up with less ability to respond than you started out with. Two halves of responsibility, when fused together, somehow tend to produce a quarter.

7. Forgiveness Factor

True forgiveness is an extraordinary event. Contrary to some opinions, it is not forgetting. It is simply choosing not to remember. As Hugh Prather (1982) suggests, forgiveness can unshackle us from the pain of the past. It does not dissolve the past, it blankets it, and it is the most creative pathway to fairness with others. It offers an opportunity for balance. Without it, we are captured by our own resentment, destined to view video reruns of our never-ending rendezvous with pain. In other words, without forgiveness we create our own torture chamber.

Well functioning families instinctively know that forgiveness is not a behaviour. It really is an consciously intended thought. To actively think forgiveness is to generate a natural state of integrity and to acknowledge that grievances are an unworthy expenditure of energy. Families that seek out and practice a variety of rituals for asking and offering forgiveness walk swiftly towards their purpose without the hindrance of resentment and judgments. Forgiveness, nevertheless, is tough, tough work.

8. Crisis Completion

Well functioning families have a strong drive not to rest until a crisis has been fully dissolved. They recognize that anything left unresolved will eventually come back to haunt the family as a whole. In a graciously uncomfortable way, the family perseveres with the upset until the upset no longer has any power over the family. Completion is an investment in family freedom.

The more specific crisis of being a parent is also well known, especially to everyone with children. My research on well functioning parents has revealed the following wellness characteristics:

Parent Wellness Characteristics

1. They treat young people as if the young people count and are significant.

2. They teach young people the value of working for what you want and how to expand your capacity to handle challenges in your life.

3. They apply clear and enforceable limits in order to minimize errors. As well, they encourage their children to make decisions for themselves and to experience the impact of their own mistakes.

4.   They model the art of give-and-take as a continuous open-ended dialogue in which participants are always poised to consider new information.

5.   They actively seek the young persons' input on issues of daily living.

6.   They encourage individuality, support uniqueness and assist in the development of competencies in the young person's chosen areas of interest.

7.   They attend to primary feelings and support full sharing of their interpretations of these feelings.

8.   They model what they want from their children.

Finally, from a young person's point of view, after surveying hundreds of them over the years, a synthesis of what wellness or competency to them means is as follows:

Youth Wellness Characteristics

1.   An ability to accept no as an answer and move on to the next challenge.

2.   A willingness to learn from mistakes without feeling bad about it.

3.   Courage to seek support from adult role models and to share their fears.

4.   Able to apologize for their transgressions and forgive the wrong doing of others.

5.   Able to ask honest questions without fear or loss of significance.

6.   Able to give up being righteous about something in favour of seeking out what works and to learn from experimentation.

7.   An engrained sense of knowing that they count, they can make a difference in what they do and they can be responsible for their behaviour.

8.   They benefit from disciplined practice and are willing to commit themselves to completing their projects.

These somewhat prescriptive lists for the family as a whole, for parents and for young persons are less than complete formulas for wellness. Actually, they are only background sketches depicting some aspects of the wellness landscape. Such an overview offers simply a beginning rough-and-ready map approximating a vast and expansive territory. To make optimal use of the lists is to use them as a guiding framework in which many variations and degrees of intensity of the various characteristics can be uniquely blended together. In this way they offer a resilient, interwoven fabric that can guide us whether we be a counsellor, young person or a parent. Collectively they can serve to stimulate the possibility of turning our crises into opportunities and our potential competencies into action.

IN SUMMARY

If the forces of competency are mobilized in a youth and family crisis, then the wellness characteristics can serve as the stable landscape that makes the crisis experience a worthwhile adventure. Even though this wellness scenario may be the space to idealistically recapture, the sad truth is that most youth and families have lost sight of this possibility altogether. Instead, they have become overly concerned with avoiding further crisis suffering. Avoidance of pain seems only to bury it for a while till it resurfaces in other forms. So the question becomes why is this so, when apparent solutions already exist and all families need to do is focus on them? Given that we all have our own journey to take, the crisis intervener predisposed to this model would do well to remember that although we can awaken and invite or even inspire, we cannot motivate or manipulate a family into setting out on a wellness journey. A wellness journey is a mixed blessing, because it inevitably requires the family to actively examine, engage, and master the sources of their suffering. Ironically, it requires the family to probe the depths of suffering in search for breakthrough possibilities. In this respect, a family must be willing to endure and learn how to master more upsets, frustration and rejection rather than less. This requires persistent action that unrelentingly seeks opportunity out of every crisis.

An attempt will now be made, in a bold and simplified way, to suggest some baseline causes of youth and family suffering. The intent here is to acknowledge the context of youth and family suffering in some way and then to offer strategies for employing the **SOURCE** formula. The aim is to facilitate the crisis intervener's discovery of ways to re-pattern the suffering framework and awaken the young person and/or the family to another way of being with crises.

YOUTH CRISES: THE FORGETTABLE JOURNEY

Some would say that the adolescent stage is crisis personified. In the few short years of adolescence, life is a continuous roller-coaster ride in which change occurs faster than is seemingly possible. Both the body and mind rapidly evolve and at times revolt against their inside and their outside world. Adolescence is a time when the past, present, and future overlap in confusing ways. It is the ending of body survival (as seen in the need for parental dependency), and the beginning of mind survival (as seen in the search for one's identity, as Erikson (1963) so well described).

Adolescence is a period of transformation or metamorphosis, in which innocence is no longer valued in comparison with responsibility, and responsibility is often experienced as doing what others want you to do. Sometimes it is as if there is still a little person existing in a big body, and at other times as if a big person inhabits a body not yet big enough. Adolescence is a period when powerful vibrations begin to unleash various forms of mind and body expressions. This raw and undisciplined power is immediately confronted with social and cultural boundaries. Thus what unfolds is an uneasy affair with power and control. Often this is typified by adolescent responses that bounce back and forth between "I don't know" and "I know everything."

Adolescence is unquestionably for most a time of turmoil and revolution. It is a time when who you are changes so rapidly that invalidation is a common experience. It chronicles the loss of childhood where acceptance is more or less taken for granted and it heralds in social pressure that

---

attempts to condition the young person to perceive worth as largely determined by one's aspirations and achievements. Disrupting this period of metamorphosis can be many buried, unresolved childhood traumas that begin to surface from the unconscious.

Moreover, breaking through childhood, the adolescent awakens to find that the next journey, as modelled by adults, is toward accentuating the materialistic self. It is a time when it becomes apparent that there are few adults who look like they have life handled and who therefore can serve as role models. From this viewpoint, adolescence is often the beginning of loss and of being lost. Not yet knowing who to become, the young person experiences an emptiness that yearns to be filled up with a defined selfhood.

Adolescence, then, tends to be the stage for fleshing out and operationalizing one's Act in life or what one portrays in order to avoid being insignificant. The Act gets played out in a trial-and-error search for some way to accentuate one's selfhood or identity. It seems that this stage of life is one easily forgotten by most adults, even when the passage may have been eventful for them. Perhaps we choose to forget this period in our life in which we naturally tested limits and explored our selfhood boundaries. Indeed, many parents with troubled adolescents can easily believe that adolescence is a forgettable journey.

To loosely summarize, adolescence is a stage (as identified by thousands of adolescents in treatment) to:

Discover a way to be your own boss;
Discover to what degree you are competent;
Discover what the boundaries are between self and not-self;
Discover how to carve out a place in your environment;
Discover how to manage a growing sense of aloneness in the world;
Discover how you can make a difference.

The most frequent responses that adolescents make to these issues are threefold: firstly, indifference, as modelled by some adults around them; secondly, scepticism, belief that opportunities will not likely come their way; and thirdly, outright hostility, to self, to others, or to their environment. These responses become more or less rigidified, depending on the particular adolescent's previous history of unresolved crises.

In reaction to the repeated, humiliating experience of having their power monitored, thwarted or discounted, adolescents in crisis invariably resist most crisis intervention efforts. In many instances they create crises that they can control to counteract crises that they cannot control.

TAMING THE TOUGHIES

Few would dispute that successful crisis intervention with adolescents is a bit like expecting or seeking out a miracle. Most adolescents in crisis are upset with the adults in their lives and do not want another adult (even a counsellor) interfering with their life. They see most adults as wanting to fix them up or change their behaviour - in other words, to "tame" them. Wanting desperately to carve

---

out their own destiny and to be "in charge" of themselves, they most often try to be tough or resilient and resist being "tamed." Most adolescents in crisis tend to be openly resistive and, at times, willing to make the crisis worse, just to experience the power that comes from being obstinant. Intervention in their crises is more often than not perceived by them as a threat to their personal freedom. They see most adults as judges, controllers, and advice-givers. Nevertheless, this very obstinence if capitalized on, can create a crisis breakthrough. The Beyond Content crisis intervener intuitively recognizes the need for adolescents to express their sense of power through crises and accordingly seeks interventions that strengthen the adolescents' control over their lives.

For handling a resistant adolescent in crisis, the **SOURCE** formula recommends the following:

Sharing

It is useful to counteract the possibility that an adolescent may fear being humiliated by actually allowing your own humility coupled with confidence to surface. To be confident and humble is to exude a sense of caring assurance that you can be of service to a young person. Ironically, those who do benefit from your support are those who recognize at some point that they can make it through the crisis on their own. Knowing this, they can choose to make use of a modicum of face-saving support from the crisis intervener to affirm that they are their own boss.

Sharing your humbleness in this way opens up the possibility your inviting them to experiment with new ways of dealing with their crises. An invitation is just that, something they decide to act on or not without obligation. Sometimes the invitation needs to be stated several times, because adolescents in crisis often initially misinterpret invitations as orders.

Convincing adolescents that they have more control over themselves than you ever can is not to suggest you would let them hurt themselves or hurt someone else. When this possibility is real, the adolescent can be advised that, while it's true that they have more control over themselves than you do, there are circumstances in which they may not have control. In these circumstances, where harm is possible, the crisis intervener must directly intervene so as to ensure the safety of all concerned.

Because adolescents are just beginning to play with logic and with their own conceptual capabilities, they know that they are no intellectual match for most adults. Consequently the Beyond Content crisis intervener is careful to stay away from sharing what's reasonable behaviour or attempting to discuss the relative goodness or not-goodness of their actions or the actions they are in conflict with. For example, to repeatedly tell adolescent drug users that drugs will kill them without equally acceptable ways to alter their state is to infer inadequacy and to inadvertently stimulate a feeling of humiliation or degradation.

What seems to be the least intrusive way to intervene with adolescents is to tell stories rich in imagery about what you have **learned** from other adolescents with similar problems and life challenges. By personalizing these experiences and by discussing what you have learned, you are, in a way, both declaring your own vulnerability to such a crisis problem, yet also communicating you have learned something about similar crises. This way of sharing sometimes communicates "an attitude of gratitude" that you can learn from them as well as possibly contribute to their self understanding in this manner. You imply confidence in that you know what you are doing, and yet you have much to learn and discover. You convey, as well, that their experiences, though they may be similar to some of your own, they are nevertheless unique. Therefore, it is important they share their views of what's going on with them.

There are many non-verbal ways to establish mutuality and a state of interdependence with them. Adolescents generally prefer to "act out" or "act in" more than to "talk out" their problems. Giving them an opportunity to share by doing something **with** their resistance is a "joining manoeuvre" that says to them that you are interested in working with them and in finding ways for their energy to really produce what they want for themselves.

Observing

Adolescents in crisis generally have a difficult time in bearing the gaze of others. Their self-image is continuously in a state of flux. As they awaken to the critical adult ways of viewing their world they easily become overly critical of themselves and highly sensitive to others seeing their fragility. A face-to-face encounter is most often perceived by a resistive adolescent as invasive. Since resistance is about boundaries, intervention starts with acknowledging their need for being resistant and their need for respect for their boundaries.

These boundaries of resistance can be detected by allowing a "soft-eyed" observation to act as an early warning system. By doing so, the crisis intervener can pick up subtle nuances when a mind/body boundary is contacted and tension begins to rise. Such tension is observable in signs such as arrested breathing, facial flushing, clenching of fists, abrupt silence, dropping of the head, increased peripheral motor agitation, and so on. The challenge at this point is to remain neutrally connected at the boundary interface. Keeping an arms-length distance from the resistance boundary indicates, once again, that you respect the energy contained in this boundary. For example, resistance may surface in the form of a boundary (such as clenched teeth) when a crisis intervener makes any family-related statements. Alternately, a promiscuous female teenager might become abruptly silent when asked about her relationship with her younger sister. In such circumstances, the crisis intervener could mirror back what is een as well as to pace and matching the current flow of energy emenating from the adolescent. Mentioning in a rhetorical way that some issues in peoples' lives are off limits to others unless they want them not to be, can assure them of your interest, while still respecting their way of resisting assistance.

Uncovering

Once the adolescent has engaged with the crisis intervener, even if it is tenous, their competencies can be highlighted. Even their resistance can be perceived in some transformed way as a competency. As mentioned in Chapter Two, Table 1 and also throughout Chapter

Six, all forms of energy, including resistance, have embedded competencies, even when the energy is manifested in destructive ways.

To accomplish this the crisis intervener, using a "soft-eyed right-brain" approach, the would create mental images of the resistance as a legitimized form of energy expression and a demonstration of some form of competency. Once two or more competencies have been revealed through this process and the sharing of them has begun to resonate within the adolescent's awareness, the crisis intervener can shift their attention towards their environment. Next, the possible resources around the adolescent are identified. Finally these resources are mobilized into action by plugging in the identified competencies as activators so thata desired resolution can be achieved.

Resourcing

Now that you have identified some baseline competencies, create around these competencies a series of inter-linked (stacked) images of them in practice that fit the adolescent's experience. Next, you can now encourage the adolescent to discover ways to have these competencies **activated** in the current crisis situation. The question then becomes how the adolescent might use these sometimes outrageous energies to teach themselves other ways to experience their significance and their aliveness. Resourcing is done to inspire the adolescent rather than to lecture. The adolescent becomes inspired when they that the intervener can turn the intervener's own tension into excitement alongside the adolescent's tension.

Completing

Contrary to what we might think, adolescents can listen to their inner intuitive wisdom as well as adults can, if not better. Being somewhat less conditioned and less sceptical, they can connect to the core Self through media of current interest, such as rock videos, games, movies, and their own self stories. Connecting with their rich imaginations, the crisis intervener probes for ways to guide them towards a synthesis of their emotions, thoughts, and experiences. They are then encouraged to use their growing sense of clarity as a stimulant or elixir for generating action statements related to their crisis. To complete successfully requires that the identified competencies by physically anchored to images and actions of acceptable role models as well as their own behavior. Having the young person repetitively mirror competencies, you can set up unique triggers using selective words, specific actions and visual images that fire off these competencies when a crisis like the current situation prevails.

Expanding

Now that the adolescent knows where theye might want to go, they can be supported to use their newly "fleshed out" competencies. Once the adolescent is able to wilfully trigger off and use her competencies, the crisis intervener would do well to get other significant adults in the adolescent's life to reinforce her competencies by acting supportively towards them. The biggest setback that can occur in this process occurs if you abandon it by allowing another crisis to interfere with it. As mentioned many times, embarking on this pathway does not get rid of crises. It just offers a more empowering way of handling them when they come along. Now for a look at the family.

FAMILY CRISIS INTERVENTION: WHERE DO WE START?

The Origin of Family Suffering

An overly simplistic or snapshot view of family suffering might suggest that being born kicks off the suffering journey and needing others (namely a mother and a family) to survive maintains it. It seems that families episodically struggle with separation and attachment as represented by the driving need for belonging on the one hand and independence or freedom on the other. This seesaw battle varies in degrees of intensity throughout family life and it is further complicated by well engrained transgenerational family survival patterns. In other words we are prone to making the same crazy decisions our parents made and their parents before them in order to avoid loss of significance within our family. It is almost as if our conditioned nature conspires against us as we implant our parents historical ways of suffering into our minds' preoccupation with our own survival. Consequently, life upsets or crises come along and are filtered through these outdated or ill-fitting family patterns.

Despite these circumstances, as Harvey White (1978) suggests in **Your Family is Good For You**, the family is the richest source of self-discovery. It is our source or origin point, although seldom consciously recognized as such; and it is where we first learn about the meaning of our own existence. In this respect our family holds the key to our freedom from suffering.

A Ticket to their Show

Intervention with a family in crisis is most often a complicated affair. If there are three or more persons involved, numerous overlapping triadic communication patterns can get generated. Not only are these interconnected triadic interactions produced by the immediate family in conflict, they are further compounded by various family-of-origin issues having an undercurrent impact on the family's disposition. This is especially so when the family is in crisis. Historically unresolved conflicts tend to re-appear in mysterious ways, making them difficult to counteract. This phenomenon is aptly captured in Henry Beacher's (1984) comment that, "What the mother sings to the cradle goes all the way down to the coffin." Figure 16, which attempts to depict the simplest triadic relationship with any given family member, offers a starting point for intervention.

Since many intricate triangulation possibilities exist, frustrated and desperate families seeking crisis assistance can easily entrap crisis interveners and ultimately use them as scapegoats to alleviate the pressures within the family. Entering into a family crisis is more often than not a costly enterprise. Not only must you risk becoming a scapegoat, but you must be perceived as helping the family out of its helplessness without allowing any one family member to lose in the process. In subtle ways, crisis interveners can get hooked by an unspoken obligation in this regard. Desirous of wanting to contribute, crisis interveners may too readily grasp at ways to sssist the family by offering sketchy advice. Crisis interveners can also end up becoming sacrificial victims as the family projects its

---

issues and helplessness on to them. They may well be "dumped on" and discounted as a resource by one or more family members.

A graphic, somewhat theatrical, analogy for this possible scenario suggests that the crisis intervener enters into a family crisis as if they were entering onto the stage of a "family theatre." As the crisis drama unfolds, the crisis intervener begins to perceive family "histories" projected in entangled ways. Some of the crisis stories or "dramas" are over-acted or presented in varying degrees of over and under-exposure. It is even possible that some members are unwilling to let the crisis intervener see their "show", for fear that the crisis intervener will be too much of a critic and perhaps "pan" them. Competition for "centre stage" and an "off" and "on" acting of the various dramas may also cast a complicated and distorted family picture. The crisis intervener usually encounters resistance even to being present in the "family theatre" in the first place. Some family members may also resist the crisis intervener's presence in order to reinforce the family crisis. Many crisis interveners can easily become jaundiced and embittered by the family's apparent lack of respect for their efforts and their desire to make a contribution.

Upon entering the family crisis theatre, the crisis intervener would do well to employ "joining manoeuvres" (in the same manner as with adolescents). By acting something like a distant uncle who has come to visit and to share in the family's stories without prejudice, the crisis intervener will often be treated in honourable ways by the family in crisis. This posture coupled with a focus on working with and through the family's resistance instead of against it, can establish a neutral yet genuinely interested connection with the family.

Linking in this way does not require mega-doses of charisma. It simply requires a willingness to focus on becoming a practicing master of ways to encourage a family make constructive use of its resistance to change.

BEYOND CONTENT MODEL APPLIED

It is worth recalling the two-phase manner in which the **SOURCE** formula can be implemented. The first phase, which consists of Sharing, Observing, and Uncovering, attends to sizing up the family crisis situation, whereas the second phase explores how to establish harmony and to discover different family interaction patterns. Sizing up, as covered in Chapter Three, focuses on determining the preferred perceptual pathways, as well as perceptual stuckness, the crisis state of integrity, and the approximate life role or Act of each family member.

Sharing, Observing & Uncovering

Families in crisis are notorious for interrupting one another. Family members will claim that they have heard it all before or that they have not been heard fully themselves and feel discounted; sometimes the interrupters simply want to be in control. In a humble, self-assured way, the crisis intervener may begin by encouraging the family to consider the idea of allowing each member to tell his or her story without interruption. Such a series of stories sets the stage for family reconsideration of others and tends to awaken mutual respect for one another. Telling one's story from beginning to end is next to impossible; yet the attempt to do so almost invariably takes less time than we or any family member might fear.

During this initial phase, mental notes can be made of any family wellness attributes that are revealed. Also, record can be made of any wellness attributes of the parents, children, or family that appear to be obviously absent yet worthy of attending to; this record is for use later in the second phase of the **SOURCE** formula. In the process of observing, the crisis intervener needs to be sensitive to the level of activation of each of the competency forces both in individual family members and in the family as a whole.

Guided by the First Order Triangle (Figure 16), the crisis intervener can begin to uncover the crisis integrity state of each family member. Next, the intervener would seek to obtain a snapshot overview of the roles or Acts of each family member, in an effort to gain an awareness of how each perpetuate his or her triangulations. Then, in an unassuming and actively neutral way, the crisis intervener can entertain the step-by-step process depicted in Figure 18, which can be described as follows:

1. Identify and connect with the family member with the highest integrity state (Step A). This acknowledges the value of starting from strength and the intent to serve as a catalyst, so that this family member can regain and maintain a state of Naturalness.

2. As the potential of this person surfaces, the crisis intervener simply aligns with the person in a supportive way, encouraging them to stay in touch with their integrity regardless of the source of the conflict. If an old family pattern is operating, the task is to have this person recognize the pattern and divert its controlling effect first from oneself and then from one's family.

3. Next, the crisis intervener works towards synergizing or potentiating, in unobtrusive non-specific ways, a stable crisis integrity state of naturalness in this first family member. Care is taken not to ignore other family members in the process. As this process begins to succeed, the crisis intervener fades into the background by encouraging this person to take on more and more of a supportive and constructive role within the family. Supportive nudges and suggestions may be used to guide this family member to operate as a co-partner in the crisis stabilization process (Step B).

4. As integrity begins to take a foothold from one family member to another (the Self-Organizing principle in effect), the triadic communications tend to collapse into a dyadic or two-way communication with the other family members.

5. The crisis intervener may entertain repeating this process with various family members as they move up and down the crisis states of integrity. Patience is essential if the crisis intervener is to capture turning-point opportunities for making a connection and thereby having her efforts diminish the family crisis state.

6.   Once one family member connects with a natural state of integrity with another member, the second triad could collapse. Now two family members can be supported to have a third family member recapture her natural state of integrity (Step C).

To move toward crisis intervention completion is to strive to achieve each of these steps to the extent that they can be achieved. In other words, to make progress one need not accomplish a state of perfect naturalness with any one family member. Sometimes, as mentioned, a family member will cycle through many states during the crisis intervention process. Consequently, several attempts may be needed if one is to maintain a foothold with a family. It may even require a number of crisis intervention sessions to move from Step A to Step B.

Clearly, other forms of clinical support can seek to achieve these same steps in a more gradual and more synthesizing way. The intent here is only to offer a guiding framework that can be entered at any point, depending on the unique style and viewpoint of the crisis intervener. Given that crises always represent opportunities, the rigor of this model is less important than the intention to capitalize on the simplest way to tease out benefit from the crisis experience.

The second phase of the **SOURCE** formula suggests movement from Step A to Step D by Resourcing, Completing, and Expanding, as follows:

Resourcing, Completing, & Expanding

7.   Once all family members (more or less) allow integrity to guide and flow through them, they can then use the crisis intervener to accentuate or highlight pathways that can be travelled towards more significant family wellness. In addition to the force of integrity, the crisis intervener can seek to mobilize the other forces of competency (Creative Intention, Self-Mastery, & Purpose). The aim would be to energize the family unit to achieve an optimal state of wellness (Step D). This final step is always to be contemplated even though it seldom is a direct outcome of crisis intervention alone. In fact, this entire process is based on going beyond coping strategies and entering and operating in the realm of breakthrough possibilities.

The crisis intervener can experiment with completing and expanding possibilities as the family's uncovered competencies are linked to concrete background family experiences. The challenge here becomes that of encouraging the family to do something **now**, in the very moment, to demonstrate its renewed sense of value. Finally, the ultimate test of the family's new-found support for one another is for its members to commit to practicing their wellness at home and, indeed, expanding to practice it with others in their community. Though it may sound idealistic to say so, it is not beyond anyone's natural capacity to make a difference. What holds us back is our attachment to the form of our suffering, to our victimized and guilt-driven positions within our family, and to our resistance to being fully competent.

FIGURE 18

THE PRIMARY FAMILY INTERVENTION PROCESS

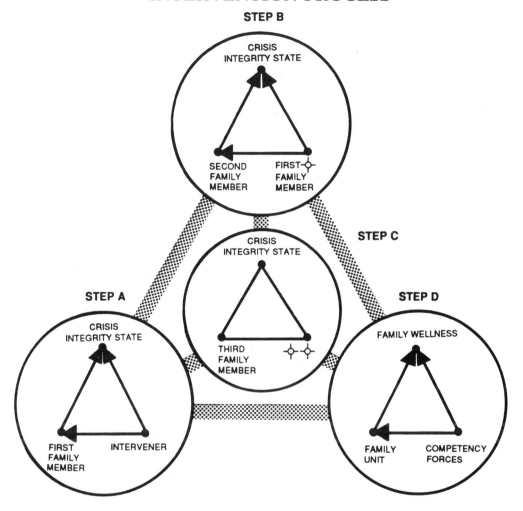

STEP B

CRISIS INTEGRITY STATE

SECOND FAMILY MEMBER

FIRST FAMILY MEMBER

STEP C

CRISIS INTEGRITY STATE

THIRD FAMILY MEMBER

STEP A

CRISIS INTEGRITY STATE

FIRST FAMILY MEMBER

INTERVENER

STEP D

FAMILY WELLNESS

FAMILY UNIT

COMPETENCY FORCES

◇ FAMILY MEMBER FUSED WITH CRISIS INTERVENER SUPPORT AND INTEGRITY

◇-◇ FIRST AND SECOND FAMILY MEMBER FUSED WITH CRISIS INTERVENTION SUPPORT AND INTEGRITY

SUGGESTED READINGS

1. **Crisis in the family,** by Umana et al. (New York: Gardner Press, 1980), systematically examines three traditional approaches to family crisis intervention. In an effort to make sense out of the disparate and conceptually vague models and practices in the fields of family crisis intervention, family therapy, and generic crisis intervention, this monograph clarifies common dimensions and reveals ways in which one might go forward and develop more effective intervention strategies. Moreover, it offers an explicate baseline from which an evolving implicate and interwoven transpersonal crisis-intervention model can be conceived.

2. An excellent Eastern philosophical educational viewpoint of family life, offered to bewildered parents in modern society, can be found in Nikkyo Niwano's friendly and upbeat book, **The wholesome family life** (Tokyo: Kosei, 1982). This readily understandable overview of ways to confront family problems through family life education is refreshingly unifying and transpersonal in perspective.

3. Inspiring essays on spirituality and family life, reflecting on ways to return to the natural rhythms of family harmony, are offered in **Lifeways,** by Bons Voors (New York: Hawthorne Press, 1982).

4. **The marriage and family book, a spiritual guide,** edited by Ravi Dass and Aparna (New York: Schocken, 1978) presents many ways to look at marriage, parenting, and family life from an eastern religious viewpoint.

NOTES

_____
_____
_____
_____
_____
_____
_____
_____
_____
_____
_____
_____
_____
_____
_____
_____
_____
_____
_____
_____
_____
_____
_____
_____
_____
_____
_____

SECTION IV

ENVIRONMENTAL CRISIS INTERVENTION

The next three chapters take a cross-sectional viewpoint of different crisis backgrounds and offer comments on how three such distinct environments generate unique environmentally specific issues. The three environments selected: schools, treatment and/or care institutions and crisis call centres, present a frame of reference requiring any employed crisis intervention model to be flexibly responsive to their mandated purpose. The Beyond Content model is presented as being able to dynamically contribute to each of these environments in a constructive competency building manner and at the same time create unusual crisis breakthrough opportunities.

Chapter Fourteen begins this section by examining the importance of schools as needing to be at the front end of managing and preventing human crises. In this respect, from an evolving holistic and developmentally enhancing perspective, a "straw man" action plan for implementing a competency based crisis intervention is put forward for consideration.

The next chapter on institutions offers suggestions on how to employ a Beyond Content perspective when confronted with the "giving-up" or "lost cause" syndrome associated with being admitted to an institution. Focusing specifically on correctional institutions as one of the most pronounced examples of how societal giving-up sets up personal as well as interpersonal discounting, suggestions are made regarding how to make the Beyond Content model workable. In addition, recognizing the necessity for institutions to be highly control-oriented, several powerful intervention tactics are described that do not violate this need. Challenged to use an expanding framework in a contracting environment, this model seeks to discover a "breakthrough in every breakdown".

The remaining chapter in this section looks at what unique skills need to be employed when offering crisis intervention support over the telephone. Presented here is a protocol for effective multi-modal listening. Comments are also made on how to verbally interact in ways that reduces vulnerability, minimizes guilt and maximizes rapport.

CHAPTER FOURTEEN

CRISES IN SCHOOLS

Transpersonal education...aims to aid transcendence, not furnish mere coping skills. It is education's counterpart to holistic medicine: education of the whole person...it is the process of exposing people to the mysterious in themselves,...it promotes friendly environments for hard tasks.

- Marilyn Ferguson

IMPLEMENTING A MODEL

Within a school environment, crisis intervention is not easily accommodated because the priority in schools is growth and development through education, not social readjustment. Many schools struggle with the increasing unrest of students who choose to reveal their anguish about being insignificant more than anywhere else, within the school environment. Crises are spawned in schools simply because this environment has the social stability to absorb the friction generated by unresolved human issues. Even though schools may put considerable effort into trying to minimize the effects of dysfunctional behaviour on the educational milieu, few schools feel confident about the sufficiency of what they are doing. Schools, in this respect, seem to be struggle with how to develop an implement a functionally effective crisis intervention model that is ecologically balanced. Most schools seek to band-aide crises and then quickly divert or them to outside resources whom they view as having the necessary expertise.

On the other hand, more and more community-conscious schools are taking on the challenge of including natural community-based crisis resources as partners in ensuring schools remain the community's centre piece of support. Those schools that do not use community resources effectively seem to either cope with crises in partially resolving ways or they become breeding grounds for momentary quick-fixes that cover up competency or make it somebody elses responsibility.

Obviously, crisis intervention self-sufficiency would be a desirable goal for schools, although somewhat idealistic given the priority that crisis intervention receives in overall school functioning. It is nonetheless possible to address crises that surface in schools without duplicating the mandates of community social support systems. Some proactive attention should first be given to the efficacy of having a crisis intervention model in the first place. A school that explores the relative utility of various models may discover them to be too limiting to cover the wide range of school based needs. What simple yet encompassing framework will work becomes the question. To begin to answer this question, a school needs first of all to clarify how its philosophy can address student upsets and what resources it needs to do so.

Once the school has established a relatively clear purpose, with concrete objectives, it might want to consider a model that uses everyone who can make a contribution as a potential resource. The Beyond Content model speaks to this possibility and can be adapted to serve schools as its contextual nature renders it adaptable to just about any environment. The contextual principles can easily be embraced within a school setting and applied by anyone, even a busy teacher. Further, the competency-based rather than problem-focused approach actually supports the underlying premise of education. In this respect, the Beyond Content model has an educational flavour to it, in contrast to more clinical or insight-and problem-based crisis-intervention models. Learning how to use the model can be done in gradual steps. As the model is holistic and systemically developed, it can be entered at any point without losing perspective of the whole. A rudimentary use of it actually promotes the learning and incorporating of it. It goes without saying that self-explorative practice done on a regular basis is necessary if mastery of this model is to be achieved. Workshops can also benefit anyone wishing to deepen their understanding of the model in order to use it with others or with themselves.

RESOURCE DEVELOPMENT

There are many actions that a school environment can take in adopting a transpersonally based crisis intervention model. Viewed as guiding suggestions, these actions are as follows:

1. Competency or Wellness Framework

The most critical step is to shift gears from a reactionary problem focus to a competency focus. At the practical level it is not really possible to assist and support someone to experience their significance if we start from an assumption that they are deficient or not good enough. Even if the behavioral evidence suggests that a person is destructive, mentally imbalanced, or self-serving, we must perceive them as competent and valuable if we are to help them enrich their lives. This can be achieved through adopting a stance that sees everyone as born with an enormous amount of potential that simply needs to be made real through action. Discovering competencies out of problems or transforming troublesome behaviour into competency traits becomes the contextual baseline for crisis dissolution. The student in crisis is actively encouraged to be awake and autonomous, to question, to seek meaning, to challenge, to self-explore in interdependent ways, and ultimately to transform as they transcend their crises.

As a preparatory exercise (or counterconditioning process, if you will), the school could develop a list of competencies important to the school setting. These competencies can be coupled with a transformed list of commonly experienced crisis symptoms (see Chapter Two, Table 1) to generate the basis for a unique approach to school crisis intervention. An example of this approach might be to take a student with a phobia for mathematics that results in fainting spells and in a planned way invite this student prior to an anxiety attack to lie down in the nursing station or medical room, close their eyes, and listen to a taped session of a math class. This technique is not meant to be curative - more comprehensive counseling or therapy may well be required. It is simply an attempt to be innovative using resistance from a competency rather than a deficiency base.

As another example of this approach, take a situation in which a student is writing swear words on the blackboard before class or passing anonymous notes that provoke disgust. A transformative approach might be for the teacher or teachers to write notes to this student acknowledging their unusual writing without attempting to correct their behaviour. The student might also be given several articles that would relate to anger management identifying a number of powerful ways to get people's attention, in this regard you would be attempting to acknowledge that it is important for people to be heard, especially when they have something they really want to say. Another possibility might be to consider having the drama teacher invite this student to participate in the drama club either as a performer or temporarily as a potential script writer. This approach may well seem to avoid or the genesis or underlying cause of the crisis symptom suggesting the possible need for more direct intervention if the student fails to naturally reveal their true needs.

For most crisis interveners the biggest barrier to employing these somewhat provocative approaches is the fear that a cry for help is being ignored. Actually though, beginning with the acknowledgement that the individual's unique way of expressing their distress, tends to leave open many pathways for them to want to seek support without the fear of further self-depreciation. The intent here is to open up thinking possibilities for a more direct and constructive way of sharing that does not produce additional resistance.

The assumption that we start from competency is the cornerstone of the transpersonally based school crisis intervention model. Acceptance of this framework in a school environment is essential if schools are to avoid becoming contributors to their student's dis-ease. Without creating such support, we become victims of our environment, over which we have little or no control. Our crises then gradually drives us further and further below the line of adequacy, landing us ultimately in the realm of the living dead.

2. The "C" Team.

Assuming that there is a modest interest in a wellness or competency frame of reference, it might then be useful to put together a competency monitoring team. This team of co-conspirators would simply become vigilant observers of major shifts in the competency level of the school due to crisies. When a significant upset occurs either in general or in relation to one student, this team would meet to discuss what competencies are being buried,

---

lost or covered up. The team could meet informally on a regular basis and discuss ways to recapture and even increase competency levels in the school. It is important that the concern level not draw the group toward seeing upsets and catastrophes as just problems and not challenges. It is extremely easy to fall prey to this contagious and insidious tendency to be problem and coping focused . Therefore it is essential for the "C" team to consciously practice seeing crises as opportunities and resistance as an invaluable source of energy to be used to dissolve crises. Moreover the "C" team would also do well to regularly practice ways of supporting each other's competencies, using the team as a barometer of the overall commitment to an ecologically balanced wellness environment.

3.   **Student Early Warning System**

In a gradual, building-block way, the "C" team might pull together a core group of students who could keep their finger on the competency pulse of the student population. Other students are usually the first to know when a fellow student is slipping. Training them to be "competency detectives" rather than "problem snitches" can be a wonderful and enriching experience. To make a difference, these students should be chosen from the general student population because of their declared commitment to self-observe and share their own competency state in a weekly guided peer-group experience. Membership in this group could also be made conditional on drawing two other students into this group over a school term. In this way, the group continues to evolve and expand, so that it synergizes a competency atmosphere around the school.

4.   **Community Crisis Support.**

Most communities that offer crisis support to schools find it awkward to optimally make efficient use of their resources when called upon to assist schools with a crisis. Fragmented and poorly articulated linkages with schools seem to be the end result despite good intentions by all concerned. Interestingly enough, this is not because well defined linkages are unworkable. More often than not, it is because of illusions that each resource has about the others. There is a natural tendency for most schools to assume that it is a sign of weakness to have a community crisis support resource come into the school territory (which often includes the student's home front) to assist in a crisis. Although it is also true that some schools view the resolution of crises as really not a school's problem, but one that should be dealt with in the home and the community.

For a linkage to really work, schools must take a proactive role in requesting such services, especially those services that are willing to focus on competency rather than symptom-based crisis intervention. Inviting agencies to participate within the school walls is much like inviting friends over for dinner. It makes sense to make them feel welcome and to encourage them to experience the atmosphere as receptive and embracing. When such an atmosphere is offered, community agencies become invaluable ancillary or adjunct support systems that can intervene before crises become chronic or overwhelming.

When a school crisis warrants immediate intervention, a crisis support service having a well defined mandate with schools can connect with the student or students in crisis in unobtrusive ways. When hospitalization is indicated, student support can be invaluable in assuming the troubled student that as a peer they would be supported in their decision to get extra support. Family contact and other social service support may be considered a natural recourse, to be expediently connected with when the school-based linkage to a crisis support service is in place.

5. A Parent Wellness Committee

Before giving over to outside resources such as social service agencies and other government-supported intervention services, a parent support safety net should be established. Committed parents need to be asked to participate in a support system that will address student crisis circumstances in both the school and the community. The primary objective will be to support and inform the school "C" team and the student early warning network of what resources are needed and which ones can be mobilized for specific crisis events.

This kind of parent group works only when the parents are given a significant role to play early in the crisis event. This parent wellness support and safety committee should primarily be used as a community "think tank" for the "C" team and the community-based crisis service. It will be necessary to offer the parent group ongoing seminar experiences on Wellness and Competency identification. School administration will need to give this committee continuous feedback on the competency status of the school environment and on what the community can do to enhance that status. Clearly, it is important that the parents remain simply advisers and guides in the school crises and not get caught up in the actual crisis direct service. Confidentiality must be honored in all cases.

IN SUMMARY

School Based Pre-crisis Intervention

General Considerations:

1. Forecast and assist the student in crisis plan for future crisis situations.

2. Continuously and persistently ask questions to clarify the degree of hopelessness, haplessness and helplessness.

3. Engage community-based emergency services (i.e., crisis mobile teams, suicide lines, community volunteer support systems).

4. Give the student an emergency aid, such as a list of telephone numbers to call, how to get immediate assistance from you, your organization or significant others.

5.	Ensure you have telephone numbers and addresses of the student and their significant others readily available.

6.	Develop a short-term agreement that stabilizes the crisis by acknowledging the resistance as a resource.

"Envivo" School-based Crisis Management

In employing the SOURCE formula and the ten crisis intervention principles, consider the following actions:

1.	First and foremost size up crisis imminent risk.

2.	Express your compassion for the depth of the person's anguish and desperateness of the moment. Validate their responses while encouraging the possibility of them perceiving their emotional storms from other angles (a challenge focus versus a problem focus).

3.	Provide a minimum of three options to their current upsetting behaviour that favour their competencies.

4.	Mobilize Creative Intention and transmute the negative energy into constructive challenge-oriented action.

5.	Plan or structure the student's time during the crisis period until your next contact.

6.	Forecast any possibility of future upset and count on a general re-occurrence of a crisis after effect.

7.	Be clear and upfront on confidentiality limits.

8.	Maintain the focus on their competencies and how they can be used to master the crisis as a challenge rather than a problem.

9.	Supportively confront the student with alternative responses that employs resources within the school setting.

This cursory outline of some raw components of a school-based crisis-intervention model is a sweeping synthesis of contextual possibilities meant only to stimulate the thinking and strategizing of a more holistic intervention perspective. Obviously, the unique needs of each school and the community it serves will dictate what specific networking requirements will work. But once we recognize that human development is much more complex, richer, and more demanding than current educational approaches acknowledge, new configurations like the Beyond Content model can be considered. The challenge is to find a way to promote this collaborative, school-and community-based, shared decision-making model, which brings together teachers, administrators, parents, students, and

---

the helping community. The Beyond Content broad-banded, coordinating approach to crisis intervention does and can work for schools. The time is ripe for bold new initiatives to promote the intelligent use of the educational environment as the centre of our personal and interpersonal competency and wellness.

SUGGESTED READINGS

1.   A thought-provoking account of how the school system needs to adopt a more transpersonal perspective is offered by Marilyn Ferguson in her milestone book, **The aquarian conspiracy** (Los Angeles: J.P. Tarcher, 1980).

2.   The journal **In context** (No# 18, Winter 1988) has dedicated an entire issue, entitled "Transforming Education", to major shifts in education. The focus in this issue on breakthrough possibilities suggests by implication ways that crisis intervention can be interwoven within a model that goes beyond schooling. The practical and upbeat ideas presented can be quite refreshing as well as inspiring to educators who are on the threshold of transforming problems into challenges.

3.   A classic account of the significance of education and of the crisis state that it is in can be found in **Education and the significance of life** (New York: Harper & Row, 1953) by the Eastern thinker, J. Krishnamurti. It offers a profound and challenging approach to education that is clear and piercingly insightful.

4.   Perhaps the richest and most absorbing current account of the crises in our education system can be found in Allan Bloom's **The closing of the american mind** (New York: Simon & Schuster, 1987). Although it tends to focus more on higher education, it reflects, by extrapolation, the grave state of our antiquated preoccupation with reason and territoriality and the resultant impact that our teachers and educators have on their students.

NOTES

NOTES

CHAPTER FIFTEEN

INSTITUTIONAL CRISIS INTERVENTION

The welfare of the people in particular has always been the alibi of tyrants and it provides the further advantage of giving the servants of tyranny a good conscience.

- Albert Camus

THE GIVING UP SYNDROME

When a person enters into an institution, whether it be a hospital, a treatment centre, a correctional facility, or a group home, the experience is almost always a fragmenting one. A fragmenting experience occurs when one's symptoms, behaviors, or deficiencies become the focal point of attention to the exclusion of one's whole being. Before the decision is made to institutionalize or be institutionalized, the person in question has likely surrendered to the symptoms. She may have given up managing themselves, or she may have taken refuge from the responsibility of living. In this respect, institutions tend to epitomize a giving up by others and a giving in (albeit often reluctantly) by those institutionalized. Giving up by others is quite prevalent as evidenced by crumbling community support and family support systems. When this happens, the institution ends up becoming the stage upon which crisis melodramas are a common occurrence. In order to survive never- ending crises, the institution in question tends to establish elaborate and often quite complex **control** systems. The seeking of the causes of crises largely becomes a search through symptoms, reflecting such concerns as hyperactivity, minimal brain dysfunction, learning disability, conduct disorder, post-traumatic stress disorder, and countless other clinically labeled syndromes. Until institutions can discover a way to give up or give back control and still function with a viable mandate, they will valiantly struggle with one crisis after another.

A CORRECTIONAL FOCUS

Commonalities exist between most institutions. They all tend to be stigmatizing, problem-focused, and dependency-creating. They easily become pre-occupied with institutional standards and tend to uniformly and rigidly apply these standards to those institutionalized. As breeding grounds where crises are acted out, institutions are forever seeking new technologies and strategies for intervening in crises. In this respect, they are fertile ground for crisis-intervention training and experience.

Though the historical focus has been on how to avoid problems and further complications, institutions are gradually waking up to ways of becoming more challenge- and competency-focused (as opposed to problem-focused). In particular, correctional institutions have perhaps out of necessity, shown increasing although cautious receptivity to the competency or wellness aspects of crisis intervention. To demonstrate how the Beyond Content model might generally apply to institutions, crisis intervention in correctional institutions will be examined. Clearly, adaptation of the Beyond Content Model to other institutions, such as hospitals, would require special attention, especially in light of the complex mandates of various departments and the differing capabilities of professional as well as paraprofessional staff. Nevertheless, for those inclined to focus on similarities as well as differences, the issues to be presented with respect to correctional institutions can have some significant extrapolative value for other settings.

THE SURVIVAL STATE

Correctional facilities, not unlike other institutions, are safety-and control-conscious, wanting to be finished with a crisis as soon as possible so that they can get on with their perceived primary mandate. Quite sophisticated crisis response protocols, around such issues as violence, drug traumas, self-harming behaviour, and suicide, are in widespread existence. Yet, these response protocols are seldom linked to an well integrated, institutionally based crisis intervention model. More often that not these protocols serve the institution first and foremost and the client second. In a sense, the institution exercises collective survival-based control to squelch or dampen down the current survival needs of the client in crisis. Correctional institutions are predominantly survival traps where crises are the order of the day. The correctional crisis intervener is almost always seen as an authoritarian figure, inextricably tied to the institution's survival needs. Consequently, the crisis intervention frequently becomes an ordeal in which a range of survival instincts results in confrontation and manipulation for power, an illusive commodity in a correctional institution. The confrontation is manifested by the clash of roles or acts rather than of genuine selves. It is these acts (both for those in custody, as well as the custodians) that are really in crisis, while one's real self lies dormant or covered up for fear of irreversible loss.

IMPLEMENTING A BEYOND CONTENT MODEL

It is a challenge to implement any crisis intervention model (let alone the Beyond Content Model) within a corrections environment. Obviously, a shift out of a crisis survival state of integrity is an essential first step. This can be accomplished by first acknowledging that the survival state not only exists for both interveners and inmates, it also predominates. Second, it is essential that any

---

model be congruent with the institutional rules and regulations, which form the platform upon which the crisis intervention model can be built.

To implement aspects of a Beyond Content Model is not impossible or wishful thinking. Clearly, safety and control must be accepted as overriding principles before any effort to transform behaviour or to connect in transpersonal ways can be entertained. Not to do so would be a little like trying to attach wings to a catapillar. Furthermore, it would be foolish to think that a crisis intervener could successfully foster responsibility, reasonableness, and constructive or higher-order aims like caring and compassion without first minimizing the errors being made in an active crisis. Efforts to go prematurely beyond endeavouring to minimize error usually result in the growth of more illusions and more resistance, as these higher-order aims cannot meaningfully be supported or sustained in most correctional environments. Often valiant efforts to incorporate them drive them further away from reality.

It is essential for the correctional crisis intervener to rid herself of false positives and, in so doing, avoid slipping into nurturing the acts of the person in crisis and inadvertently perpetuating and reinforcing this person's minimal self. Before a transformative and wellness perspective can be fully activated, a thorough exploration of negative, calculating, or surface thinking has to occur. A focus on the resistance arising from the breakdown in a crisis can reveal breakthrough possibilities. This approach strongly advocates that mastery of resistance is the cornerstone of institutional crisis intervention.

THE BALANCING OF POWER AND CONTROL

It is quite evident that those who enter institutions lose considerable control over their lives and seemingly have at least as many crises within a correctional institution as they did outside. Almost invariably, the more control they invite, the more power they have to unleash through their crises experiences. In other words, the more victimized they are, the more they create crises to attract rescuers. Also, the more rebellious they are, the more they cause tyrants to surface in their crises. Unable to get direct control in powerful ways, they generate upsets that episodically disturb the institutional control state. For example, the more institutional control that is exercised over self-injurious behaviour, the greater the likelihood that the person will become more self-destructive. The more that restraint is given, the more it seems to be required. This is true even with depressed or apathetic behaviour: the more it is confronted, the more it tends to prevail.

The Beyond Content approach to this dilemma is to seek ways to maintain a balance of control and power by supporting and molding power expressions in the form of emotional expressions during crisis events. This approach is not what traditionally happens. Traditionally, the wish to extinguish crises quickly leads to smothering the emotions, forcing them to smolder underground, only to resurface as re-occurring flash fires. As in a gas well, the excess pressure or power must be continuously released, or the inmate will eventually explode. The Beyond Content perspective adjusts to the survival state of both the institution and the client, recognizing that a balance must be maintained.

Implementing the Beyond Content model with institutionally controlled clients starts with re-adjusting the balance of control and power to the extent that the primary aim is to minimize any further deterioration. Three of the Beyond Content contextual principles stand out as significant in this process. They are, On Immediacy, On What Works, and On Self Organizing (see Chapter Two). Extraordinary attention needs to be paid to unifying these principles. The intent is to create a driving wedge that guides the crisis intervener towards accentuating or mobilizing the competency force, **Self Mastery**. This competency force stands out as the most critical of the four forces (Chapter Three) for correctional institutions.

More specifically, **Immediacy** of response to a crisis is essential if control is to be maintained at the lowest possible level. Continuous adjustment to doing **What Works** to minimize error keeps the confrontation to a minimum. Continuous adjustment also supports the person in crisis (in a neutral, sensitive, and mature way) to recover her balance and to **Self Organize** without losing face. These contextual principles can form a supportive and resilient background for crisis intervention in a correctional institution. As the stabilizing background, they allow the crisis intervener to focus on various ways to address the fragile, off-balance needs for self-mastery.

Continuous focus on self-mastery serves to guide the person in crisis towards her own wisdom, allowing her to discover face-saving escape routes out of the crisis situation. For example, the crisis intervener might encourage this person to recall what has worked before when she was at risk of losing as she is now. Appeal to her ability to uncover ways in which the crisis can be de-fused until she has generated a list of possibilities and her imagination seems exhausted. By the use of this subtle process, you can generate a movement towards compromise without having to force it to happen.
There are numerous ways, depending on the nature of the crisis, to approach reducing the need for control by allowing incremental increases in power during a crisis. Some of these power tactics will now be briefly discussed.

POWER TACTICS

To give a sense of how these power tactics work within a correctional setting, five of them have been selected for review. They are the following:

1. **Co-opting**
2. **Short-Circuiting**
3. **Image Re-structuring**
4. **Distorting Distortions**
5. **Mobilizing Humour**

Before discussing these power tactics individually, a disclaimer is necessary. As techniques, they ought not be used indiscriminantly. Unless they are sensitively and compassionately adjusted to fit each unique crisis, they can actually stimulate the crisis to grow worse. In other words, they should not be used prescriptively, because some circumstances which appear to be similar may not respond similarly to the use of the same power tactic. The power tactics are described here only to facilitate self-awareness and self-exploration possibilities for those working in crisis institutions. An institutional crisis intervener would be well advised to seek approval from the institutional authorities for use of any facsimile of one of these power tactics before trying it on.

1. Co-opting

Co-opting essentially means to take in, assimilate or absorb within an institutional culture those who are in conflict with it. This power tactic is multi-faceted: it actually encompasses or blends together a number of institutionally-based crisis intervention approaches. In this regard, it has been used more as a process than as a technique.

Those well-schooled in institutional positive peer cultures and therapeutic communities will likely be familiar with co-opting as a natural outcome of shifting the counterculture of institutionalized persons toward a contra-culture or one that actually advocates prosocial goals. Co-opting is often used **within** a therapeutic community or as a special form of generating a positive peer culture. It is notable for how provocative it can be for both the institutional authorities and for the incarcerates, especially as it accentuates the competencies of both. Co-opting can produce extraordinary results if it is effectively and wholeheartedly used.

Cooperation through addressing the crisis as a challenge rather than a problem from the inmate in crisis is the primary context to be created using the co-opting process. From a Beyond Content perspective, the primary competency force attended to is Self Mastery, as manifested by the individual first and secondly by the peer group or the institutional community. Some of the major aspects of co-opting are the following:

* Inmate-centred acknowledgement that they actually do have control capabilities over the **interactive** functioning of the institutional environment, whereas the institution controls the economic, political, and external social forces. From this focus, the aim is to resource those in crisis and not the crisis per se, so that those in crisis are encouraged to control themselves. It is viewed that they can control themselves individually and as a group much more powerfully than can any sanctioned program or crisis intervention approach.

* Inmates are invited to be collaborators or cohorts in the crisis resolution process. They are immediately recognized as competent in something related to the crisis event, and they are viewed as able to respond in a responsible, accountable, disciplined, and committed way. It is the very resistance they display in a crisis that needs to be used to activate their competency resources. For example, unpredictability can be activated as creativity, and unreliability can be perceived as some form of flexibility.

* Co-opting in an institutional crisis encourages the crisis interveners to adopt more of an anthropological approach, allowing their curiosity to override the need to exercise control. Essentially, they demonstrate a fascination with the crisis, seeking to learn as much as possible from those in crisis. They do not take control unless they absolutely have to. Instead they seek out ways to make the inmate a collaborator in the crisis resolution. At every possible crisis

---

turning point, the power to dissolve the crisis issues is given to the inmate, emphasizing that the inmate, not the crisis event or the crisis intervener, has the power.

* Co-opting seeks to "de-label" or "de-pathologize" a crisis event. By focusing on client competencies, prosocial skills and personal strengths within a cohort or collaborative framework, crisis interveners can counteract negative self-fulfilling prophecies caused by problem labeling. Crises are seen as opportunities for purposeful clarification and consequent alteration of outdated responses to troublesome life events.

* This process also acknowledges the role of inmate peers as advisers and potentially (with training) as assistants, collaborators, and even educators with their peers around their crises. The increased significance that they gain in this way does not mean that they are given any authority over others or any special privileges. Rather, they are encouraged to see themselves as more and more able to assist their peers in crisis.

* Finally, the key to this process is to continuously educate inmates in ways to avoid "mis-takes" by learning how to master their institutional interactive environment within their peer structure. The control skills practiced with one another within the institution can be invaluable to them when they later regain their freedom.

Co-opting is not disguised manipulation, in order to take control over the inmate. It is also not a form of paradoxical intention to achieve behavioural change, although change and cooperation can be achieved as a natural outcome of the co-opting process. Furthermore, it is not intended to generate an artificial culture of care. It is simply a bold attempt to personify, uncover, and revitalize competencies that already exist within and between others in the institution.

Co-opting certainly is not without its drawbacks, To begin with, it cannot be done without developing a clear, well worked out approach for gradual implementation. Contingency arrangements based on how and when to abandon this process must be clearly understood, as well as authorized by the institutional hierarchy. Despite the value of co-opting, it is uncommon for an institution to grant a commitment to experiment with this process. Ironically, if such a commitment is granted, the very advantages of the approach can also cause it to be aborted. Positive results in a negative environment can easily get lost, buried, or even sabotaged, because such results often reveal the shortcomings of the institution and thereby threaten the status quo. Given that co-opting can reveal institutional shortcomings, it is best not to consider it as a technique unless it can tolerate being vulnerable as it opportunistically learns through it's mis-takes.

2.   Short-Circuiting

This power tactic diverts attention away from a crisis by cutting through a confrontation and commandeering the power of those in crisis and then redirecting it. Take

---

for example a situation in which two offenders are being verbally and physically aggressive towards one another. A short-circuiting approach would attempt to disrupt their oppositional pattern by creating a temporary state of confusion. This disruptive technique is characterized by a highly energized, yet neutral response to the crisis conflict. For example, giving one of the inmates a cigarette, a blanket, or anything that doesn't fit the crisis circumstances tends to short-circuit their current oppositional behavior causing them to be somewhat confused by this benign form of disruption. Capitalizing on their confusion, the crisis intervener then guides the two individuals away from each other. Next, the inmates are directed to express their aggression in other ways that are both justifiable and satisfying. Short-circuiting can also be effected by drawing their attention dramatically towards a concern of yours that demands immediate attention. One way in which this can be done is to loudly broadcast a fuss about something quite neutral, such as television privileges. By the crisis intervener remonstrating their upset over the need for routine and structure, they can short-circuit their attention towards the concern that television privileges are in jeopardy and that their input is needed if these prvileges are to be retained. Their attention is re-directed towards this issue, so that their blaming and oppositional behaviour becomes transferred to the crisis intervener. At the same time, the crisis intervener calmly and in a low voice guides them away from each other, appealing to their self-mastery capabilities.

Once these two in crisis have been short-circuited, they must both be given sufficient opportunity to verbally vent their frustration towards one another at a safe distance. No attempt should yet be made to reason with either of them about the issue of conflict. Once both have been somewhat de-fused, the SOURCE FORMULA can begin to be applied, taking care to heed the intervention guidelines on encountering violence outlined in Chapter Ten.

3.   **Image Re-structuring**

To survive in an institution, the individual almost invariably adopts a survival-based image of themselves, which gets expressed in the form of an ACT. Such an image imprisons the individual and actually stimulates additional behaviors that reinforce the image as a means of protecting against further loss. Since such an image is artificial and territorial, it easily gets into conflict with images of others in the institution, obviously including the institutional authorities. As a result, the image is likely to be continuously in conflict even though its intention is to protect the inmate from further anguish. Image confrontation or manipulation ensues, and the result is frequent crises. These various images can easily be identified as masks, such as those outlined in Chapter Five. Cloaking these images in institutional jargon, descriptive examples of some of them are:

*   The **"Heavy Dude or Wheel"** manipulates people by intimidation. Such people tend to be loud and pushy. They act as though nothing scares them and nothing would stop them if they were provoked; but inside they are very scared, particularly of their feelings, although they would never admit it.

*   The **"Con Man"** is pseudo-mature, declaring experience and wisdom they do

not really have. Such people think they can get whatever they want because of their cunning. They are like chameleons, wearing many different masks interchangeably in order to manipulate and control others. They tend to be self-centred and highly materialistic.

* The **"Ice Man"** is a person who has an uncaring attitude towards others and a "know-it-all" stance. This gangster type would rather be a someone's crime partner or dope partner than a genuine friend. They thrive on conflict and the suffering of others as a way of experiencing their aliveness as the value of manipulation exceeds the value of their existence.

* The **"Tragedy Queen"** looks as though an accident is always just around the corner. What such people say and how they act draw aggressive behaviour from other inmates towards them. They fear they are insignificant without a steady diet of upsets. They will even resort to self harm.

These institutional face ACTS mask the real individuals underneath, preventing those individuals from experiencing and expressing true emotions. As a result, they become extremely lonely and go without **real** relationships with other people. To live behind a false mask or ACT is to remain in prison.

Image restructuring is a power tactic that recognizes that more than one mask is possible for the incarcerate, the patient, or the client. The crisis intervener begins by searching for ways to subtly restructure a person's image in the crisis moment. The intervener then attempts to expand the new image to add new ways to react that are just as powerful but, not as destructive as the person's currently practiced ways.

For example, when encountering an "Ice Man" acting out aggressively, the crisis intervener might look for opportunities to expand the "know-it-all" attitude even further. One possible response the crisis intervener could make would be to suggest that, because they know what is happening here better than anyone, then they are the most appropriate ones to forecast the outcome. The crisis intervener could then add that, because they (the inmate) are experts about this crisis issue, they will also know how to turn this upset into a humorous affair and how to use have it to get more of what they want. In employing this tactic the crisis intervener attempts to accentuate the inmate's perception of themselves as being even more macho, or more capable than they even think they are. The outcome desired is to have such persons discover for themselves other ways to act by talking to them as if they already knew what these ways were. Careful attention is paid not to appear to be legitimizing violence or anti-social behaviour. While the potential for anti-social behaviour is acknowledged, the emphasis is placed on how to divert the person's competency to other and perhaps gradually more powerful and genuine forms of behaviour.

Restructuring the Tragedy Queen's image might be to get them to fantasize what it would be like to be a famous actor or actress given their unique life experiences to date. Exploring further the crisis intervener would attempt to enhance the Tragedy Queen's image by gradually re-structuring it with a competency based framework well accepted as an art form worthy of expression. This "value added" approach to their ACT tends to diminish the inmate's need to be so rigid in their patterned interaction of the moment.

4.   Distorting Distortions

It seldom works to tell inmates in a crisis that they are distorting the facts. Such a suggestion is often deprecating, and suggests they are to blame which they invariably cannot accept. Crises are inherently distortions - otherwise they would not be crises. The power tactic of distorting distortions is one way of using the crisis resistance as a resource. Essentially, this tactic acknowledges that crisis distortions are purposeful and it embellishes them even further. In this way it adds power to the distortions, giving them more licence to distort. Take, for example, a person in crisis who exclaims that she will never pass at school. Recognizing signs of a tragedy queen, you can explore ways of expanding this distortion. For instance, you can ask if she has a very special kind of deficiency that causes her to do poorly, or you can tell her that school failure is obviously what she wants or what others want and that she seems destined to be a victim in any educational pursuit.

In another case, someone refuses to stop taking drugs. This rebellious stance can be supported by suggesting that it is good to stand up for oneself even when doing so will eventually kill them. Giving this kind of rebel more power can take the form of telling them when they are about to harm themselves, that what they are about to do can almost never be prevented and that attempts at prevention usually only make things worse. Recounting in a lucid and thorough way how attempts at prevention usually lead to increased self-harming behaviour quite often serves as a way to reduce the need they might feel to have to continue to self-harm. In this way, the internal need for attention can undoubtedly be met by externalizing the need such that the crisis intervener's embellished story telling acts as a replacement experience.

There are countless ways to distort distortions. Of paramount importance is to ensure that this power tactic is delivered with respect and acknowledgement of the individual's need to save face in any reconsideration that they may make about their current behavior. Furthermore, the tactic of distorting distortions is intended solely to give the person a broader perspective on their behaviour, not to taunt them with the gruesome results of disaster.

5.   Mobilizing Humour

Humour is an extremely powerful antidote to a crisis. Used as a power tactic, it draws a person in crisis out of their preoccupation with either the disasters of the past or the doom of the future into a state of present awareness. Delicately employed, especially in situations that are taken too seriously, humour releases both physical and psychological tension, encouraging the person in crisis to shift away from their outrage to a lighter, more balanced stance. It diminishes the feeling of being alienated or disenfranchised. Humour is compelling and influential; it alters people's mindsets so that they become more suggestible and more compliant.

In an institution, humour, when practiced without intent to ridicule, is one of the few acceptable ways of expressing non-verbal warmth and positive regard. The masks that people wear in institutions can be acceptably revealed through humour. If the crisis intervener can use the mirror of humour to get the person laughing at themselves, they can then more easily tolerate losing face in a crisis. Combined with image restructuring, humour offers avenues for a quick recovery of significance without apparent catastrophic loss. Furthermore, this combination can uncover ways of broadening one's response capabilities by lessening the rigidity of one's face masks.

The benefits of humour obviously are too many to recount; yet humour is easily forgotten in a crisis, especially in a correctional institution. More often than not, humour is experienced as a way of diminishing others rather than of supporting them to recapture their flexibility of thinking, feeling, and being.

As an example of the use of humour as a power tactic in a correctional institution, consider an offender who is threatening to beat up somebody or to destroy something because of loss of privileges. In engaging this hyperventilating, over-exaggerating offender, the crisis intervener might attempt to gradually lighten the mood by recalling how the offender's anguish is a little like the roadrunner cartoon in which, no matter how hard the wolf tries to get the roadrunner, his traps backfire. The intent here is to get the offender to explore even further his clandestine intentions, only in a manner that is laced with humour rather than anger. In this respect, humour is actually being combined indirectly with the power tactic, distorting distortions.

Calculated humour often gets awkwardly transmitted and can be perceived as silliness or even as manipulation. But when it is spontaneously offered rather than prescribed, humour has a way of catching people off guard. Humour used in a confrontative way short-circuits the current resistance state, getting the attention of those in crisis for the moment. Take for example, the "Tragedy Queen" inmate who is creating an escalating spiral of anguish over their fear of physical violence from other inmates because they are accused of being "snitches". Confronting them by humorously startling them with a remembered comic-strip joke or by showing them something you think is humorous can shift them out of their tragedy state.

Because this type of person is easily lost in self-made traumas, the challenge is to elicit resistance to your attempts to catastrophize their plight and in so doing to reduce their hyping-up behaviour. Thereafter, ways can be sought to dissolve the crisis completely.

IN SUMMARY

The examples cited suggest that the small number of power tactics mentioned can be blended together in various combinations as is suited to the special needs of each crisis. Once again, power tactics are meant to restore a balance between loss of control and personal power. The biggest drawback to their use is the fear of giving the offender the upper hand in a crisis, at the expense of the institution. In fact, this only happens only when the reigns of power over oneself extend to having authority over others. Obviously, a true understanding of the interrelationship of power and control must precede use of any of these power tactics. Following such understanding, there must be a commitment to a crisis model if innovative and life-enhancing crisis intervention is ever to be an ongoing possibility in a correctional institution. These requirements represent an enormous challenge indeed to our established institutional systems.

SUGGESTED READINGS

1.   An excellent account of brief intervention techniques for therapists that is also quite relevant to the work of crisis interveners is Jay Haley's **Uncommon therapy** (New York: Norton, 1973). This easily digested overview of the extraordinary work of Milton Erickson chronicles the beginnings of a more transpersonal approach towards human suffering that uses hypnosis in uncommon ways.

2.   Ross & McKay, in their book **Self-Mutilation** (Toronto:Lexington Books, 1979), offer a thorough review of institutional self-harming behavior, specifically related to young girls in a training school. In particular, their chapter on Co-opting reveals how this rather provocative power tactic can be useful in correctional institutions.

3.   Farrelly's & Brandsma's book **Provocative therapy** (California:Meta Publications, 1973) presents an excellent review of the value of humour in treatment. These authors, viewing humour as an absolutely essential component of healing and offer numerous examples of how humor can serve to re-establish personal balance after a crisis.

4.   An extremely thought provoking analysis of how powerlessness corrupts and of how self-empowerment is thwarted by self-defeating attempts to over-control social conditions is presented in Micheal Lerner's **Surplus powerlessness** (California:Institute of Labor & Health, 1986). This unique book is indispensible for anyone interested in exploring ways to create meaningful transformations in our social institutions.

NOTES

NOTES

CHAPTER SIXTEEN

CRISIS CENTRE CALLS

There are really only two questions. Questions that have no answer
are all the same. They request only that you become uncertain and
conflicted. All other questions arrive at a single answer and ask that
you accept relief. Real questions answer themselves . . .

- Hugh Prather

GENERAL ISSUES

Being on the receiving end of a crisis telephone call is, by its very nature, an impoverished and therefore risky affair. More often than not, a telephone crisis call can leave the crisis intervener feeling incomplete and vulnerable to abuse or misuse. The telephone is an incredibly powerful instrument, with the capability to cut across many crisis barriers (Miller, 1973). In crisis circumstances, the telephone quickly bypasses time and space issues. Persons in crisis choosing to call out for support through the use of the telephone can transmit their anguish in bits and pieces, without feeling the same inhibitions that face-to-face encounters would bring. These persons in crisis can easily develop expectations of the crisis intervener or feel dependent after having their voices connect. Spared the need for any social restraint and interpersonal "ice breaking", they can spill out their anguish with seeming impunity. Furthermore, they are really the ones in control of the interaction, because the calling was up to them in the first place, and it is within their power to end the contact at any time.

Since the communication is largely restricted to auditory information, the crisis intervener is also at the mercy of the willingness of these persons in crisis to share. This vulnerability, like a magnet, tends to draw the crisis intervener towards trying to rescue or be helpful, depending upon the crisis story heard. Words become the imperfect medium with which the crisis intervener struggles with to communicate, and these words always seem woefully inadequate. The crisis intervener, not in a controlling position, treads lightly, often fearful that his or her words will hurt even though the intention is otherwise. Ironically, such sensitivity frequently prepares the ground for the person in crisis to perceive the crisis intervener as a source of hope in their moments of hopelessness. The people in crisis can quickly gravitate towards demanding that the crisis intervener absolve their of the responsibility for their present crisis. In short, a transference relationship can easily become an outfall of the process of telephone crisis call intervention.

Further complicating this auditory affair is the distortion of information that can easily occur because of the restricted visual and affective information available. It becomes risky for the crisis intervener, because they may fall into the trap of attempting to complete their understanding of the crisis using their own visual and affective data arising from their own past experiences that appear similar to the presently shared crisis story. That is, the crisis intervener may be tempted to fill in the blanks of the crisis story with information from their own point of view, generated from their own past experiences. In this way, a "personalized" simulation of the current crisis is developed from very limited information. This simulated picture is often quite useful; yet it is limited, restricting, and sometimes tangentially misleading.

Moreover, it is not uncommon for the crisis intervener to quickly become somewhat attached to the person in crisis. This apparently happens as it is extremely easy for the crisis intervener to become naturally intrigued with the similarities of their own unfinished life crises with that of the person in crisis. The result is that the crisis intervener tends to easily develop a loosely imbedded investment in the crisis melodrama. Though counter-transference possibilities such as this are common and can occur in any crisis situation, telephone crisis intervention offers one of the most provocative mediums for this to occur. For those interested in a thorough review of these hazards and of other issues related to telephone crisis intervention, both Miller (1973) and Lester, et. al. (1973) have covered the issues in detail.

A BEYOND CONTENT APPROACH

It is interesting to note that, although most crisis interveners perceive a crisis caller as the one out of control, the crisis intervener is usually more out of control than the caller. As already mentioned, the caller largely controls the intervention. On the other hand, the crisis intervener is often perceived by those in crisis as having extraordinary powers to help them out of their helplessness. The challenge for the Beyond Content crisis intervener is not to get trapped into a rescuer-victim scenario, in which control becomes the primary way to stabilize the crisis. To avoid entrapment, it is essential to adhere to the principle of psychological neutrality while maintaining a posture of compassionate support.

Those involved in daily crisis calls, would do well to regularly review the ten contextual crisis intervention principles over a five-or-ten minute pre-work preparation period. Doing so tends to mobilize the essence of these principles through one's voice in a natural, quite conscious way. Trying to remember these principles when entrenched in a crisis call can create awkwardness and communicate a lack of assurance that the crisis will come to a successful conclusion.

Guidelines to consider when using the SOURCE formula with crisis calls will now be outlined. Since previous chapters have covered many crisis topics in detail, using the SOURCE formula, the guidelines offered here are meant to be generic. For easy reference, they are listed in point form.

Sharing

1. Making a connection in a crisis call starts with the very first words of introduction. If you preface the introduction with your first name, you become identifiable at least by label, and increases chances of making a connection. Avoid using introductory phrases such as "How can I help you?".

2. Within the first five minutes, encourage the person in crisis to give you, at the very least, their first name and optimally their telephone number.

3. Preface all communication with the first name of the person in crisis. Doing this repeatedly will further personalize the sharing and will tend to generate a sense that the person in crisis is important.

4. When someone is acting like a tyrant or rebel, hear their whole story without interruption until they begin to repeat themselves. Then share your curiosity about key words they use, and confirm with them that you are hearing the story correctly.

5. Share that it is evident to you they trust themselves enough to make this call (a competency acknowledgement).

6. Share your purpose as soon as possible, and indicate any restraints around your availability.

7. Upon encountering someone acting like a victim seeking consolation, share slowly and intersperse dialogue with moments of silence in a patient, non-demanding way. Be concrete and neutral in your statements. Allow your patience to ward off any frustration that you might feel about not hearing enough from them. Encourage one-or-two word answers by preceding questions with statements such as "John, when I hear someone say they don't know what to do anymore, it makes me want to support them to uncover what they need to do about their situation. Do you want me to do that?"

8. Share yourself as someone balanced and open by pacing along with the person in crisis (maintaining roughly the same energy rhythm) and trying to match their predominant perceptual way of being. Doing this will deepen a trusting connection.

Observing

1. To observe in a telephone-call situation is a challenging task to say the least, since by virtue of the circumstances the visual mode is unavailable. Get the person in crisis to

describe to you in visual terms what their crisis is like. Encourage themher to do this by commenting on possible analogies to their situation.

2. Observe by listening with "soft ears." Start by being psychologically neutral and dis-identifying with the crisis issue; then listen for rhythm, flow, and context as opposed to the meaning of the words shared.

3. Observe by listening to the crisis story as a rough inadequate facsimile or map of the unfathomable crisis territory. Keep reminding yourself that usually more than three quarters of what is said is not what is really meant. Allow the words to flow past, and tune in to shifts in tonal affect. Note such shifts in tonal affect as signals of underlying emotional trouble spots relating to the crisis event. This will allow you to stay focused on the pattern of communication rather than the content of the crisis story. By focusing on undercurrent patterns of dissonance the true crisis need can be discovered with less confusion and needless attention to secondary issues.

4. Observe by listening as if you were them speaking, allowing your own intuition to create a visual awareness of what is possibly missing or what is needed to resolve their crisis. This way of listening is often experienced by the person in crisis, as if you were really experiencing their inner as well as their outwardly expressed anguish.

5. Observe by listening for turning points in their emotional stability when they become more aware of the possible options for resolving the crisis.

6. When listening, be aware that a natural tendency to look down at the telephone predisposes our dialogue to focus on internal affective concerns. It is useful to initially adopt this downward-looking posture to get a "felt sense" of the emotional state of the crisis. Once this is obtained, shift your body to allow your visual field to expand upwards and around, keeping a scanning profile with all your senses operating. This change in body state tends to encourage the person in crisis to odopt an alignment to a more visually upbeat mind as well as body state.

Uncovering

1. Ask to talk on the telephone with any others immediately available and involved in the crisis, if any, and check to make sure that you don't leave anyone out. In so doing, you ensure that all resources that each person might bring to the crisis situation are identified or uncovered.

2. Check for crisis integrity state, evaluate what roles or acts are being portrayed, and determine the primary perceptual mode of communication.

3. Assess the risk level of harm to self or other's and, if appropriate, call in supports such as relatives, neighbors, friends or the police. Whenever police involvement seems warranted, have the call made by someone directly involved or immediately available

---

and knowledgeable about the situation. Advise whoever is able and willing to call the police on what to say about the level of risk and what form of assistance from the police would be most beneficial. Check afterwards to make sure this support person was satisfied with the outcome.

4. In an unobtrusive way, allow your natural curiosity to thoroughly uncover what dangers exist in the immediate environment, such as guns, drugs, alcohol, automobiles, bridges, and other such environmental hazards. Do not let shyness or fear of upsetting the person in crisis deter you from inquiring about the risks.

5. Discover if at present or in the past if the person in crisis has called any other resources, such as hospitals, clergymen, community support organizations, drug and alcohol programmes, school counsellors, therapists, treatment centres, or distress centres.

6. Find out whether any important anniversary dates related to past tragedies or milestone events are upcoming.

7. Almost always, the person in crisis wants something to happen immediately. Discover what this might be.

Resourcing

1. Through the process of speaking individually to all those involved in the crisis, determine what competencies could ameliorate the crisis situation. Encourage the natural use of community resources first, before suggesting the potential availability of professional resources.

2. Invite the person in crisis to tell you if you can be of assistance through a home visit (if any are able) or in a meeting at a neutral place as appropriate. With respect to a home visit, offer yourself or your crisis team to all those involved and state that you need everyone's consent. If the people in conflict with this person in crisis would or do not consent to a home visit, you may consider asking this person to consider a place outside of their residence.

3. After creating a visual picture of the crisis situation through the uncovered information, have at least three mutually established or agreed-upon client competencies either implicitly or explicitly be considered as resources for use in alleviating some of the crisis stress.

4. Ensure that immediate relief is experienced by the person in crisis from employing or activating some of the resources that have been uncovered.

5. As the need arises, offer suggestions of possible resources to further resolve the crisis. Such suggestions should be given only when it is perceived that the person or persons

in crisis can hear them as possible resources and be open to entertaining the idea of making contact with them.

Completing

1. Completing on the telephone entails patiently persevering until the person(s) in crisis make(s) a commitment to a recovery course of action.

2. Completing the crisis involvement, entails calling back after two or three weeks, or, in some cases, two or three days, to see if anything else is needed.

3. To terminate the call, offer a summary of the agreements and undertakings made and request that each person state their understanding and acceptance of what is next.

Expanding

1. Since nearly all crises handled by telephone are efforts to establish a beginning level of support, rarely does one go significantly beyond the pre-crisis state of stability.

2. When the opportunity does present itself the crisis intervener could suggest ordeals that would serve to carry the person towards achieving a transformative experience. Such ordeals include home or community work that focuses on the persons learning something or uncovering something about their life circumstances. Such ordeals are usually quite simple, yet they require a willingness on the part of the person in crisis to exert some effort. For example, a person unable to sleep may be asked to get up every time their sleep pattern is interrupted, and iron clothes for at least one hour. Expanded awareness need not be achieved immediately. Often if a seed is planted in the form of a suggestion, a delayed reaction results in an awareness breakthrough sometime after the crisis event.

IN SUMMARY

In summary, listening to someone's crisis on the telephone involves much more than just hearing it. Listening requires an open and empty mind, free to recognize subtle changes in communication. In an effort to lead the reader to some kind of awareness of how it might be for the person on the other end of the telephone, a dialogue is now presented. This dialogue has been synthesized from many readings, may crisis calls, many written and spoken statements of others, and from my own transpersonal learnings. As such, its authorship belongs to countless others.

ON LISTENING: BETWEEN YOU AND ME

Don't be fooled by what I say.
What comes out of my mouth almost never has anything to do with what is going on with me.

For I wear a mask, many masks that I am afraid to take off, yet none of them are really me.

Beneath lies my mind's voice that tells me to hide my confusion, my fear, my aloneness; to sometimes run away, and to sometimes strike out.

That voice inside seems to rule me. It tells me that being myself is not enough!

I don't want anyone to know this.
I panic at the though of being vulnerable and fear being exposed.

I am afraid you'll think less of me, that you will laugh at me, and that your laugh will kill me.

I am afraid that deep down I'm nothing, that I am no good, and that, as in the past, I will be abandoned and rejected by you.

I play out my ACT, my desperate melodrama, in search of relief from my felt sense of awkwardness, ugliness, and worthlessness. I try hard, hard as I can to win, to show you, to beat you to the punch. And so begins a parade of masks.

I'll tell you everything that really is nothing. So, please read between the lines. Hear what I am not saying. Do not listen to literal meanings.

Listen for my essence. My voice reveals in many subtle ways: My incomplete sentences, my innuendos, my omissions, my preoccupations, my excitement. Listen and you will know what I am really saying.

I want you to hold out your hand, even when that's the last thing I seem to want or need. I really want your essence to call me to my own aliveness.

It doesn't make sense, I fight against the very thing I cry out for. Don't give up, even if I do.
Your freedom is also mine. We are related.

SUGGESTED READINGS

1. In addition to the two references mentioned in this Chapter (Brockopp, 1973; Miller, 1973), Everstine & Everstine, in their book **People in crisis** (New York: Bruner Mazel, 1983), outline some of the major crisis call issues encountered by an Emergency Treatment Centre. Chapter three, in particular, describes how the Emergency Treatment Centre responds to the first telephone contact with a person in crisis and what to do in case of an emergency.

2. Another very practical account of telephone intervention is available in **Crisis counselling** (New York: Continuum, 1984), by Eugene Kennedy. In this book, Kennedy covers concerns related to chronic callers, the importance of records, special problems, and also the way in which the telephone generates its own unique crisis-intervention concerns.

NOTES

NOTES

SECTION V

TOWARDS COMPETENCY

The final two chapters essentially focus on how to take action so as to produce meaningful results with the Beyond Content model. It might be said that knowledge without disciplined action is the beginning of delusion. On the other hand, disciplining yourself to take action creates breakthroughs in competency. Putting it another way, as Bob Dylan suggests, "He who is not busy being born is busy dying".

Chapter Seventeen begins the journey towards competency by outlining ways to enhance and maintain crisis intervention skills beyond just "coping" or getting by. In this respect, it covers three main topics: crisis consultation, crisis debriefing and crisis teamwork.

Beginning with crisis consultation, it supports the view that consultants are essential allies to ensuring the crisis intervener's competencies flourish and make a difference regardless of the degree of difficulty encountered in a crisis. More importantly, it ensures the crisis intervener stays on track with their natural integrity, remains clear about their purpose, seizes every opportunity to be innovative and competency-focused and demonstrates how to be in charge of life's dilemmas rather than the dilemmas being in charge of them. Guidelines are offered for crisis consultants on how to maximize their value to crisis interveners and correspondingly suggestions on how to program the use of consultants is also presented. This chapter goes on to outline step-by-step ways to make crisis debriefing an invaluable process with other crisis intervention associates. Completing this chapter are suggestions for those who team up with others in their intervention work. These suggestions focus on working styles, teamwork preparation and ways to support each other.

Chapter Eighteen concludes this book by reflecting back on the basic assumptions of the Beyond Content model and compares this model with generic broad banded traditional crisis intervention assumptions. In light of the differences and similarities comments are offered regarding the limitations of the Beyond Content model. These comments are followed with a discussion on the perils of travelling on the Beyond Content pathway. Issues such as maintaining a personal commitment to wellness, how to address personal burnout, what to do about the lack of consensus support for a contextual approach to crisis intervention and how to share this model with others are discussed.

Finally, the question of what to do next with this approach to crisis intervention is posited. In this regard, suggestions are offered on specifically how to incorporate this crisis intervention framework into one's daily practice. As well, what's next speaks to the need for an enthusiast to regularly discipline herself to practice the evolving art of self-observation, to seek out associates who are willing to be co-conspirators along the path of competency self-mastery and to form networks of support for the journey. Completing the step beyond is some indication of the immeasurable sense of empowerment and self-mastery that can be achieved when one begins to discover how to forecast outcomes in one's crisis intervention work.

CHAPTER SEVENTEEN

SELF MAINTENANCE AND SKILL ENHANCEMENT

Nature attains perfection, but man never (in his view) never does. There is a perfect ant, a perfect bee, but man is perpetually unfinished. He is both an unfinished animal and an unfinished man. It is this incurable unfinishedness which sets man apart from other living things for, in the attempt to finish himself, man becomes a creator. Moreover, the incurable unfinishedness keeps man perpetually immature, perpetually capable of learning and growth.

- Eric Hoffer

This chapter explores three process oriented activities that are invaluable to crisis interveners if they are to remain flexible, vibrant, and in balance. Essentially, they serve as de-contaminating processes and promote on-going enhancement of the effectiveness of the crisis intervener's work. Beginning with the activity of crisis consultation, several primary tasks are outlined in an effort to clarify how to most effectively use crisis consultation. Also discussed are example questions that might be asked by a consultant, along with format possibilities for presenting a crisis scenario to a consultant. The aim is to support the meaningfulness of crisis consultation as an enriching resource, significant in its value as a process that can facilitate fine-tuning of crisis intervention competencies.

The second activity, a cleansing process referred to as crisis de-briefing, is not to be confused with crisis consultation. While crisis de-briefing can occur simultaneously with crisis consultation, the two activities actually form different, though inter-linked, aspects of the crisis intervention self-maintenance and skill-enhancing fabric. De-briefing is a process that needs to occur after every crisis as a completing experience. De-briefing minimizes the ingraining of limiting crisis response patterns and reduces the buildup of counter-productive stress in the crisis workplace. De-briefing can be done by a colleague, by a supervisor, or, as already suggested, by a consultant. In an effort to clarify how crisis de-briefing can be of value a de-briefing protocol is offered as a rough guide. It is designed to be used, modified, and expanded upon in accordance with each individual's unique crisis intervention needs and the needs of the sponsoring organization.

The third activity is about how to establish a synergistic team approach to crisis intervention. This chapter offers suggestions on how to function as a co-leader or guide.

CRISIS CONSULTATION

Re-Tracking

Unquestionably there are many detours and hazards which undermine effective intervention and tend to diminish the competency of the crisis intervener. The territory of crisis intervention, by its very nature, contaminates those who enter into it. Eventually, such contamination throws even the most dedicated crisis intervener off balance, causing her to become side-tracked, dead-ended and exhausted by the apparent inability to make a difference. Crisis consultation can be one way out of this darkness when used effectively.

There are many obvious benefits of crisis consultation, not the least of which is its capability to move us from the dangerous ground of surface or calculated thinking to deep thinking or primal awareness. Calculative thought is "bound-up" or "re-presented" thought, habitually re-constructed from our cultural and personal memory experience. Consultation can free us from this bound-up awareness and the consequent inner mind conflict. When it works well it serves to open us to a unifying vision of our natural wisdom working in harmony with our practice. By modeling centredness and balance consultants can really act as a reflection, showing up how we have disowned or covered up aspects of ourselves. An effective crisis consultant reveals to us our shadow and encourages us to make use of it by re-incorporating it rather than fighting or avoiding it. Crisis consultation can stimulate our contemplative nature, awakening us to many ways of thinking and perceiving a crisis situation.

While crisis consultation can assist us out of dead-ends by enriching our viewpoints and adding depth to our service, it can also awaken dormant or uncover clouded over intuitive skills. These re-vived skills can be re-tracked to expand the options available, so that many intervention possibilities begin to surface. Yet, all too often, operating out of respect and recognition of a consultants' expertise the tendency is to reluctantly use consultation without a clearly extablished, previously worked out, and mutually accepted frame of reference. This results in the consultation process often being a "hit or miss" experience. Nevertheless, the mechanics of operationalizing crisis consultation are simple and straight forward when guided by the crisis intervention principles suggested in Chapter Two. The crisis intervener or crisis service would be well advised to clarify these mechanics with a prospective consultant prior to implementing a consultation process.

Some suggested baseline operational needs from the consultation process will now be briefly mentioned, as a guide to stimulate clarification of these needs. These requirements include guidelines for both the consultant and for the crisis intervener using the consultant.

Consultant Guidelines

From a Beyond Content framework perspective, a crisis service and a prospective consultant would likely want to come to some agreement around how and the service needs or the program mandate could be enhanced by consultation. The primary needs might generate the following

---

consultant guidelines:

1.   Provide, in a supportive and augmentive way, ongoing affirmation of the crisis intervener's competency and further, that success can be achieved when one remains committed to a wellness based crisis intervention approach.

2.   More specifically contribute by assisting the crisis intervener by focusing on refining current intervention strategies.

3.   Stimulate the **natural** wisdom of the crisis intervener. This is an awakening task with the aim of stimulating deep thinking or primal awareness.

4.   Offer educational information when crisis intervener experience suggests the need for more information than presently known.

5.   Add professional and diagnostic treatment expertise in the form of concrete and utilitarian suggestions in accordance with the ability and experience of the crisis intervener.

6.   Clarify the worst fears of a crisis intervener and offer suggestions on how these fears can be addressed in a vital yet opportunistic way.

7.   Identify how and when both client and crisis intervener disloyalty and confrontation impact on crisis intervention effectiveness. Also, offer suggestions on how the intervener can be decontaminated from the after-effects of a crisis.

The most effective consultant is one who stimulates exploration when there appears to be nothing left to explore. This kind of consultant serves not as an expert but as a guide only offering their own specific experience about crises as a secondary aspect of the consultation process. By modelling an inquisitive yet contemplative stance, the consultant can often inspire crisis interveners make a shift towards expanding their awareness by viewing the crisis as an opportunity to make a contribution to others.

Agreeing on the approach to be employed by a consultant is one matter. Actually making effective use of a consultant is another. Some pitfalls, as well as suggestions for the effective use of the consultant by the crisis intervener, will now be considered.

Using A Consultant

Crisis consultation is often considered to be either a luxury or a service that cannot be easily integrated within the chaotic workspace of a crisis service. Ironically, it seems that there is an underlying tendency to avoid crisis consultation, as the concept suggests to some crisis interveners that they are less than adequate in some crisis situations. Since this suggestion is generally considered to be intolerable, the crisis intervener is likely to overlook the need for consultation as a way of reducing the possibility of showing any vulnerability. When clear awareness of this territorial-like tendency is experienced, the challenge is to overcome it by boldly designing the service to have

---

consultation be mandatory. When this type of crisis intervener maturity prevails, consultation can enhance intervener competency immeasurably. When it does not, often a crisis intervener or crisis service gradually loses vibrancy and increasingly becomes burdened with the contamination of unresolved crisis-intervention experiences.

The process of discounting the utility of crisis consultation is often subtle, covert, and insidious. The discounting is frequently done silently and justified by a pseudo-caring reason that is really not necessary to burden anyone with some unresolved issues of the past. In this regard, it is not uncommon for crisis interveners to minimize their crisis experiences and consequently argue that it is unnecessary to use up the consultant's valuable time by bothering them with inconsequential issues. A crisis intervener, in a respectful-like manner, might be heard discounting with statements such as:

* It's too late to bother the consultant now.
* It's unnecessary, as nothing is going to change anyway.
* I forgot.
* I will wait until I have more information.
* I don't think that anyone can help in this crisis.

The crisis intervener needs to counteract these perceptions with a well-anchored injunction that self-understanding and personal power as an intervener are almost always significantly enhanced when consultation is sought. Consultation can act as a powerful catalyst to generate more options, produce more crisis turning points for change, and generate a renewed sense of competence. The impact on those in crisis can be immeasurable.

Crisis consultation needs to be a two-way sharing process. It is important not to let professional status or posturing interfere with this process. Therefore, openly declare what you want from a consultant, and consider the request for both scheduled and impromptu consultation to be a mutual privilege for both parties.

Scheduled consultation generally produces a clearer and more educationally focused understanding of the crisis than does impromptu crisis consultation. It can serve to better prepare the crisis intervener for follow-up intervention as well as to expand awareness of how to act more effectively in similar future crises. For most consultations, it is important to know that it is not necessary to share all the details of a crisis event. Besides, such sharing often takes up too much valuable time. While the crisis story might be interesting, the consultant is of most benefit when responding as a receptive and humble detective, searching for patterns and information gaps. In searching and probing, the aim of the consultant would be is to uncover new resources as well as pathways out of the crisis maze of the moment.

The emphasis in consultation should be primarily on the present, although the future as well as the past should be addressed insofar as they contribute to the present crisis need. Moreover, the consultant would do well to highlight both the disruptive as well as the harmonious patterns of interaction of those in crisis. In so doing the correlation of these opposite conditions often reveals previously unconsidered strategies for intervention.

Some possible questions that a consultant could consider asking are the following:

* What are the primary presenting problems?
* What resources are lacking?
* Who, primarily, is initiating the crisis?
* Who is most controlling, most powerful in the crisis situation?
* Who is most out of control?
* What resources have been tried and might be tried?
* What is unclear and what is presently clear about the crisis situation?

The crisis consultant might also perception-check the understanding of the crisis intervener with questions such as these:

* Can this (intervention technique) work for you?
* This (outcome) may happen. What would you do then?
* Some possible interventions might be . . . Which ones could you see fitting for you in this crisis?

Knowing ahead of time the answer to some or all of these questions does not preclude the need for a consultant. Often the crisis intervener can benefit from hearing their own responses broadcasted aloud rather than just inside their head. This process serves to reveal gaps in information, to synthesize insights, and to release personal blockages that interfere with the intervener's committed purpose. Knowing what questions might be asked actually reinforces the experience of an aligned yet independent partnership with the consultant. Developing this type of arm's length partnership can greatly enhance the efficiency of the consultation process, with both parties able to quickly move towards the same objectives. Therefore it would be wise for a crisis intervener to sit down and roughly identify the questioning framework that the consultant would use. Developing an understanding and acceptance of the process can serve to de-mystify as well as increase confidence and acceptance of this consultation process.

Finally, to make best use of scheduled crisis consultations, the crisis intervener needs to come prepared with well thought-out questions that they want to explore within a framework that makes best use of the consultant's time and expertise. From a generic perspective a crisis review format with a consultant might include the following:

* A brief statement about the person(s) in crisis, covering their age, living situation, physical, mental, emotional status, the crisis state of integrity and their predominating mode of operating in the crisis event.

* The presenting problems, who they affect, the recurrences of problems, current status, risk level.

* A statement about what purpose does the crisis serve; emphasizing the payoff to those involved.

* An account of the resources available, both tried and untried.

* A review of the interventions tried by self and others.

* An account of the presently identifiable competencies related to the crisis event.

Presenting in a thoughtful and disciplined way exemplifies a commitment to pursue excellence and honors the consultation process. Such presentation produces an excitement about the consultation process based on the expectation of meaningful results. This excitement can be contagious, spreading to those co-workers around a crisis intervener and ultimately fostering a co-creative environment aimed at getting results.

In summary, crisis consultation can operate as a kind of "third eye" for a crisis intervener. It can allow for quick recovery of the resources available in the environment and can be of immeasurable value in supporting the competency of the crisis intervener. As a mirroring process, it can reveal blind spots in the crisis interveners' vision, allowing for a continuous and growthful development of crisis intervention skills.

CRISIS DE-BRIEFING

To begin with, it is important not to confuse crisis consultation with crisis de-briefing even though these two activities are often inter-linked with the consultant and the de-briefer often being one and the same person. As a retrospective cleansing process, de-briefing is more likely to be done by a colleague or a supervisor and can be a significant aspect of team-building.
More crudely speaking, crisis de-briefing is a little like regurgitating your food. It is not something that you necessarily relish doing. In fact, it is normally repressed whenever possible. Yet, when done, it almost always reduces tension and re-establishes a sense of balance for those involved in crisis intervention.

To counteract our mind's pre-disposition to be lazy, slothful, and ignoring requires a commitment to go beyond our limitations. Crisis de-briefing challenges us to do that. It supports our taking what is good for us, even though it may not be judged good by our mind. For crisis de-briefing to be meaningful, it must be done regularly-like jogging. When done regularly it pays off, even though on some days we would rather do anything else but. In your work space, make a commitment to it and do it religiously. Condition yourself to do it by regularly rewarding and acknowledging yourself and others who follow-through with this process.

As part of your professional development, advocate for compulsory de-briefing. Have it sanctified. Better yet, encourage or even demand that it be modelled by those responsible for the development of your service area. Do not be satisfied with just a written incident report form of de-briefing. This linear mapping of a crisis event is at best an impoverished viewpoint, easily misinterpreted and highly prone to critical judgement rather than acknowledgement. More often than not, written reports primarily serve organizational survival rather than crisis intervener aliveness.

A DE-BRIEFING PROTOCOL

If you and your service area rise to the occasion and commit to de-briefing your crisis interventions, what about working guidelines? From the contextual Beyond Content model, a generic protocol is suggested. Clearly, this protocol is less than sufficient to fit the uniqueness of most work settings. Therefore, you will have to reflect from time-to-time just how you might adopt or adjust the protocol or even use it to stimulate you to develop your own protocol. This protocol can be initiated with the assistance of the following guidelines:

* First, schedule the de-briefing to occur as soon after the crisis event as possible. Leaving it longer than a day after immeasurably diminishes its value.

* Establish a daily ritual around it, like clinical rounds in a hospital, and make the ritual mandatory.

* Unless it is absolutely essential, do not let minor crises in the workplace take precedence over de-briefing.

* Agree to a process that efficiently uses the time available to complete current de-briefing needs. If need be, allow all crises handled by those involved in the de-briefing to be mentioned, knowing that some are on-going and that continued review will be necessary. Ensure that those crises that are still incomplete are priorized for later review.

Now the protocol for de-briefing presented here includes five steps. They are:

1. Establish Time Limits
2. Allow for Crisis Story Telling
3. Support Frustration Release
4. Conduct Perception Checking
5. Engage in Appreciation Sharing

1. **Establishing Time Limits**

Before beginning, the de-briefer in consultation with the crisis intervener would agree to a set period of time for the complete de-briefing process. Within this time alloted a sub set of time would be established for story telling part of the debriefing process. Once this is done, uninterrupted story telling or rehashing of the crisis event can be entertained without risk of the story telling drifting and becoming overly time consuming. Optimally, there should be no more than ten minutes for story telling, in the interests of making effective use of valuable time. However, on rare occasions, more time may be essential, because of the need for further intervention clarity. On such occasions, it is wise to reach an agreement with all concerned that such time is needed at the expense of other tasks.

---

2. Crisis Story Telling

From a crisis context, sharing the crisis events with another person is usually an uncomfortable experience and one often avoided. Often huge gaps in information occur because the crisis intervener naturally leaves out parts that might reflect negatively on her competency or bring back feelings of discomfort. Most crisis stories tend to be explanations of why the crises turned out the way they did. They are almost invariably told to make the crisis intervener look right and others wrong, confirming the intervener's superiority of understanding or their authority. Interestingly enough, none of these reasons told through story-telling ultimately generate a sense of satisfaction. Story-telling is nonetheless very valuable for cathartic reasons alone. Moreover, it can stimulate us to awaken our underlying natural capabilities to deal with future similar crises.

Telling the story in an uninterrupted fashion gives the crisis intervener breathing room and the opportunity to self-explore in a less defensive manner. The same artful listening skills used in sizing up a crisis can be practiced in the de-briefing process by the de-briefer. Remind yourself as a crisis de-briefer that less that 30% of the story can actually be accurately told. So listen for congruence in the flow of the story and patiently wait until a full sense of the crisis story has been shared before seeking clarification of incongruence or of fragmented issues. No attempt should be made to question or advise at this point. The crisis de-briefer can best facilitate this being a natural interactive process by periodically offering encouraging acknowledgements of congruent aspects of what is shared. After the story has been fully heard, questions can be asked. The questions should be designed to invoke or stimulate the relief of bound-up frustrations and resentments.

3. Frustration Release

By encouraging the release of pent-up frustrations in an abreactive way, de-briefing can be of significant value in de-contaminating the crisis intervener after a crisis experience. The process is simple and educational in focus. It is meant to support venting rather than to be a form of therapy. Examples of questions that the crisis de-briefer might wish to ask at this stage are as follows:

* What was said that frustrated you?
* Did you experience any dissatisfaction from those in crisis about your intervention efforts?
* What losses were you trying to avoid, as the crisis intervener?
* Did you experience being resented? If so, how did they demonstrate this?
* What did you want to work and it didn't?

These and other questions like them, are more challenging of unfinished personal issues than most people anticipate, for they provoke "self-remembering" as well as "self-exploration" of current personal limitations. As the de-briefer, exercise patience

---

and acknowledge the crisis intervener as often as they risk sharing their vulnerability. As this process unfolds, a releasing effect will likely be experienced. Clues evidencing this might be body reactions such as sighing, changing to a more laid-back body position, adopting a contemplative aura, or reflecting a "talked out" state. After allowing this shift to settle in for a few minutes, the next step could be to "perception-check" to see if anything else needs to be shared, uncovered, or added in order to dissolve any residual resentments or frustrations.

4. **Perception-Checking**

This is a straight forward matter of the crisis de-briefer's asking a number of open-ended questions. Some of these might be:

* Is there anything unfinished for you?
* Is there anything you need or want to say to someone?
* If you are incomplete in any way, can you or are you willing to complete without having the person(s) in question there?
* What would you like to do now to advance your competency as a crisis intervener?
* What is next for you?

The final step taken to complete the debriefing experience is to engage in the delightful, energy-charging process of appreciation sharing. The manner in which the crisis intervener responds to questions such as these will reveal the degree to which they have recaptured a natural state of integrity. A fully recaptured state will be self evident to the crisis intervener and obvious to the debriefer as it will be hallmarked by a renewed sense of vigor and enthusiasm for taking on new challenges.

5. **Appreciation-Sharing**

This process starts with the de-briefer encouraging the crisis intervener to reflect back on their crisis intervention experiences from an altogether different perspective. This shift in focus involves the crisis intervener, firstly, creating a visual re-run of the crisis event with themselves in it. Then as a compassionate witness they begin teasing out of the crisis experience; any actions no matter how small, that warrant appreciation. In specific terms this retracing of the crisis experience, as guided by the crisis de-briefer, involves a careful recounting of the comments or actions that were made to them that were really implicit forms of appreciations. For example, a person in crisis might have listened attentively for a moment, accepted a suggestion, opologized for outrageous behavior, demonstrated some level of patience, showed some fleeting signs of compassion or consideration for others or even reluctant cooperation. If little or nothing surfaces in this scanning process the de-briefer encourages several re-runs until overlooked or covered-up possibilities surface.

Shifting the focus of this mental reenactment onto the part played by the crisis intervener, the de-briefer encourages the crisis intervener to entertain appreciation-based self-examination. Questions that could be asked in achieving this outcome are:

* What were you appreciated for verbally by others?
* What were you appreciated for non-verbally by others?
* What did you appreciate about yourself?
* What did you want appreciation for?
* What do you want appreciation for right now?

It is extremely important that the de-briefer persist with these types of questions until an emotional response is emitted reflecting a willingnesss to accept praise and self acknowledgement. Care is also taken in this process to ensure the crisis intervener avoids discounting statements, succombing to shyness or alternatively to entertain false pride.

Once revealed, the appreciations need to be anchored initially as examples of the crisis intervener competencies. For example competencies such as consideration and calmness can be physically anchored in the crisis intervener's body by repetitively having them reenact calmness as they breathe out and consideration as they breathe in. At the same time visual reminders of how they looked at the time as well as what looks they received from others can be used to strengthen the felt sense of appreciation. Anchoring these acknowledgments is absolutely essential to re-establishing balance after a crisis event and to ensure that benefit is gained from the crisis experience. Successful anchoring requires sensitive and repetitive effort on the part of the de-briefer to first, generate a positive emotionally charged state and secondly to discover unique trigger points (words, emotions or visual stimuli) that can re-generate the desired competency state.

The crisis de-briefer, in addition to acting as an appreciation detective for all concerned seeks to complete by reviewing the de-briefing process itself so as to reveal the contributory value of different parts of the process. To conclude the de-briefer could declare the obvious by acknowledging how the willingness to de-brief does make a difference. Often this can be accomplished by simply offering "thank-yous" to all concerned. While this is obvious, declaring the obvious is necessary, for the tendency is to assume that the obvious is understood when it may not be felt that way. The process of crisis de-briefing is really a gift of mutual learning between those involved. The crisis de-briefer would therefore do well to acknowledge the crisis intervener's contribution to the debriefer as well as the intervener's willingness to share in the process. Appreciation-sharing can, if we let it, open up expansive thinking and being. When allowed to become an integral part of crisis work, it has a refreshing, yet tranquil, effect on those who participate.

CRISIS TEAMWORK

Whether you work in a hospital emergency ward, community out-patient clinic, drop-in centre, school, correctional facility, or any setting in which more than one of you have a mandate to serve others in crises, the opportunity to **team up** can be richly rewarding. It is a helping art form we have yet to fully master - to deeply connect, collaborate, and cooperate psychologically with colleagues while serving someone extremely troubled by life's circumstances. All the gurus, the masters, the supervisors, the professors, and professionals can do little for us compared to what true partners can do for and with each other when they align. This is not a state of instant intimacy or in any way an invasion of a person's privacy. It is a state driven by a common purpose. Contrary to what we might think, our individuality, as well as our competency, is actually enhanced when we dare to work as a collective. When we work alone, we often shadow-box what we cannot see in ourselves. In teams, we have an opportunity to exponentially diminish as well as de-energize one another's shadows or projections. Working inter-dependently with another crisis worker is like operating as two sides of the same coin, neither casting shadows on the other.

When two or more crisis interveners have a common purpose, each can experience a synergy effect wherein the partnership is bigger than the individuals alone. Crisis teamwork has the potential to uncover many more real breakthrough possibilities for those in crisis than can be achieved by one person alone. It also models how mutual support actually works. The impact of cooperative effort tends to instill in individuals struggling with their crisis a confidence that people can contribute to one another. Such modelling also fosters an atmosphere of assurance that freedom from suffering is possible.

Speaking frankly,, failure to team up with a friend or colleague when the opportunity arises is really an act of disempowerment of the other. This disempowerment is disguised in contra-indicating statements such as the following:

* I don't really know the person well enough yet.
* I'm not sure who would be best at doing what.
* We really can't afford to use two people when one can adequately do the job.
* I'm not ready to work that inter-dependently with my colleagues just yet.

Unfortunately, these tactics tend to win out in the polite game of personal and professional territorial etiquette. Few of us gravitate towards capitalizing on team-work possibilities. For many it seems reoccuring fears of our own inadequacy have created a barrier that protects ourselves from experiencing failure with others. This barrier or boundary is built on an illusion, which can be recognized as such when we come out from behind our historically generated masks. These masks are similar to the ones covering up those whom we serve in crises.

Ultimately, we need social support to sustain on going change. Teamwork builds this in, capitalizing on the moment as well as inspiring others to seek ways to grow in their relationships. Unless you are a natural and confirmed hermit (in which case it is highly unlikely you will be a crisis intervener), your challenge is to rally around a flag of enriching differences with others, of shared capacities, of mutual viewpoints, and of greater degrees of freedom to be collectively provocative while fostering stability in a crisis event.

Having said this, what preparatory effort is required to actualize the team work, and what about working guidelines: the do's and don'ts of crisis team work?

TEAMWORK PREPARATION

After starting with a thorough grounding in self-preparation practices (See Chapter 3), the next step is to challenge yourself to double up with a colleague. Begin by asking your prospective partner to spend half an hour with you to discuss your teamsmanship.

1.   Perceptual Modes

Your first task will be to declare to one another which one of your perceptual modes predominates in a crisis ituation: visual, kinesthetic or auditory. (See Table 3, Chapter Five) You can start by discussing with one another experiences you have had that were mildly stressful and discovering in that way which perceptual modality each of you operates in when under stress. In short, simply by paying attention to your dialogue with each other and to the way in which you interpret the world, you can discover your predominant perception modality. It is also quite possible that your partner in this exercise will be able to tell you which modality is dominant for you without too much difficulty.

Continuing to share with your partner after establishing perceptual preferences, experiment for a few minutes with matching perceptual modes of operating with one another. In other words, if your partner tends to be visual, then attempt to visually align with him. Take turns inter-changing in alignment with one another, particularly if your perceptual dominancies are different. Matching in this way will produce a pleasant, balanced, and easily revealing conversation. If the two of you are already matched, you will notice how easy it is to be with one another. Continue the exercise by shifting to a less dominant modality, and again practice getting into alignment with one another. This may stimulate you to uncover new aspects of one another which were previously overlooked.

There are strengths and weaknesses both to being aligned and to being complementary in perceptual modes for crisis intervention work. Alignment allows you to offer a unified, dramatically synergized connection with the other. However, alignment makes your weaknesses less prone to surface and tends to compound one another's blind spots. In such a situation, your joint blindness can cancel out your joint synergistic capability. If you know this, you can be sensitive to training yourself to have each other break stride, so that one maintains a focus in one modality while the other shifts to matching the modality of the person or persons in crises. This gives those in crises the benefit of a clarifying multi-modal viewpoint of their crisis concerns. Offering a variety of perceptual combinations can enrich awareness by pinpointing or highlighting numerous pathways towards self-sufficiency. Sensitivity to the various combinations minimizes the number of dead-end adventures or inadvertently movements from one perceptual tunnel to another.

Having uncovered your perceptual dominancy, you may wish to briefly discuss with your partner how the two of you might act in unison to assist others recover a state of perceptual balance. When perceptual balance is restored for those in crisis, it tends to open up fresh viewpoints and reveals valid ways of dissolving a crisis.

You may find the original time you allotted for sharing with your colleage is all used up by now. Decide if you wish to continue on now or to set a later time for developing your working relationship further. Time and complacency will be your enemies here, even though you know that doing this with your partner may pay handsome dividends. Commit yourself to continuing, and hold each other accountable for this task.

2.   Knowing Your Acts

This next exercise is extremely challenging, for it requires a disclosure to a teammate, of how you act or how you operate in life in order to avoid losing. Discovering, much less declaring, one's ACT requires an extraordinary commitment to self-observation. The degree to which you are clear about your ACT depends upon how willing you are to reveal your persona or your shadow to you. The most difficult step to take in this regard is to give yourself permission to be vulnerable both with yourself and your teammate or colleague. Once the step is taken, the frightening aspect of being transparent melts away and is replaced by a sense of expansion and curiosity. It is interesting to know that those who have dared to open themselves to being aware of their own ACT can perceive the ACTS of others much more readily. As with perceptual dominancies, knowing your own ACT allows you to steer away from hazards or road blocks set up by people you work with in crises. Now consider doing the following Act-revealing exercise with your partner.

Begin by sitting directly in front of your partner. As you close your eyes, allow yourself to reflect on how you avoid losing in life. Recall at least three significant life events where you were required to do something in order to survive as a person. Now share these events, with one another. Take care not to interrupt the other - just listen. Endeavour to be attentive to the perceptual mode being used by one another. Allow about fifteen minutes each for the sharing of your past events; and acknowledge each other for sharing. Remember, thanking one another for sharing is too often taken for granted. Acknowledge that the other person's story is worth sharing. Remind yourself also that deep down you know that the map or story is not really representative of the territory. The territory is much more expansive. In any event, what is important here is the experience of one another's essence through their stories. Next, let yourself speculate with one another on the nature of your primary ACTS. Sharing in this way is like taking off one's mask. Take what you have now shared, and begin a dialogue on the usefulness of these ACTS or masks in your life. Once these ACTS have been revealed, there is a tendency to want to discount them in search of a more open way of being. Allow yourself to recognize that your ACTS have been of value to you in some significant way; and consciously recognize how this has been so. Allow yourself to laugh about your ACTS, tell humorous stories about them, and be light about them.

Take the situation where you are both working together, assisting someone who has just taken an overdose of pills. Imagine how both of your these ACTS or masks harmonize or conflict with one another and discuss how you would act in this situation with one another, and comment on whether you would react to your partner's behaviour in critical or opinionated ways. Notice whether or not you have a "canned wrap" about certain problems. A "canned wrap" is simply a well-defined position about an issue which you have spoken to over and over again. You know it's a "canned wrap" when it comes out of you repetitively in the same way, from one occasion to the next. Hearing yourself play this old tape is the first clue to knowing that the force of your ACT is surfacing. Complete by sharing

---

your revelations and then acknowledge one another for your mutual willingness to self-explore.

You will know that you have completed sharing with your partner when a sense of movement is evident. Making a solid connection with your partner is an exhilarating experience. Often this sense is quite profound. It is as if your willingness and openness has stimulated an extraordinary sense of your both being bigger than your limitations.

TEAMWORK BASICS

1. On Guiding

A team approach to crisis intervention suggests a need for clarification of roles in the intervention process in order to prevent possible problems, such as duplication of effort, the overlooking of certain issues, and conflicting approaches to crisis concerns. Such problems can be much more easily addressed when a decision is made about who would be a leading guide and who would be secondary. A leading guide would be in charge of focusing upon foreground issues. A decision on who is the leading guide should be made prior to entering into a crisis situation. Before deciding, consider various factors: each individual's experience with the type of crisis at hand, the readiness of each member to explore new territory, and the goodness of fit of each member's predominant perceptual mode and ACT with the crisis situation. The other role, just as important in its own right, focuses on background or completing issues. Both the background and the foreground roles are essential to a holo-systemic approach to crisis intervention. Neither one is sufficient alone. "The Lone Star" crisis intervener has the demanding task of taking both roles. This is quite possible, but it is not as powerful and empowering as the efforts of a two person coordinated team effort.

The leading guide's first task is to explore the component issues related to a crisis. The task is to examine the lay of the crisis land: it is to scout out and identify the risks, the resources not used, and the pathways already travelled. This is best done while avoiding judgement. The leading guide needs to be a consummate inquirer continously asking questions. This is not to say they don't interact interspersing statements of their own in a mutually engaging way.

The completing guide in a complimentary manner, focuses on the background and notices what has been made clear and what could be woven together to develop new possibilities. The completing guide clarifies multiple viewpoints of the same landscape. This guide invites clients to share their understanding of the crisis landscape. As a completer, this guide resonates with the leading guide, inviting the leading guide to highlight the significance of resources against the background landscape of the crisis scenario. The completing guide offers background assurance that stability can be achieved in completing or tying up loose ends.

In many ways, this teamsmanship is akin to an optimal mother/father relationship within a family. It is a balancing act in which unconditional support is mutually given. This balancing act allows compassion, peacefulness, and sustenance to backdrop enthusiasm, meaningful confrontation, and complementary action.

---

2.   On Mis-takes

Often during a crisis intervention event the pathways taken by the crisis intervention team members diverge. Despite committed effort by team members to work in synchrony it seems they can easily become prey to attractive side issues shrouding the crisis event. These side issues camouflage and protect those in crisis from further loss by acting as decoys to shift the pressure away from themselves. For example, one crisis intervener can get detoured and dead-ended by becoming preoccupied with a substance abuse problem while the other team member might be drawn into unemployment as the primary issue. While both issues are prevalent the primary issue might be an ungrieved family suicide. The crisis team in circumstances such as this would do well to remember that it's efforts will, in a trial and error manner, continuously converge and diverge as a natural aspect of the intervention process. Despite this tendency they need to remain assured and confident that the combined efforts they make will nonetheless periodically generate opportunities for them to recapture their teamsmanship balance. In fact, it is the very mis-takes they collectively make, when acknowledged and actively focused on that lead to effective intervention. Moreover by making "mis-takes" without fear of perceived incompetency the crisis team can effectively model for those in crisis how humility, curiosity, and flexibility as desirable attributes in solving their crisis situations. Therefore making "mis-takes" ought to be perceived as a natural component of crisis intervention work and actually should be encouraged as an experience.

As a crisis team you are urged to consult with one another frequent throughout the crisis event. It is amazing how those in crisis will give you the time to get your "ACTS" together if you dare to do so. Consulting with one another can also be a way to short-circuit the chance that one intervener will make the other irreversibly wrong during intervention.

3.   On Being Dis-connected

When it happens that you feel wronged, judged, or disempowered by your partner, allow yourself to rally around your big self and humbly let the wrongdoing settle for a moment without trying to rectify it. Encourage yourself to gracefully support your partner even more! Your partner may not be aware that their ACT is plugged in and needs to be de-energized by your own willingness to let your teamsmanship go slightly off course for a while. Confide in yourself, knowing "mis-takes" are disguised opportunities. At the earliest possible time, let a time-out consultation with your partner be used to get you back on track. When you and your partner are successful in getting a time to re-group allow your awareness of your primary purpose for intervening to overide your mis-alignment and reinforce your efforts towards re-establishing a cohesive partnership. Furthermore as you would seek to achieve a "coincidence of opposites" with those in crisis let this principle also guide you towards achieving closure with your partner. Doing this will allow your partner to be empowered in ways that allow communal wisdom to be re-captured at crisis de-briefing time.

In summary, teamsmanship is a preferred journey to take. Take it by preparing yourself through self-revealing examination of your perceptual viewpoints, your primary ACTS, and your strength as a team. Committing yourself to a team approach produces personal dividends that enhance your functioning capabilities as a crisis intervener.

SUGGESTED READING

1. An indispensible book for those who lack extensive professional training in crisis intervention, but who nevertheless are confronted with a wide variety of troubled people, is Eugene Kennedy's **On becoming a counsellor** (New York: Seabury Press, 1977). As well as covering the basic ground rules for sound and effective counselling of a multitude of human problems, it offers numerous suggestions on how to escape, avoid and actively make use of crisis entanglements through reflection and self evaluation.

NOTES

NOTES

CHAPTER EIGHTEEN

THE STEP BEYOND

Come to the edge, he said.
They said: We are afraid.
Come to the edge, he said.
They came.
He pushed them . . . and they flew.

- Guillaume Apollinaire

It is high time we shed ourselves of attachment to old forms and eased
the flight of the unfettered human mind.

- Marilyn Furguson

BASIC ASSUMPTIONS

Throughout this book, right from the beginning persistent attempts have been made to differentiate between the Beyond Content crisis intervention perspective and the predominant, yet fragmented, array of crisis intervention models more commonly referred to by crisis interveners. As said in many different ways already, the Beyond Content model is different from other approaches and yet also quite similar. By now it will be obvious to you that the Beyond Content model is a perspective that can embrace any model or framework, though at the same time, it seeks to go beyond the ordinary and beyond consensus thinking. As a contextual approach, it is largely intangible, yet it is a synthesizing approach, and coherently tolerant of reductionistic approaches to crisis intervention. In this regard the Beyond Content model has sought to incorporate numerous strategies originating from more commonly known crisis intervention models within its transpersonal frame of reference. Moreover, the model also attempts to offer approaches that add value to these strategies with the aim

---

GENERAL CRISIS-INTERVENTION ASSUMPTIONS	BC CRISIS-INTERVENTION ASSUMPTIONS
Crisis as a problem, as a breakdown of competency.	Crisis as an opportunity to breakthrough, have untried competencies mobilized.
Concern with abnormal behaviour.	Concern with competent and natural behaviour.
Emphasis on stabilization, returning to a pre-crisis state of functioning.	Movement beyond stabilization to include a higher state of congruence with self, others, and one's environment.
Resistance as a barrier to learning and recovery.	Resistance also seen as a resource for transformation.
Focus on symptom removal and explicit disorder issues.	Exploration of symptom boundaries and implicate flow of energy patterns.
Intervention approach primarily structured, instrumental and delineated by well established protocols.	Holistic and wellness based integrating protocols within a relatively flexible and expanding framework.
Emphasis on coping skills.	Emphasis on competency skills.
Crisis intervener tends to be emotionally responsive.	Crisis intervener tends to be psychologically neutral.
Client seen as dependent needing to be directed towards independence.	Client seen as autonomous and spontaneously capable of being interdependent.
Encouragement of self-acceptance.	Encouragement of self-transcendence.
Intervener as knowledgeable, advice giver, teacher, and fair judge of character.	Intervener as an associate guide, pilot, or opportunity partner. Egalitarian in approach, permitting candour and dissent.

Body, intellect, and emotions are distinct and separate human paradigms with the sum seen as unfathomable, yet greater than the parts.	The essence or higher self embraces all human paradigms and exists within each part, such that with the part exists the whole.
Mind seen as the primary pathway to solving the crisis.	The mind/body and environment seen as an ecologically imbalanced holosystem striving to evolve.
Prevention largely seen as what not to do (smoking, over-eating, harbouring resentment, and so on).	Prevention seen as coming from solutions about what doesn't work.
Delivered as a skill, measurable by contracts, behaviourial indicators, and crisis termination.	Delivered as an attitude, a way of perceiving others from strength and a willingness to go beyond certainties.
Manipulation and helping to function better are practised, in order to get rid of the problem.	Serving and assisting to recover natural competency are practised, in order to transcend the problem.
Distorted thinking is addressed largely by analytical, linear, left brain thinking.	Striving for whole brain awareness. Augmentation of left-brain rationality and distortions by right brain intuition and imagination.
Crisis healing through eradication of symptoms.	Crisis healing through self-healing. Comes as a direct result of re-capturing whole-ness.
Addresses getting past crisis barriers and side-stepping stress, ignoring or avoiding it.	Addresses going through crisis barriers and using stress by paying attention to it as a resource to learn from.
Change is a desired end goal.	Transformation is the primary goal.

of continuously fine tuning their potential for making a difference in a wide array of crisis circumstances. A synthesized overview of the basic assumptions of the Beyond Content model compared with the more traditional or generally known assumptions underpinning crisis intervention practices is now offered. The intent here is to summarize and clarify the qualitative differences as well as to highlight the distinctive nature of the Beyond Content approach to crisis intervention.

Arising out of the transpersonal paradigm, the Beyond Content approach to crisis intervention is embedded in sound science, systems theory, an understanding of the integration of the various aspects of the mind and body, knowledge about the spectrum of consciousness and the potential for altering and expanding our awareness. Rather than emphasising reductionistic problem identification it searches for meaningful patterns by endeavouring to observe using full spectrum awareness. It supports the search for meaning, the re-capturing of competency, and a sense of harmonious connection with our environment. It promotes an environment of acceptance for absorbing and using the power in chaos and dissonance. It is meant to be contextually complementary to other crises intervention models, as well as being quite dynamic and at times paradoxical. Yet we are nonetheless in the morning of our understanding on how to use a transpersonal approach to crisis intervention. In an inspired and embryonic way, the Beyond Content framework for crisis intervention is obviously a hybrid offshoot of the transpersonal paradigm. It is clear that the transpersonal perspective does not need crises in order to manifest itself. However, it is increasingly evident that our crises do need the transpersonal perspective.

So as not to create an illusion of the completeness of this model and of the approaches shared in this book, some aspects missing from the model will now be discussed.

WHAT'S MISSING?

First of all, this book is not meant to offer an exhaustive compendium of the overwhelmingly expansive field of crisis intervention. Many very significant topics have not been addressed, such as natural disasters, hostage scenarios, crises of the aging, and terminal illnesses, to name a few. The intention has been to offer a broad-banded overview of crisis issues and to demonstrate the various aspects of the Beyond Content Model in relation to these issues. Trusting that common threads run through most crises, it is modestly suggested that the model can be extrapolated to fit the wide spectrum of crisis issues not covered. Also, if your awareness of the extraordinary realm of intuition and forecasting has been stimulated, you the curious crisis intervener, are encouraged to read between the lines of the information shared in this book and apply what you will, as it fits.

The techniques and strategies described in this book are meant as snapshot examples of possibilities. These techniques and strategies are by no means held out as the only, or even the most, effective ways to generate movement out of the crisis maze.

The past few decades have seen the proliferation of countless innovative crisis strategies and techniques. These strategies and techniques have been introduced by reputable leaders from many helping disciplines and they are gradually weaving their way into widespread acceptance in the helping professions. Nonetheless what is missing is a focused effort to link the various strategies and techniques together into a coherent framework that can be readily absorbed and adopted by those

---

seeking to make crisis intervention their field of competence. In many ways, these strategies and techniques result in only the partial resolution of crises. All too often those in crisis (valiantly aided by the crisis intervener) stumble out of the crisis battlefield as the walking wounded somewhat incomplete and unclear about what to do next.

Since the Beyond Content model is a developing framework still in its infancy, you as the maturing crisis intervener will need to experiment and adapt your "strategies of choice" as you see fitting with this model. One's current understanding of the transpersonal perspective and it's implications for the Beyond Content model will no doubt largely determine the value experienced in implementing this model.

If you have read this far, you will likely have experimented already with many of the "state of the art" strategies, often labelled by buzz words such as "paradoxical interventions", "awareness processes", "metaphors", "re-framings", and so on. For those wanting to explore the use of some of these techniques further, a list of suggested readings is offered at the end of the chapter.

What is also missing from this book is a legitimatizing way to use this model. An important, unanswered question is, "Does the model fit for a crisis intervener whose mandate requires a chartered or registered approach sanctified by some socially approved organization?" Regardless of how embracing of traditional approaches this model is and regardless of how attractive aspects of this model might be, applying the model can be at the very least frustrating and at worst, destructive for those who need to honour well-established territorial mandates. Moreover the model can be quite dangerous to those straddling between the two paradigms. The approach, when it is reduced to the ordinary coping realm, can easily be distorted, abused, and rendered unworkable. This problem is further compounded by the esoteric, difficult-to-describe-in-words foundation of the model. In fact, as already mentioned, describing it really offers only an approximation, a rough and crude roadmap of an enormously vast, multi-dimensional territory. Because the framework is metatheoretical and, at times, metaphysical, endeavouring to capture its essence is a little like trying (as Ken Wilber [1979] suggests,) "to grab the ocean with a fork." Furthermore, efforts to press what is viewed as a "holosystemic" model into a linear expressive model can seriously debase its' contextual framework. Therefore a note of caution is offered to those who strive to adopt aspects of the model without generating genuine experiences of it for themselves. The journey cannot be taken literally!

On the other hand, it is madness to mix the dominant linear mode with a less practised and less understood transpersonal mode unless one is able to integrate the two. The dilemma for the crisis intervener springs from the fact that the alternative, namely limiting oneself to the Cartesian mode of perception alone, is also madness. To go beyond our symptom preoccupied and culturally conditioned madness, it is necessary to focus on developing a genuine, balanced interplay of both paradigms. To take this kind of pathway you will need to have an affirmative attitude towards life, to emphasize the present moment over the past and the future, and to generate a deep awareness of the spiritual underpinnings of our existence. Stepping onto this pathway is our biggest challenge.

Those so inclined may wish to refresh their awareness of the basic aspects of the model. To examine the efficacy of weaving the different strands together, you may wish to review Figure 10 and the accompanying outline of the basic components of the Beyond Content model, located in Chapter

Six. Also, reviewing the brief summary of comparative assumptions earlier in this chapter can further refresh your memory of the distinctive nature of this paradigm.

The Beyond Content model is meant, then, to serve as a platform for further exploration. Perception of the transpersonal aspects of the model is possible for anyone, even though embodying the model in its fullest is a rare occurrence. Before we can fully use the model, however, we need to discover ways to let go of our outdated maps and be willing to take an inner journey of self-observation.

Once such a journey is embarked upon we encounter numerous risks that shake the model's foundation. Some of these perils of the pathway will now be briefly discussed.

PERILS OF THE PATH

Staying on the Beyond Content pathway requires an enormous personal commitment to continually self-explore and to examine one's own integrity. It is easy to catch onto the essence of the model, only to quickly drift back to a consensus reality, drawn into our own melodramas by the predominant cultural, professional, and practitioner minimal self reality. Because taking this pathway requires the crisis intervener seek out light amongst the shadows of our crises, the crisis intervener must be deadly serious about catching oneself before possibly drifting into a preoccupation with darkness or, in other words, a problem focused approach. The commitment to self-explore can easily be shelved. We can easily be seduced into searching outside ourselves for ways to become competent. Staying awake to this fact is essential.   It may be obvious to you now that existing well established paradigms cannot embrace the transpersonal paradigm without first letting go of some of their antiquated aspects.

It is also likely that personal commitment will be shaken by the discounting actions from others, projected onto the crisis intervener in the form of resistance after declaring a transpersonal stance. This resistance will come from clients, colleagues, and helping organizations. It will surface in the form of mockery, coolness or outright hostility. Even though mounting data point to our readiness for a transpersonal paradigm, some people will hold out against it until a shift in awareness of crisis proportions shocks them out of their consensus trance. Thus, the Beyond Content crisis intervener needs to be willing to handle discounting statements and not take them personally.

On Burnout

The preoccupation with burnout is one of the most insidious and somewhat contagious aspects of the currently predominating consensus reality, that can draw the crisis intervener into a survival state. Burnout is a factor when the crisis intervener perceives that there is not enough of oneself to go around when crises start to pile up. Consensus once again operates to condition the average crisis intervener not to go all out, for fear of being abused or over-used. More often than not, to protect against being sacrificial, the crisis intervener can lean towards creating a catastrophe around the risks of burnout, embellishing them and giving them more power than they deserve. Underlying this concern is the crisis intervener's lack of clarity of purpose.

Armed with a well fleshed-out purpose, developed and fine-tuned through continuous self-examination, the crisis intervener can shift the context of burnout to the concept of "burnthrough". To "burnthrough" is to be, like a dedicated laser, able to cut through malignancies and to stimulate aliveness and excitement. To "burnthrough" completely is to burn thoroughly, leaving nothing behind but ashes, so that there is nothing unspent, all is completely transformed. This possibility is without a doubt alien to most crisis interveners. Interestingly enough, burning through is like breaking through. Ironically, the possibility of breakthrough seems to most often surface spontaneously when the crisis intervener overcomes the fear of being empty, finished, all used up. When this fear is mastered the crisis intervener can experience a wonderful sense of freedom and actually become rejuvenated by a commitment to unconditionally serve others in need without being sacrificial. To discover this state is to give oneself permission to experience it. This state is most impressively captured in the following statement about the true purpose in life:

> This is the true joy in life to be used for a purpose recognized by yourself as a mighty one, that being a force of nature instead of a feverish selfish little cloud of ailments and grievances complaining that the world ought to devote itself to making you happy. I am of the opinion that my life belongs to the whole community and for as long as I live it is my privilege to do for it whatever I can. I want to be thoroughly used up when I die for the harder I work the more I live, I rejoice in life for its own sake. Life is no brief candle to me. It is a sort of splendid torch which I have got a hold of for the moment and I want to make it burn as brightly as possible before handing it on to future generations.

> - George Bernard Shaw

The greatest benefit of "burnthrough" is an enhancement of the quality of our lives. Crises then become springboards for discovering more innovative ways to experience our aliveness.

On Discounting Workability

Another remarkable peril of the pathway is that its workability "the actual value it produces" may be underplayed and even discounted. Although, obvious breakthroughs do occur when resistance is used as a resource and when wholeness represents the matrix for health and well-being, many people still feel the need to defend and retain an obsolete paradigm of reality. Letting go of the past entails giving up outdated dogmas, structures, and beliefs, and becoming our own children again. Before this happens, an unsentimental form of awakening has to occur. Otherwise what works will continue to be ignored or not seen, even when it is blatantly obvious. The discounting experiences of those leading-edge crisis interveners challenging themselves with "breakthrough" possibilities surfaces in the form of being branded as hopelessly idealistic or being ignored and unrecognized for their efforts. Before this scenario changes a major crisis of awareness will have to occur. A new awareness, like a "groundswell", will be the coming generations' legacy. Our ongoing task is to minimize the effects of our past conditioning, to discover ways around our preoccupation with survival, and to learn how to get out of our own way long enough to be able to, in impactful ways, serve others in crisis.

On Teaching Others

In contradiction to what I have long thought to be the case, numerous workshops have revealed to me that the majority of those working in the crisis field find little difficulty in accepting this new paradigm. Yet only a minority are able to act on their new-found awareness. It seems that our teaching approaches do little more than debase the paradigm by trying to convey an understanding of concepts rather than an experience of them. Our teachers are often vague and unclear about what a paradigm shift means, let alone how to demonstrate it. And few teachers have incorporated the basic principles well enough to be able to model them.

To teach this approach requires the educator adopt an experiential, "learning how to discover" approach, as opposed to a more traditional pedagogical or instructional approach. Far too many teachers are fossilized around time-honoured learning procedures which generate very little excitement about the field. As well, it seems most of our established schools are still far too entrenched in curriculum and taxonomies to be able to respond effectively to our contemporary needs.

For a teacher, the challenge is to attract and inspire interest without creating a following that depends on the teaching or the teacher. Fears of charlatanism, cultism, and brainwashing have a tendency to mellow even the most competent teachers of a "holosystemic" approach to crisis intervention. Fortunately, interdisciplinary approaches to crisis intervention are becoming more and more common. As crisis breakthrough in the various disciplines begin to converge, teachers or guides are surfacing who have an experientially demonstrated commitment to wellness and to treating the whole person. Such teachers, because they are largely self-taught, respect the value that one can be ones' own teacher. Teachers then, are primarily used as reference guides to assist the crisis intervener stay on track and committed to the journey of self-exploration.

Making the Implicit Real

In writing this book, it often occurred to me how futile it is to tell someone who is suffering from an overwhelming sense of inadequacy or impotency that despite such feelings they are actually quite competent, and capable of being self-sufficient. For those perched on the cliff above the abyss of insignificance, such a message is like getting pushed off the cliff by ignorance. For those who are obviously deluded, lost in their cumulatively destructive life-events, out of touch with reality as others know it, or indelibly imprinted with a pervading sense of worthlessness, telling them otherwise is to deny their reality. Clearly, the challenge is to honour their current state of being and at the same time to watch for occasions when their natural competency leaks out of the crevices of their crisis melodrama. Behind their diminished self is the larger self or essence that is suffocating and dying from lack of attention. To draw this out is to restore aliveness and competency. How to do it is the unknown territory that can become known through practicing the functional aspects of a transpersonal crisis intervention framework. I am convinced that the essence of competency must be experientially communicated over and over again, in humble yet provocative ways, until a glimmer of essence is let loose from those entangled in a web of restrictive conditioning.

Now perhaps somewhat more wary of the hazards of the path, yet still open to explore the vast and largely unexplored transpersonal territory you may well be at a crossroad. What's next is the operative issue for those who have read this far.

WHAT'S NEXT?

Incorporation

Willingness to experiment and practice gets one into the Beyond Content ball park. By simply modelling the model, the crisis intervener can connect with its depth of field and discover exactly what kind of practice is required if the approach is to become incorporated. Starting as a practicing master, rather than as a master practicing, one can get glimpses of one's inconsistencies, one's barriers to aliveness, and one's mindless conditioning. Since we have for the most part disconnected from our higher selves, it takes great effort to get re-connected to our natural inheritance. As mentioned numerous times already, self-observation is essential to get us on the pathway, to sustain our growth, and to guide us along the path.

On Self-Observation

Self-exploration or self-observation opens the door for this contextual approach to become a coherent experience. Self-observation is extremely hard work. It involves learning how to be aware of awareness, how to be psychologically neutral, how to generate willingness rather than wishfulness, how to detect the ways in which thinking gets in the way of being, how to admit one's mistakes, and how to explore our fears fearlessly. Daily discipline is essential; otherwise we fall again into the traps of our more subtle forms of conditioning. Even with daily discipline, the crisis intervener needs to observe their practice of self-observation, to make it refreshingly different so as not to get overly conditioned by it and subsequently fall asleep again.
Though it is wise to be your own guru, sorcerer, pilot, or guide you need co-conspirators, associate guides, and even teachers if you are to sustain the process of self-exploration.

On Associate Guides

Once you have recognized that there are few credible guides available to support you to become your own sorcerer, the question becomes how you can make a connection with one. Before searching it is important to examine whether you have any undercurrent resistance to being guided. Most often we are clouded by our own imperfections and crazy ideas about free will, such that even if a guide were available we would sabotage our true intent to be inspired or led by one. When one's own resistance is acknowledged and a clear willingness to go beyond our barriers is established, a truly workable guide will become available. Such guides are drawn to us as we are to them when we are appropriately ready.

On the other hand, when we search prematurely and are driven by an undercurrent need for attention and affirmation, we will find many guides who have significant flaws. Frequently, such a linkage serves only to amplify one's own pathology and to foster dependence. To avoid such guides, it is essential to confront both oneself and one's potential guides.

Guides ought not be gurus or to be so charismatic that you lose yourself in their magnificence.

Powerful and empowering guides are like you, on a continuous journey of transformation. Such guides are noticeable for their humility and for their willingness to give away their power to others. As guides demonstrate more power, they also demonstrate more responsibility. Ironically, such guides seek power by giving it away. Empowering guides recognize, through persistent self-exploration, their own impurities, their own desires and their own clingings. They are ever mindful of their own shadow or the unconscious aspects of themselves that make them fallible. These kinds of guides vigilantly watch for signs that their teachings are being taken too seriously by themselves and others.

Being more seasoned travellers of the pathway, such guides can teach you how to avoid trouble spots, because they know from experience. Yet they are seemingly not invested in needing to teach you. They are true associates, who recognize when you need reinforcement to develop your own competency. The maturing crisis intervener will recognize worthy guides by their action-oriented congruence with holistic wellness. The way they walk, talk, and resonate a vibrant form of caring about life ought to be carefully examined. True guides need to be free of hidden agendas, and they needs to model what works.

Exuding peaceful auras, such guides also appear more awake than you. When you connect with such persons, study them well, and they will mirror or reveal to you false aspects of your personality or your Act while having no apparent investment that you change.

Network Supports

In addition to guides, it is valuable to have a support network that actively practices wellness and competency ways of being. Creating such a network can support you to stay tuned to your purpose, to further cultivate and reinforce self-exploration, and to clarify just how you slip back into an automated de-energized space. Because in our cultural life-space integrity is easily lost and creative intention easily short-circuited by basic survival needs, a support network can serve to awaken you by contrast and by example. This type of network is not to be confused with a social support network in the general sense. Instead of social accommodation and approval, it practices caring confrontation. Its purpose is to support a chain reaction among its members, so that each experiences a continuous energy flow towards staying awake. In this regard, members are encouraged to confront one another to practice self-observation, to share pitfalls they encounter in staying on track, and also to share any breakthroughs they experience in their crisis-work and self-work.

Getting such a group together is just as difficult as getting together with an effective guide. Often these two aids go together, with a group naturally forming around a guide. This latter development can in itself ensure continuity of purpose and accelerate one's self-actualization movement. Pumping crisis iron alone leaves the crisis intervener impoverished in the long run. Connecting with others committed to the wellness pathway and expanding it to include our living community is essential to our survival.

On Forecasting

On the leading edge of this field is the scientific experimentation with our ability to forecast what can and will happen through the use of altered states of awareness. This may become a new

---

and challenging frontier for the transpersonally oriented crisis intervener. The capacity to forecast is unquestionably a well buried talent that we all possess,and ways are being discovered or uncovered to resurrect this ability, which some loosely referred to as intuition. The Beyond Content model boldly suggests that predicting the crisis weather is possible when the dynamics of competency are forged together, creating a conduit between essences of the person in crisis and the crisis intervener. Like child's play spontaneous awareness springs out of non-attached connectedness which allows the rhythms of knowing to be revealed as patterns and flow. This state of being can best be cultivated through self-exploration. During the past few decades, many different processes that facilitate self-exploration have been identified. The exercises and examples mentioned throughout this book are just some of the useful guides to consider.

Crisis intervention from a Beyond Content perspective, must as repeatedly stated, be perceived as an adventure in self-exploration. The step beyond is to trust the healing journey by being open and adventurous, without expectations. To follow the flow of experience within a "holosystem" is to recognize that self-healing will naturally come about, "with a little help from our friends". When the person in crisis and the crisis intervener each let go of their roles and acts and begin to explore unknown territory together, the outcome can be no less than magical.

In venturing to the step beyond, you will be pressed to handle the biggest crisis of all--our ingrained need to depend on a mechanistic conception of reality. Therefore, my plea to you is to **practice, practice, practice**. **Practice** discovering your competency. **Practice** self-observation. **Practice** seeing beyond content; and allow the strategies and formulas presented in this book to stimulate you and to generate your own congruence with your integrity.

Finally, do this with humour because levity graces our souls and makes the serious work of crisis intervention an act of enlightenment. As Susuki Roshi says after one has become committed to the transpersonal path, "The only thing left to do is to have a good laugh."

NOTES

REFERENCES

Anderson, C., Stewart, S. **Mastering resistance: a practical guide to family therapy**. New York: Guilford Press, 1983.

Ardell, D.B. **High level wellness**. Emmaus, P.A., USA: Rodale Press, 1977.

Assagioli, R. **Psychosynthesis**. New York: Penguin Books, 1965.

Assagioli, R. **The act of will**. New York: Penguin Books, 1974.

Bohm, D. **Unfolding meaning**. New York: Routledge & Kegan Paul Ltd., 1985.

Brockopp, G.W. **Crisis intervention: Theory, process and practice**. Springfield, Ill.: Charles C. Thomas Ltd., 1973.

Brown, M.Y. Discovering the self, **Psychosynthesis Digest I**, 20-38, 1981.

Brown, M.Y. **The unfolding self**. Los Angeles, Cal.: Psychosynthesis Press, 1983.

Buber, M. **I and thou**. New York: Charles Scribner's & Sons, 1970.

Caplan, G. **Principles in preventive psychiatry**. New York: Basic Books, 1964.

Caplan, G. **Support systems and community mental health**. New York: Behaviourial Publications, 1974.

Capra, F. **The turning point**. New York: Bantam Books, 1982.

Castenadas, C. **The teachings of don juan**. New York: Ballantine Books, 1968.

Castenadas, C. **The eagle's gift**. New York: Simon & Schuster, 1980.

Carkhuff, R., **Beyond counselling and therapy**. New York: Holt, Rinehart and Winston, 1976.

Cochrane, C.T., and Myers, D.V. **Children in crisis**. Beverly Hills, Ca.: Sage Publications, 1980.

Cohen, S. **The drug dilemma**. New York: McGraw-Hill, 1969.

Debono, E. **PO: Beyond yes and no**. New York: Simon & Schuster, 1972.

Emery, S. **Actualizations: You don't have to rehearse to be yourself**. New York: Doubleday Press, 1977.

Erickson, M., and Rossi, E. **Experiencing hypnosis: Therapeutic approaches to altered states.** New York: Irvington, 1981.

Erikson, E. H. **Childhood and society.** New York: Norton, 1963.

Everstine-Sullivan, D., and Everstine, L. **People in crisis: Strategic therapeutic interventions.** New York: Brunner/Mazel, 1983.

Ewing, C. **Crisis intervention as psychotherapy.** New York: Oxford University Press, 1978.

Farley, G.K., Eckhards, L.O., and Hebert, F. **Handbook of child and adolescent psychiatric emergencies.** New York: Medical Examination Pub. Co., Inc., 1979.

Farrelly, F., and Brandsma, J. **Provocative therapy.** California: Meta Pub., Inc., 1974.

Favazza, A.R. Why patients mutilate themselves. **Hospital and Community Psychiatry,** 40(2), 137-145, 1989.

Fromm, E. **The art of loving.** New York: Harper and Row, 1956.

Fields, R., Taylor, P., Weyler, R., & Ingrasci, R. **Chop wood carry water.** Los Angeles, Ca.: Jeremy P. Tarcher, Inc., 1984.

Ferguson, M. **The aquarian conspiracy.** Los Angeles: J. P. Tarcher, 1980.

Gendlin, E. **Focusing.** New York: Bantam Books, 1978.

Getz, W. Wiesen, A., Sue, S. & Ayers, A. **Fundamentals of crisis counselling.** London: Lexington Books, 1974.

Goble, F. **The third force.** New York: Crossman Inc., 1970.

Gordon, K., Eckhardt, L., and Herbert, F. **Handbook of child and adolescent psychiatric emergencies,** New York: Medication Examination Publishing Co., 1979.

Gorman, P., and Ram Dass, **How can I help.** New York: A Knopf Co., 1985.

Grof, S. **The adventure of self discovery.** New York: State   University, 1988.

Grof, S. **The adventure of self discovery.** New York: State University, 1988.

Haften, B., and Peterson, B. **The crisis intervention handbook.** Toronto: Prentice-Hall, 1982.

Hampden - Turner, C. **Maps of the mind.** New York: MacMillan Pub. Co., 1982.

Hayward, J. **Perceiving ordinary magic.** Boulder, Col.: New Science Library, 1984.

Hill, R. Generic features of families under Stress. In: Parad H.J., **Crisis Intervention: Selected Readings.** New York: Behavioral Publications, New York, 1973.

Houston, J. **The possible human.** New York: Jeremy Tarcher Inc., 1982.

Hyman, S. ed. **Manual of psychiatric emergencies.** Toronto: Little Brown & Co., 1984.

Jantsch, E. **The self organizing universe.** New York: Pergamon Press, 1980.

Jung, C. **The undiscovered self.** New York: Mentor, 1957.

Jung C. Synchronicity: and causal connecting principles. In: **Collected Works,** Vol. 8., Bollingen Series XX., Princeton University Press, Princeton, N.M., 1960.

Jung, C. **Memories, dreams, reflections.** New York: Pantheon Books, 1961.

Kaplan, D. Observations on crisis therapy and practice. **Social Casework,** 49, 151-55, 1968.

Kardner, S. A methodologic approach to crisis therapy. **American Journal of Psychotherapy,** 29, 4-13, 1975.

Kennedy, E. **Crisis counselling.** New York: Continuum Pub. Co., 1984.

Kohlberg, L. Statement sequence: the cognitive-developmental approach to socialization. In: **Handbook of Socialization Theory and Research** (ed.), Goslin, D., Chicago: Rand McNally, 1969.

Korzybski, A. (cited) Wilber, G. **No boundary.** Boulder, Col.: New Science Library, p.27, 1981.

Krishnamurti, J. **Education and the significance of life.** New York: Harper & Row, 1953.

Krishnamurti, J. **The awakening of intelligence.** New York: Harper and Row, 1974.

Krishnamurti, J. **Exploration into insight.** New York: Harper & Row, 1980.

Kroll, J. **The challenge of the borderline patient.** New York: Norton & Co., 1988.

Kubler-Ross, E. **On death and dying.** New York: MacMillan Pub. Co., 1969.

Kubler-Ross, E. ed. **Death: The final stage of growth.** Englewood Cliffs, N.J.: Prentice-Hall, 1975.

Leonard, G. **The silent pulse.** New York: E.P. Dutton, 1978.

Leonard, G. **Education and ecstacy**. New York: Delacorte, 1968.

Lester, D., and Brockopp, E. eds. Crisis intervention: theory, process and practices. In: **Crisis Intervention And Counselling By Telephone**. Springfield, Ill.: Charles C. Thomas, 1973.

Levine, S. **Healing into life and death**. New York: Double Day Press, 1987.

Lindemann, E. Symptomology and management of acute grief. **American Journal of Psychiatry**, 101: 141-148, 1944.

Lowen, A. **Bioenergetics**. Middlesex Eng.: Penguin Books, 1967.

Madden, D. and Lion, J. **Rage-hate-assault and other forms of violence**. New York: Spectrum Publications, Inc., 1976.

Maslow, A. **The farther reaches of human nature**. New York: Viking Press, 1971.

Maslow, A. **Towards a psychology of being**. Princeton: Van Nostrand, 1962.

Miller, S. Dialogue with the higher self. **Synthesis** 2, 122-139, 1975.

Miller, W. The telephone in out-patient psychotherapy. **American Journal of Psychotherapy**, 21:1, 15-26, 1973.

Mitchell, J. and Desnick, H. **Emergency response to crisis**, London: Prentice-Hall, 1981.

Nietzche, F. Composition of thus spake zarathustra. from **Ecce Homo** in Bo Ghiselin, ed., **The Creative Process**. Berkley: University of California Press, p.201-203, 1952.

Parad, H., ed. **Crisis intervention: Selected readings.** New York: Family Service Association of America, 1965.

Parad, H., & Parad, L. A study of crisis-oriented planned short-term treatment: part I and II. **Social Casework**, 49, 346-55, 418-26, 1968.

Parad, H., **Emergency and disaster management**. Bowie Md.: Charles Press, 1976.

Peck, S. **The road less travelled: A new psychology of love traditional values and spiritual growth**. New York: Simon & Schuster, 1978.

Perls, F. Gestalt therapy and human potentialities. In: **Explorations in Human Potentialities**. ed. H.A. Otto, Springfield: CC Thomas, 1968.

Perry, P. and Kufeldt, K. **Safety Net II - 1988. Community in metamorphosis: implications for youth.** Calgary, Can.: U of C Press, 1988.

Piaget, J. Piaget's theory. In: **Carmicheals' Manual Of Child Psychology,** ed. P. Massess. New York: Wiley, 1970.

Progoff, I. **At a journal workshop.** New York: Dialogue House, 1975.

Querido, A. The shaping of community mental health care. **British Journal of Psychiatry,** 114, 293, 1968.

Ray, S. **Loving relationships.** Melbrae, CA.: Celestral Arts, 1980.

Rogers, C. In retrospect: forty-six years. **The American Psychologist,** 29, 115-123, 1974.

Rapoport, L. The state of crisis: some theoretical considerations. **Social Service Review,** 36, 1962.

Rapoport, R. Normal crisis family structure and mental health. **Family Process,** 2, 68-80, 1963.

Ross, R. and McKay, H. **Self mutilation.** Lexington, Mass.: Heath & Co., 1979.

Rossi, E. **The psychobiology of mind-body healing.** New York: Norton, 1986.

Satir, V. **The new people making.** Mountain View Cal.: Science & Behaviour Books, 1988.

Schneidman, E. Crisis intervention: some thoughts and perspectives. **Crisis Intervention.** (Spector, G.A. & Claiborn, W.C., eds.). New York: Behaviorial Publications, 1973.

Schneidman, E., Farberow N., and Litman, R. (eds.). **The psychology of suicide.** New York: Science House, 1970.

Schulberg, H., and Sheldon. The probability of crisis and strategies for preventative intervention. **Archives of General Psychiatry,** 18, pp. 533-58, 1968.

Selye, H. **The stress of life.** New York: McGraw-Hill, 1956.

Simonton, O., Mathews-Simonton, S., and Creighton, J. **Getting well again.** New York: Bantam Books, 1978.

Smith, L. A general model of crisis intervention. **Clinical Social Work Journal,** IV, (3), Fall, 162-171, 1976.

Smothermen, R. **Transformation #1.** San Francisco: Context Publications, 1982.

Smothermen, R. **Winning through enlightment.** San Francisco: Context Publications, 1980.

Spangler, D. **Revelation: the birth of a new age.** Findhorn: Findhorn, Foundation, 1977.

Tart, C. **Waking Up.** Boston: New Science Library, 1987.

Taplin. J.R. Crisis therapy: critique and reformation. **Community Mental Health Journal,** 7, 13-24, 1971.

Toffler, A. **The third wave.** New York: Bantam, 1981.

Truax, C., and Carkhuff, R. **Towards effective counselling and psychotherapy: Training and practice.** Chicago: Aldine, 1967.

Webster new world dictionary college edition. Toronto: 1966.

Wicks, R., Fine, J., and Platt J. **Crisis intervention: a practical clinical guide.** New York: Charles B. Slack, 1983.

Wilber, K. **No boundary.** Boulder, Col.: New Science Library, 1979.

Wilber, K., Engler, J., & Brown, D. **Transformations of consciousness.** Boston: New Science Library, 1986.

Wilber, K. **The spectrum of consciousness.** Wheaton, Ill.: Theosophical Publishing House, 1977.